Contemporary Theories and Practice in Education

by

Yves Bertrand

Magna Publications, Inc.
Madison, Wisconsin

Contemporary Theories and Practice in Education
by Yves Bertrand

Translation and adaptation of the third French language edition, copyright 1993 by Agence d'ARC (Groupe Éducalivres inc), Laval, Québec. Théories contemporaines de l'éducation

© 1995 by Magna Publications, Inc.

Magna Publications, Inc.
2718 Dryden Drive
Madison, WI 53704-3086
608/246-3580

Translated by Jean-Marc Poisson

Edited by Robert Magnan

Design by Tamara L. Cook

Library of Congress Cataloging-in-Publication Data

Bertrand, Yves.
    (Théories contemporaines de l'éducation. English)
    Contemporary theories and practice in education/by Yves Bertrand;
    (translated by Jean-Marc Poisson).
        p. cm.
    Includes bibliographical references (p.   ) and index.
    ISBN 0-912150-41-6
    1. Education--Philosophy.   2. Educational Psychology.
    3. Educational sociology. I. Title.
    LB14.7.B37 1995
    370'.1--dc20   95-42307
                                                            CIP

Table of Contents

Introduction..*1*

Theories of Education.. 1

Classification of Educational Theories 2

Chapter 1 Spiritualistic Theories............................*9*

1.1 Spiritualistic Revival... 9

1.2 History and Problems... 10

1.3 Principles of Spiritualistic Education.................. 13

1.4 Conceptions about Education......................... 16

    1.4.1 Maslow's Theory 16

    1.4.2 Harman's Theory 20

    1.4.3 Leonard's Theory 22

    1.4.4 Ferguson's Theory 25

    1.4.5 Fotinas's Theory... 27

1.5 Conclusion.. 28

Chapter 2 Personalist Theories........................... 29

2.1 On Becoming a Person...................................... 29

    2.1.1 History and Problems 30

    2.1.2 Two Trends 34

2.2 Nondirective Education..................................... 34

    2.2.1 History and Problems 34

    2.2.2 Principles 35

    2.2.3 Strategies... 35

2.3 Neo-Humanistic Theories 38

   2.3.1 History and Problems 38

   2.3.2 Principles.. 39

   2.3.3 Strategies... 40

2.4 Interactive Theories
of Personal Development 43

   2.4.1 History and Problems 43

   2.4.2 Principles.. 44

2.5 Open Education 46

   2.5.1 Problems 46

   2.5.2 Principles.. 47

2.6 Conclusion.. 50

Chapter 3 Psychocognitive Theories 51

3.1 The Construction of Knowledge 51

3.2 Constructivist Didactics.................................... 51

   3.2.1 History and Problems 51

   3.2.2 Prior Conceptions.................................... 54

   3.2.3 Some Constructivist Didactics 57

   3.2.4 Allosteric Model 59

   3.2.5 Epistemological Disturbance................... 64

3.3. Pedagogical Profiles 66

   3.3.1 La Garanderie's Model 66

   3.3.2 Pedagogical Profiles and the Teaching
of Mathematics 69

3.4 Conclusion.. 73

Chapter 4 Technological Theories 75

4.1 Salvation through Technology 75

4.2 Two Main Trends.. 78

4.3 Systemic Trend 79

   4.3.1 History and Problems 79

4.3.2 Instructional Design 81

4.4 Hypermedia Trend.. 84

4.4.1 Evolution of the Hypermedia................... 85

4.4.2 Organizational Principles
of Hypermedia Environments................. 88

4.4.3 Examples of Open Hypermedia
Environments... 93

4.5 Minimal Training 97

4.6 Conclusion.. 101

Chapter 5 Social Cognitive Theories............... 103

5.1 Transactions between Individuals
and their Environment 103

5.2 Social Cognitive Theories
of Social Learning 107

5.2.1 History and Issues................................. 107

5.2.2 Principles... 108

5.2.3 Pedagogical Strategies........................ 111

5.3 Social Cognitive Conflict Theory 114

5.3.1 History and Issues................................. 114

5.3.2 Principles... 115

5.3.3 Pedagogical strategies 118

5.4 Vygotsky's Sociohistorical Theory 118

5.4.1 History and Issues................................. 118

5.4.2 Principles... 120

5.4.3 Pedagogical Strategies........................ 121

5.5 Contextualized Learning Theories 122

5.5.1 History and Issues................................. 122

5.5.2 Principles... 123

5.5.3 Pedagogical Strategies........................ 126

5.6 Cooperative Teaching
and Learning Theories 128

5.6.1 History and Issues.. 128

5.6.2 Principles.. 130

5.6.3 Pedagogical Strategies............................. 132

5.7 Conclusion.. 137

Chapter 6 Social Theories 139

6.1 Social Theories of Education 139

6.2 Institutional Pedagogies 140

6.2.1 Psychosociological Trend...................... 141

6.2.2 Psychoanalytical Trend 143

6.2.3 Institutional Pedagogy
and Nondirectivity 144

6.2.4 Paradox of Institutional Pedagogy 145

6.3 Conscientization Pedagogies......................... 146

6.3.1 Freire's Ideas 147

6.3.2 Pedagogies of Liberation..................... 151

6.3.3 Critical Pedagogy 156

6.3.4 Social Pedagogy
of Self-Development............................. 166

6.4 Eco-Social Theories of Education 174

6.4.1 Systematic Education in an
Ecosociety.. 176

6.4.2 Experiential Education........................... 179

6.4.3 Curriculum for the Future..................... 182

6.5 Conclusion... 186

Chapter 7 Academic Theories 189

7.1 Quality Education: A Problem 189

7.1.1 Barbarians at Our Gates! 189

7.2 Two Trends 192

7.3 Traditionalist Theories...................................... 193

7.3.1 History and Problems 193

7.3.2 Principles.. 197
7.3.3 Curriculum of a Classical Education..... 200
7.4. Generalist Theories 201
7.4.1 Problems of Quality Education.............. 201
7.4.2 Principles of General Education........... 202
7.4.3 Pedagogical Strategies......................... 212
7.5 Conclusion... 215

Chapter 8 General Conclusion *217*
8.1 Questions about Education 217
8.2 The Best Theory.. 218
8.3 For a New Eco-Social Competence.............. 222

Contemporary Theories and Practice
   in Education Matrix *223*

Bibliography...*227*

Index..*271*

Contemporary Theories and Practice in Education

Theories of Education

This book provides an introduction to the principal contemporary theories of education. In particular, we analyze those that, in recent decades, have marked thought about what education should be. They generally include an analysis of the problems of education and proposals for change. Most are accompanied by reflections about the goals of education, the roles of instructors, the place of the student, the scope of course content, and the sociocultural relevance of education.

We will use the following expressions interchangeably: theories of education, educational models, approaches to education, educational paradigms, and philosophies of education. Of course, each of these expressions has a particular meaning that distinguishes it from the others. However, we would like to remain at an introductory level and avoid getting lost in epistemological considerations of the differences among these expressions.

The term "theory" generally means a set of ideas, more or less systematically organized, about a given subject. However, the degree to which education theories are systematized varies greatly: some authors emphasize the philosophical foundations for their theories, while others show greater interest in pedagogical strategies. We have tried to reflect these differences.

We would like to stress that any theory of education is partly subjective, in that it is based on a perspective of educational reality and is thus subject to interpretation. We should also note that when a theorist emphasizes certain aspects of education, this does not mean that he or she is neglecting other aspects. For example, most educational theorists who stress development of the student's autonomy are also concerned with the successful integration of that student in society.

Classification of Educational Theories

We need to classify educational theories because there are so many that it is difficult to understand them and to choose directions and make changes in education.

The proposed classification consists of seven categories:

1. Spiritualist

2. Personalist

3. Psychocognitive

4. Technological

5. Social Cognitive

6. Social

7. Academic

Of course, there are different ways to categorize theories and practices in education. Among the typologies that have been proposed in the last twenty-five years that we could cite: Daniel Hameline (1971), Georges Snyders (1973), Elliot Eisner and Elizabeth Vallance (1973), Guy Avanzini (1975), Diane Lapp *et al.* (1975), Louis Not (1979), Jacques Ardoino (1980), Georges Lerbet (1980), ElizabethVallance (1986), Jean Houssaye (1987), Bruce Joyce, Marsha Weil, and Beverly Showers (1992), and Yves Bertrand and Paul Valois (1992).

The system of classification proposed in this book takes into consideration the dizzying evolution of the cognitive and social cognitive movements and research into the processes of knowing, information technologies, and sociocultural didactics.

Finally, it should be noted that any classification only serves to organize the confusion and allow us to see characteristic and representative forms. It is in this spirit that the reader should understand this classification, which organizes according to four polar elements (Figure 1.1):

1. The subject (the student)

2. The content (subject area, discipline)

3. Society (others, the world, the environment, the universe)

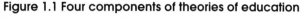

Figure 1.1 Four components of theories of education

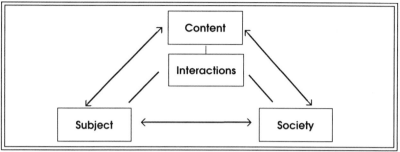

4. Pedagogical interactions among these three poles
(the instructor, communication technologies)

Here is a preliminary description of the characteristics that allow us to associate theories with one of these poles.

Subject Pole

At the subject pole we find two major trends — spiritualist and personalist. The spiritualist trend focuses on the transcendental and spiritual relationship between the individual and the universe. The human being, through his or her intentions and intuitions, reaches a spiritual dimension in relationship with the universe. Metaphysical religions and philosophies guide this sector of educational thought. The personalist trend — also called humanistic, libertarian, or organic — is characterized by its focus on the internal dynamic of the person: needs, aspirations, desires, impulses, energy, etc.

Society Pole

To the society pole we can attach the social theories that define the objective of education as the significant transformation of society, usually in a perspective of greater social justice. Education is fundamentally a question of social and cultural structures. It should play an important role in the transformation of society and culture. We will see that numerous social educational theories propose educating people to change society.

Content Pole

With the content pole are associated the academic theories for which the subject areas to be taught — such as classical literature and mathematics — have a structure that is objective and independent of the student and of society. These values and these contents exist in themselves; human psychology and social structures hardly matter. Traditionalists are interested in the return to classical values. Generalists, on the other hand, stress skills such as critical thinking and logical reflection.

Interactions among the Three Poles

Among the three poles are located the interactions that form the bases for the more didactic theories. We discern three trends:

- The technological theories are essentially interested in the modeling of interactions among subject, society, and contents; the human being is defined as an entity that processes information and is fed through media.

- The psychocognitive theories analyzed in this book relate essentially to the constructivist didactics conceived through the psychology of learning.

- The sociocognitive theories are most particularly interested in the impact of cultural and social factors on learning.

Figure 1.2 summarizes contemporary theories of education according to the four components. The following is a brief summary of each of the seven major trends that we can discern in contemporary theories of education.

Figure 1.2 Contemporary theories of education according to the four components

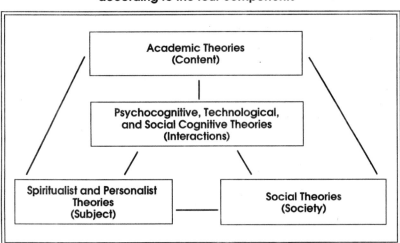

Spiritualistic Theories

An old educational trend emerged from its ashes in the early 1970s. This is the spiritualist current, also called metaphysical or transcendental, of interest particularly to people concerned with the spiritual dimension of life on this earth and by the meaning of life. Proponents of the spiritualist theories of education focus on the relationship between the self and the universe in a metaphysical perspective. These theories are often situated within the "new" sociocultural trend, called "New Age," although they are more concerned with the values described in often millennial texts. Eastern religions and philosophies provide much of the basis for educational thinking: Zen Buddhism and Taoism are often cited as dominant sources for this educational current.

In this spiritualist current we find the educational theories of Willis Harman, Constantin Fotinas, Abraham Maslow, George Leonard, and Marilyn Ferguson, centered on the so-called spiritual, metaphysical, or transcendental values. The individual should learn to liberate himself or herself from the known and go beyond his or her limits in order to rise to a spiritual level that is considered higher. The individual should master spiritual development by using his or her internal energies and channeling them into such activities as meditation and contemplation.

Energy comes from within. It appears under various names, such as God, Tao, the Invisible, Divine Energy, and so forth. The human being should enter into contact with the divinity that is present everywhere and try to attain through intuition that divine and spiritual nature that should guide him or her and in which he or she should trust.

Personalist Theories

Personalist theories — also called humanist, libertarian, nondirective, organic, impulsive, free, or open — are based essentially on notions of self, liberty, and personal autonomy. The individual who is in a learning situation should master his or her education by using internal energies. The educational theories grouped in this category emphasize the role of facilitator that the teacher should play in relation to the students. The teacher should continually focus on the self-actualization of the child. Carl Rogers still remains an excellent example of this vision of education. In the U.S., Quebec, and France, we continue to refer to his concept of education, which stresses the freedom of the student and his or her desires and willingness to learn. In the 1960s and 1970s, free or open or "alternative" schools proliferated, inspired by an approach based on the complete development of the student.

Psychocognitive Theories

Psychocognitive theories are concerned with the development of cognitive processes in the student, such as reasoning, analysis, problem-solving, representations, prior conceptions, mental images, etc. The foundations of these educational theories are often to be found in the cognitivist psychological research that investigated diverse aspects of learning.

The cognitivist theories are more interested in the internal processes of the mind, whereas the behaviorists are more interested in the effects of the environment on learning and, more specifically, in functional relationships between the organization of the pedagogical environment and human behaviors. We will limit ourselves in this book to the constructivist theories that accentuate the construction of knowledge.

Technological Theories

Technological theories, also called technosystemic or systemic, generally focus on improvement of the message through the use of appropriate technologies. The word "technology" is taken in a very broad sense. It covers procedures such as we find in systems approaches and in instructional design. It also covers instructional material for communicating and processing information: computer, television, VCR, tape recorder, videodisc, compact disc, etc. The recent trend is in hypermedia, computer-assisted learning environments, and interactive software. Objectives consist, for example, of creating new hypermedia environments using artificial intelligence concepts and tools, of simulating real scenarios, such as laboratory experiments with devices such as compact discs containing phenomenal quantities of images and commentary.

Most of this research is relying on the impressive capacity of computers to process information. Computers can easily manage multiple sources of information, whether they are in the form of images, sounds, or text. This is what we call hypermedia.

Research is also exploring ways to improve the quality of interaction between human and computer. This research is making an impact on pedagogy, although these changes are penetrating slowly into the school world, that is, the "real world."

Social Cognitive Theories

This trend of education stresses the cultural and social factors in the construction of knowledge. The focus is on the social and cultural interactions that form pedagogy and didactics. This dynamic trend is particularly strong in France, the U.S., and Canada, where numerous researchers are questioning the domination of the cognitivist trend in research. They note most particularly the problems caused by a vision of education that is overly psychological, and they put great emphasis on the social and cultural place of knowledge.

Social cognitive theories describe the social and cultural conditions of teaching and learning. Some theories dwell on the analysis of social interactions of cooperation in the construction of knowledge and propose a cooperative pedagogy in order to sensitize students to this way of working. Others stress the cultural foundations of education and propose that pedagogy include the necessary cultural dimension. These theories are thus opposed to the cognitive movement — which is rather individualistic — and concerned with the very nature of the process of knowing.

Social Theories

Social theories are based on the principle that education ought to allow us to resolve social, cultural, and environmental problems. The primary mission of education, then, is to prepare students to find solutions to these problems. The favorite themes of these researchers are social and cultural inequalities, social and cultural heredity, different forms of segregation, elitism, problems of the environment, the negative impact of technology and industrialization, and the deterioration of life on our planet.

Academic Theories

Academic theories — also called traditionalist, generalist, and classical — focus on the transmission of general knowledge. They generally oppose the domination of specialized education. Two groups of thinkers are in the academic trend — the traditionalists and the generalists. The traditionalists want education to transmit a classical content, independent of current cultures and social structures. The generalists emphasize general education that stresses a critical mind, flexibility, an open mind, and so forth.

In both cases, the role of the teacher consists of transmitting this content and the role of the student consists of assimilating it. Academic theories rely on teachers exposing knowledge that forms the heart of a general education. They often rely on constant striving for excellence and putting maximal effort into study and work. The values they convey are discipline, hard work, respect for tradition, and democratic values, as well as a sense of civic responsibility.

Chapter 1

Spiritualistic Theories

The spiritualist trend focuses on the transcendental and spiritual relationship between the individual and the universe. The human being, through his or her intentions and intuitions, reaches a spiritual dimension in his or her relationship with the universe. Metaphysical religions and philosophies guide this sector of educational thought.

1.1 Spiritualistic Revival

The spiritualistic educational movement is probably one of the oldest on the planet. Like the tide, it always returns.

In the past twenty-five years, we have witnessed a very strong resurgence of this spiritualistic movement. Industrialized civilization has failed to fulfill a fundamental human need to understand our presence on Earth. We have a lot of information, but little explanation about the meaning of life.

People have always wondered: "Does life have a meaning?" Hence the proliferation of spiritualistic movements that answer positively: "Yes, there is another world, an unnameable world with a thousand names that we must experience." The goal of spiritualistic education is to familiarize the individual with this spiritual reality — also called mystical or metaphysical.

One could say that the spiritualistic theories of education follow two trends. The first is more traditional and involved with handing down religious knowledge. This book will not analyze that trend. The second, described in the following pages, is further removed from traditional religions, their institutions, and their conventions. It tends to consider any form of theology or institutionalized religion as an escape from life.

This quote by Jiddu Krishnamurti (1970, p. 12) sums up perfectly this second trend, which is more preoccupied with the relationship between the individual and the Universe than with the real and objective existence of a superior and divine reality:

> The question of whether or not there is a God or truth or reality, or whatever you like to call it, can never be answered by books, by priests, philosophers or saviours. Nobody and nothing can answer the question but you yourself and that is why you must know yourself. Immaturity lies only in total ignorance of self. To understand yourself is the beginning of wisdom.

This educational trend is not religious either, in the institutional meaning of the word, and is not associated with a particular religious persuasion or church. It is more cosmic, in the meaning Mircea Éliade (1965) gave to the word when he said that the Cosmos is now inaccessible to Christians living in a modern town. Their religious experience has become private and is no longer open to the Cosmos. The Cosmos has become opaque, inert, silent: it does not send any message; it bears no significance. Now, Éliade says, any surpassing of the human condition means abolishing the personal Cosmos in which we have chosen to live.

1.2 History and Problems

The spiritualistic movement, which is so popular nowadays, really took off at the beginning of the twentieth century. In 1980, however, Marilyn Ferguson published *The Aquarian Conspiracy: Personal and Social Transformation in the 1980s*, which established the movement by presenting a synthesis of what had been done and written on the subject. Ferguson drew a lot of her inspiration from the work of Willis Harman at the Stanford Research Institute, especially at the beginning of the 1970s.

Indeed, Harman probably contributed the most to popularize the idea of a New Age culture, as well as the notions of the industrial paradigm and the emergent paradigm. The researcher wrote at the beginning of the 1970s that we were on the verge of a sociocultural revolution. We would leave behind, he said (1972a), an industrial vision of the world to go toward a transcendental one, that is, a vision of the world based on spiritual values that have remained throughout the ages.

Obviously, the idea of a spiritualistic vision of the world is not new. It stems from Platonism and Neo-Platonism, from Hinduism and the Oriental religious philosophies such as Taoism and Zen. The people most referred to are Meister Eckhart, Richard M. Bucke, Arthur Koestler, and Aldous Huxley.

Bucke wrote an important book, *Cosmic Consciousness*, which has been fueling the debate on the transcendency of consciousness since it was first published in 1901. In his book, Bucke suggests the notion of cosmic consciousness. He argues that the human race is taking on a new form of consciousness that goes beyond simple consciousness and self-consciousness. He analyzes on a psychological level the notion of the Universe's divine unity in such central figures as Jesus Christ, Gautama Buddha, Paul, Plotinus, Mohammed, Dante, John Yepes, William Blake, Walt Whitman, and many others (forty-three cases in all).

Bucke finds that the importance of rational consciousness is overestimated and should be less important. Cosmic consciousness is the most important form of consciousness and is distinct from learning, imagination, conception, and speculation. It is characterized by a feeling of belonging to the Universe and by such emotions as joy, happiness, a feeling of immortality, and moral high-mindedness. It is a form of ecstasy that happens suddenly and temporarily and that, after it is gone, has brought about a virtually permanent change in the individual.

One should also stress the influence of Taoism, which was developed by Lao-Tzu in the sixth century B.C. The work that is usually referred to is *The Book of the Way and Its Virtue*, a short but dense book of aphorisms and paradoxes. In their presentation of the book, François Houang and Pierre Leyris (1979) rightly stress that Taoism is the cosmic principle that is immanent in any human existence and in any activity in Nature. It is the fundamental and undifferentiated unity in which all the contradictions and all the differences of human experience and thought resolve themselves, and that we can reach only through a mystical intuition.

This book had an enormous influence on the American counter-culture of the 1950s: Allen Ginsberg, Jack Kerouac, and William

Burroughs. John Rowan (1976) argues that Lao-Tzu's book influenced humanist psychology, especially its remarks on the use of the qi (chi) energies coming from the source ('tan-t'ien') within the individual. Taoism continues to have a lot of influence on today's spiritualistic counter-culture.

The spiritualistic movement seeks to answer the problems of the individual. These problems are defined as follows. Several authors who share a spiritualistic vision of the universe — Ferguson, Constantin Fotinas and Michel Henry, Harman, Hazel Henderson, George B. Leonard — agree on the source of our problems: the industrial organization of life on this planet. They talk of the *industrial paradigm* as the basis for society's macro-problems. Harman (1988) defines paradigm as the fundamental structure of perception, thought, and action that partakes of a specific vision of reality that cannot be questioned without producing fundamental changes in the thought process. To change your paradigm is to change your vision of the world.

The predominance of the industrial paradigm means that people wrongly think that industrial progress is the only way to envision life. Each of us is literally and dangerously hypnotized by industrial progress, Harman (1988) warns us. The industrial paradigm is nothing but the reflection of the culture of human domination over the universe and possesses the following characteristics (Harman, 1988, 1972a; Bertrand and Valois, 1992; Henderson, 1993):

- Development and application of a scientific method; union of scientific and technological progress

- Industrialization of the organization and division of labor

- Predominance of the consumer society and the work ethic; belief in unlimited material progress

- Effort to control Nature; positivist theory of knowledge

- Individualism of a society, which is considered an aggregate of individuals pursuing personal interests; predominance of personal interests over collective ones

Spiritualistic education seeks to answer these problems. We will now see the fundamental principles of this education.

1.3 Principles of Spiritualistic Education

Spiritualistic education, which is also called metaphysical or mystical, offers a culture and an educational approach centered on a transcendental vision of the relationship between the individual and the Universe. The Universe is fundamentally divine, sacred, and transcendental. We are a part of this totality, and spiritual values transcend the particular situations of individuals.

Spiritualistic education makes a distinction between the levels of consciousness. Indeed, the individual has within himself or herself a cosmic consciousness, which has access to an invisible spiritual reality. It is believed that this consciousness enables us to have a mystical experience.

We will now see how some authors (Ferguson, 1980; Leonard, 1987; Harman, 1988; Bertrand and Valois, 1992; Fotinas and Henry, 1993; Henderson, 1993) describe the main values of the spiritualistic vision of education:

- Complementarity between physical and spiritual experiences: acceptance of all explanations as being only metaphorical; use of different non-contradictory levels in order to explain physical, biological, mental, and spiritual realities

- Teleological conception of life and evolution: ultimate reality considered as one and transcendental; any physiological act acquires a human value when it assumes a spiritual dimension

- Discovery of fundamental values through the inner experience of the hierarchy of the levels of consciousness; possibility of supraconscious and subconscious influences

- Life goals: conscious participation in individual growth and in the process of evolution; development of the individual through the community; integration of work, play, and growth

- Goals of society: to encourage development of the transcendent and emergent potentialities in the individual

Spiritualistic education is based on a vision of the Universe that usually makes itself understood through paradoxes (Éliade, 1965; Leonard, 1981; Ferguson, 1980). Zen literature is basically made up of paradoxes turned around on themselves. However, Éliade (1965) points out, the modern Westerner feels uneasy when faced with certain manifestations of the sacred. He or she finds it hard to accept that a stone or a tree can be a manifestation of the sacred. Éliade (1965) says:

> We will never stress enough the paradox that constitutes any hierophany, even the most elementary. Being a manifestation of the sacred, any object becomes something else, without ceasing to be itself, for it continues to be part of its cosmic environment. ... In other words, for those who have a religious experience, Nature as a whole can reveal itself as a cosmic sacrality.

Éliade's remark is the key to the spiritualistic vision, the paradoxical aspects of which will be presented in the following pages.

Spiritualistic education refers to an eternal and universal philosophy. Traces of it can be found in the traditional legends of primitive peoples almost anywhere in the world. The fully developed forms of this philosophy can also be found in all major religions. The first version of this philosophy, which is common to every theology, dates back more than twenty-five centuries. Many religious traditions have borrowed its principles, in all of the main languages of Asia and Europe.

Huxley had already written in 1946 about the *Eternal Philosophy*. According to him, the original expression 'philosophia perennis' (or eternal philosophy) characterizes what is common to the metaphysical philosophies (p. vii):

> Philosophia Perennis — the phrase was coined by Leibniz; but the thing — the metaphysic that recognizes a divine Reality substantial to the world of things and lives and minds; the psychology that finds in the soul something similar to, or even identical with, divine Reality; the ethic that places man's final end in the knowledge of the immanent and transcendent Ground of all being — this thing is immemorial and universal.

Huxley's reflections on the paradox of the eternal and divine self that is within every one of us, or, in other words, the paradox of the immanence of the transcendency or divine character of the human being, were to inspire in particular Harman and Ferguson in their descriptions of the new vision of the world.

Harman (1972a, 1988) states that this vision assumes a form of transcendent spiritual order, distinct from the individual and perceptible in the human experience of each of us. Life has a teleological meaning, and evolution has a finality in itself that can be found in each of us. From this premise, Harman (1972b) draws three important conclusions that allow us to clearly understand the specificity of the transcendental vision of the world:

1. The essential proposition of the eternal philosophy is as follows: each of us can, if we want, reach the level of cosmic consciousness. We can reach a cosmic consciousness and be aware of a reality underlying the phenomenal world, also called Divine Reason, Brahma, etc. The creation and development of an individual as well as his or her participation in the process of evolution are considered to be determined in the end by a supreme center called Atman, the self of Vedantic writings, the super-soul.

2. The basic hypotheses of positivist science have the same relationship with eternal philosophy as does Newtonian physics with the physics of relativity. They are part of a more general and more global theory. Therefore, one should not see in positivist hypotheses any contradiction, or even opposition, but rather a complementarity.

3. The eternal philosophy is both old and new. It does not begin with the 1960s. What is remarkable is the generalization of this form of metaphysics in the culture of our times. Spiritualistic philosophy, which used to be limited to such theories as Emerson's Transcendentalism or Bergson's Creative Evolution, is now more popularized and less esoteric. It is now possible to

take a course in Eastern philosophies, Zen Buddhism, Taoism, and transcendental meditation — philosophies previously limited to a few initiates.

To sum up, the individual is characterized by the transcendental faculties of his or her consciousness. This consciousness, the powers of which we hardly know, can in particular rise to a transcendental level, and this level constitutes a superior level of consciousness. Human beings are fully human when their consciousness assumes this cosmic and transcendental dimension.

1.4 Conceptions of Education

We will now look at different conceptions about education focusing on the works of Abraham Maslow, Harman, Leonard, Ferguson, and Fotinas.

1.4.1 Maslow's Theory

Maslow's thinking went through three stages: behaviorism, humanism, and metaphysics. Maslow admits to being a behaviorist when he first started his research, but the birth of his child made him change from behaviorism to humanism. The birth of his child made him understand that education must encourage the self-actualization of the individual, that is, the possibility to become fully human and to develop to the fullest of one's potential.

Maslow then became opposed to behaviorist learning as a general model of learning and criticized 'efficient' education, the purpose of which was to hand down knowledge to children and allow them to adjust to the industrial society. In a behaviorist perspective, Maslow said, the child rapidly learns in school that he or she has to please the teacher. The child also learns that creativity and a critical mind are not highly valued.

Maslow went through a second stage: he asserted that self-directed learning or self-actualization is more important than other-directed learning, that is, memorization of facts, rules, etc. This, in turn, led Maslow to talk about the ideal college. In this college, there would be no credits, no degrees, no prerequisite courses. You could study whatever appealed to you. Moreover, anyone could register at this college and anyone could teach.

Education would be non-stop in this educational retreat, where you could find what you wanted and thus find yourself. The goals of this education would be the discovery of your identity and your vocation.

Maslow was definitely an important spokesperson for humanistic psychology. But his last writings show that he wanted to go beyond this psychology, which was too preoccupied with the individual, and go toward a more mystical vision, which he called the Z Theory.

When he came into contact with mystics, Maslow sought to go beyond humanistic psychology. Maslow found in books by Daisetz Teitaro Suzuki, such as *Mysticism: Christian and Buddhist* (1957), a broader explanation of what he was trying to develop in his psychology of the Being.

Suzuki had a lot of influence on the North American counter-culture of the 1950s and 1960s. At a conference Maslow organized in Cambridge in 1957 as head of the Research Society for Creative Altruism, Suzuki gave a lecture on the Zen vision of human values. He explained very clearly the paradoxical and altruistic nature of love, that is, to forget the self in giving to another (Suzuki, 1959).

Thus, by getting acquainted with Zen literature and studying such authors as Bucke, Huxley, Rudolf Otto, and Éliade, Maslow was finally able to found the psychology of transcendency. "I am Freudian, behaviorist, humanist," he said (1970), "and I am developing a more globalizing fourth psychology: that of transcendency."

He then tried to go beyond the concept of self-actualization and to replace it with the notion of human plenitude. He made his concept of *peak experience* synonymous with the Zen concept of *satori* and Bucke's concept of *cosmic consciousness*. In doing so, Maslow intended to describe, in psychological terms, the mystical or religious experience.

He was then led to distinguish between two kinds of knowledge of the Being: cosmic consciousness, defined by Bucke (1901) as a feeling of belonging to the whole Universe, and the narrow perception of a particular element, such as a flower or a butterfly, a perception in which the subject forgets himself or herself as a subject and becomes "other." Cosmic consciousness implies a fusion between the subject and the Universe within an intuition that is often viewed as religious. But Maslow insisted on the fact that this intuition, this transcendency of the consciousness, is natural.

However, and this is the first paradox, the discovery of the 'I' leads inevitably to the discovery of a self that is independent from the 'I' or the ego, a holistic, global consciousness — that is, our belonging to the human species and to life. To look for idiosyncrasies — what makes us different from each other — enables us to return to the common human dimension.

The second paradox can be summarized this way: to find the divine meaning of the Universe through mystical communion is to find oneself. It is to discover the divine dimension of the individual. This important theme in mystical theology was very popular among American transcendentalists, and in particular with Ralph Waldo Emerson.

The third paradox is as follows (Éliade, 1965; Maslow, 1976): it is the experience of life that is fundamentally religious, while conventional religions are not. Atheists are sometimes more religious than those who practice a religion, for the latter have objectified the sacred and have reduced life to its earthly dimension. The transcendental religious experience is in no way related to religious institutions, since it is a dimension of life, a characteristic of every individual as such. Your everyday life is sacred when you fulfill your meta-needs and when you have a sacred vision of life. Later, Maslow stated that authentic religious experience is often inversely proportional to the degree of organization of the religious institution.

Maslow identified a set of values, the values of the being, which he placed beyond self-actualization. They are characteristics of reality and not feelings or emotions. These values, which he called "meta-needs" (or "growth needs"), include (Maslow, 1970 and 1976):

- Truth
- Beauty
- Goodness
- Unity
- The transcendency of dichotomies

- Vital energy
- The uniqueness of the individual
- Perfection and necessity
- Interdependence
- Justice
- Order
- Simplicity
- Good-heartedness
- Gracefulness
- Playfulness and humor
- Independence
- Liveliness

People who enjoy their work very much and who make it their vocation will not establish a dichotomy between their work and their life. They will regard their work as an expression of their talents. Consequently, the dichotomy between joy and work disappears and is replaced by a fusion between the two.

The purpose of education is, in a way, to facilitate this knowledge of yourself in relationship to the Universe. The point is to learn who you are, to listen to your inner voices, to discover the meaning of your life (1970). To discover your identity, Maslow says, is to discover your vocation. By acquiring a knowledge of your inner self, you can derive a set of values.

However, this inner knowledge is in no way similar to the existentialist project of Jean-Paul Sartre. It is more a rediscovery of your own subjective biology insofar as all human beings have a spiritual life. Education must be centered on discovering this subjective biology and satisfying the meta-needs. We should learn that life is precious and should enjoy it.

Now, the educational system, with its current structure of crowded classrooms, is not favorable to the experience of joy, on the contrary. We have to forget this behaviorist form of teaching, says Maslow (1976). Meditation and contemplation techniques should be central to education, he adds.

Teachers must be open: they must have a positive outlook about their students. Above all, they must help their students find themselves. They must meet the fundamental psychological needs: security, a feeling of belonging, love, respect, and esteem. Ultimately, the best way to teach a subject — whether mathematics, history, or philosophy — is to facilitate the student's intuitive perception of his or her relationship to the Universe. The student must be able to have the Zen experience, which consists of seeing the temporal and the eternal simultaneously, perceiving an object in its profane and sacred dimensions. In short, the goal of education should be to encourage the individual to acquire knowledge of the Being.

1.4.2 Harman's Theory

Harman (1972, 1974, 1988) describes a conception of human knowledge that corresponds to a metaphysical vision of life. The main characteristics of this conception are as follows:

- Knowledge will be inclusive and no longer exclusive. The distinctions among science, religion, and humanism will be attenuated. As much importance will be given to subjective experience as to objective experience.

- Science will be eclectic in its method and in its definition of science. Controlled experimentation will no longer be the only way to find the truth. Complementarity and relationships will be sought; reductionisms will lose their intrinsic value.

- The new paradigm of knowledge will be open to all attempts to systematize subjective experience.

- Science will no longer be based on the dichotomy of observer/observed or investigator/subject. Rather, we will encourage trust in collaboration and shared research.

- Science will no longer seek objective neutrality and will assert itself as moral and connected to human life.

- Science will try to reconcile such dichotomies as freedom/determinism, materialism/transcendentalism, science/religion.

- The new paradigm will take into account the levels of consciousness as well as appropriate concepts and metaphors.

- The metaphysical paradigm will encourage a total vision of diverse experiences such as creativity, intuition, mysticism, religious experiences, and psychic phenomena.

We will now look at the teaching strategies recommended by Harman. Harman maintains that the education peculiar to the new society must strongly emphasize the quest for the divine center. Its goal is therefore the search for the absolute and it is based on a "technology that changes the individual," which facilitates this quest for the absolute by ensuring the development of the multiple aspects of consciousness. According to Harman, education should serve the individual, allow him or her to accomplish an inner journey, and make it easy to come out of his or her shell.

With a different approach, education would be a transition toward a superior form of knowledge. Harman (1974) mentions several authors who wrote about the unidimensionality of our everyday perception of things, including Eckhart, Huxley, and Plato. He also cites Arthur Koestler who describes in *The Invisible Writing* (1954) the three stages of knowledge: first the sensorial perception, then the conceptual world, and finally the extra-conceptual world or the occult. Each level includes the previous one: the second stage fills the gaps of the first one and gives a meaning to the absurd disparity of the tangible world; the third stage demonstrates that the spatio-temporal limits of the self are purely an illusion.

Finally, Harman (1974) takes up Bucke's thoughts (1901) with regard to the cosmic consciousness at the highest level. Perception of life and the order of the universe are accompanied by an intellectual enlightenment, a moral exaltation, and an indescribable feeling of joy. It is called the sense of immortality or the consciousness of eternal life.

Harman (1974) conceives of educational activities as a technology to change the individual according to a philosophy of existential transcendentalism. Chart 1.1 presents some elements of this technology and its results.

Obviously, the organization of educational activities is centered on the student. The goal is to promote the growth of the individual. Because the main agent of education is the student,

Chart 1.1 Metaphysical technology

Elements of the technology	Results
Meditation, yoga, psychedelic drugs, hypnosis, self-hypnosis	Awareness of the spiritual dimensions of the transcendental self
Sensorial awareness	Openness to sensations, emotions, beauty
Self-awareness exercises, group therapies	Honesty, openness to human relationships
Training groups, Gestalt therapies, sensitivity training	Spontaneous response to experience, to self-expression, to individual autonomy, to emotional freedom
Psychodrama	Release of the feelings of guilt and fear rooted in religious experiences
New theatre, underground press	Repression of the self by social institutions, radicalization of conflicts

students determine the desirable pedagogical progress. They choose the courses that, in their opinion, will help their personal development the most. They evaluate their own progress and choose the necessary corrections. The teacher is a resource and helps the student, whatever his or her request, cognitive or affective. In short, the organization of educational activities is characterized by the flexibility and multiplicity of the services provided for the student.

1.4.3 Leonard's Theory

You cannot function, writes Leonard (1968), in an educational system that is conservative, repressive, boring, and based on evaluation. The current system impedes learning. It hypnotizes the students by making them absorb the current social values and makes it very difficult for any form of criticism or liberation. The students have the illusion that they are learning, and sitting in the classroom, they have the impression that they are working and acquiring personal discipline.

Paradoxically, Leonard notes, the traditional system causes passivity and irresponsibility. Order is only a matter of appearances in a classroom where all the students are busy taking notes.

The teacher is a slave to a system: he or she perpetuates it and does not dare question it.

Leonard (1968, 1971, 1978, 1981, 1987) proposes an approach to education that is connected to enjoyment and to life. Following the same line of thought as Maslow, Alan Watts, Krishnamurti, and John Rowan, Leonard states that the natural condition of the human organism is joy. You can feel yourself being swept away by a new force, he says, a new energy that shows through ecstasy.

Ecstasy is a state in which individuals find themselves transported outside of themselves and out of the tangible world, into contact with the Consciousness of the universe. They free themselves from an anthropocentric vision and move toward a cosmic vision: they are no longer the center of the universe. They forget about their trifling domestic troubles to return to the fundamental rhythm and *joie de vivre*. And it is this *joie de vivre* that stirs up an ecstasy.

This 'new' vision of life necessarily requires an ecstatic conception of education. One must find, says Leonard, other educational settings, more joyful and less repressive than the current schools. Ecstatic education allows us to feel pleasure in learning and, at the same time, reconciles learning and life, reason and emotions.

Education in the joy of learning, says Leonard (1987), is based on a mystical approach to our interactions with the universe. Mystical education is founded on a body of texts coming out of humanistic psychology, on the literature of Eastern philosophy, and on mystical texts. According to Leonard, mysticism should be interpreted as the belief in a unification of the self in a bigger whole, called God or the unity of the universe. Although the names vary according to each religion or philosophy, this fundamental belief is generally based on an intuitive, metaphysical, or ecstatic experience that is hard to describe, since it happens within the individual.

Education must carry out two tasks. The first one is, in a way, a liberation from the everyday considerations that limit education to merely technical and utilitarian learning. It includes a phase of liberation from the educational system in its present conception. This phase of liberation is difficult but essential. To escape the traditional frames of thought and to learn to function creatively requires a lot of effort.

The second task of ecstatic education is to help the student acquire an inner discipline similar to that of the creative artist, a new sense of the cosmic responsibility and the intuitive knowledge most often called wisdom. The student must learn to base his or her life on such principles as sharing, creativity, friendship, cooperation, empathy, and openness. And it is the student who controls his or her learning.

Meditation and the reading of sacred texts and mystical works are the favorite pedagogical strategies of ecstatic education. Meditation is an exercise that allows the two spheres of the psyche, separated at birth, to find each other again in a certain unity. These two spheres are the conscious and the unconscious: the conscious is the element that marks difference and individualization in a person, while the unconscious is the element that unites the individual to the cosmos.

Unification of the two elements through meditation is the principle on which this form of education is based. The unconscious has to be inseminated by the conscious that lies within it. Thus, the unconscious, activated and combined with the enriched conscious, reaches a supra-personal mental level in the form of a personal and spiritual renewal. This renewal then leads to a progressive inner differentiation of the state of consciousness into autonomous structures of thought.

The last phase of meditation leads to the obliteration of all differences. This integration phase produces a liberation of all the oppositions that the individual faces every day within himself or herself. From then on, there is no more distinction between subject and object. There are no more dichotomies in the mind.

Transcendental education results in liberation from the dichotomies between the individual and the universe, to find a direct access to unity, without any categorization. These dichotomies are a source of ignorance. To concentrate on the self, says Leonard, leads directly to ignorance.

To sum up, according to Leonard, education must be mystical, full of energy and joy, even ecstatic, and it must liberate us from all dichotomies. It should allow the birth of a new individual in each of us and of new, more cosmic relationships with the universe.

1.4.4 Ferguson's Theory

Ferguson (1980) also proposes a description of the transpersonal education necessary to that spiritual renewal. We must reject, she says, the current conception of education.

Our system of education is bureaucratic, more preoccupied with correctness than with openness. Schools are the instruments of a truncated vision of reality. They break up experience and human knowledge into subject areas and undermine the continuity of knowledge. They impede the growth of young people. Ferguson (1980, p. 34) protests:

> Young minds are dampened and diminished every day in numbers too great to bear thinking about, forced through a system that stunts the capacity for a lifetime of growth. In contrast to insects, as someone said, human beings start out as butterflies and end up in cocoons.

Organization of education, in a transpersonal perspective, must be in line with the following principles (Ferguson, 1980):

- Transpersonal education can take place anywhere because it is independent of the educational system. It does not need schools. But it can also be provided in the current system. It is also independent from time: education is a process that continues throughout an entire lifetime.

- Transpersonal education starts with the students, their desires and their needs. Learning is viewed as a journey, an inner experience, a transformation of the self. Ferguson tells us:

  > In transpersonal education the learner is encouraged to be awake and autonomous, to question, to explore all the corners and crevices of conscious experience, to seek meaning, to test outer limits, to check out frontiers and depths of the self (p. 287).

- Transpersonal education "emphasizes the continuum of knowledge, rather than 'subjects' " (p. 288). It opposes too much theorization of content matter, compartmentalization into subject areas, required programs, and separation into age groups. It includes field trips, demonstrations, and visits to specialists.

- Transpersonal education does not prioritize the acquisition of knowledge. It focuses on learning to learn. One should learn to ask the right questions, to find information, and to be open to new concepts.

- Transpersonal education likes analytical thought but is more interested in divergent thought, imagination, and, above all, intuition.

> Without intuition, we would still be in the cave. Every breakthrough, every leap forward in history, has depended on right-brain insights, the ability of the holistic brain to detect anomalies, process novelty, and perceive relationships (p. 297).

This is why, Ferguson notes, keeping a diary of dreams, 'concentration' exercises, and the exploration of feelings should be encouraged.

- Transpersonal education does not impose learning. The teacher respects the autonomy of the student and yet avoids laxity. Ferguson says:

> The open teacher helps the learner discover patterns and connections, fosters openness to strange new possibilities, and is a midwife to ideas. The teacher is a steersman, a catalyst, a facilitator — an agent of learning, but not the first cause (p. 292).

Ferguson concludes that school cannot by itself provide a holistic education. The whole community has to get involved, as in Plato's times:

> Educators are belatedly examining a holistic Greek concept, the *paidea* [paideia]. The paidea referred to the educational matrix, created by the whole of Athenian culture, in which the community and all its disciplines generated learning resources for the individual, whose ultimate goal was to reach the divine center in the self (p. 307).

1.4.5 Fotinas' Theory

Fotinas presents a metaphysical theory of education in several works, the most important of which is *Le Tao de l'éducation*

(1990). Drawing his material from the great Muslim, Buddhist, and Hindu traditions, and especially from Lao-Tzu's *The Book of the Way and Its Virtue*, Fotinas has abandoned a personalist pedagogy to build a theory of education that he calls metaphysical or transpersonal (Fotinas and Henry, 1993). Fotinas defines this theory as "any condition that, by its structure and its functions, promotes and facilitates the growth of the Individual according to his or her nature and which aims to better Education and the Learner."

Adopting the style of Taoism and taking up completely the principles of *The Book of the Way and Its Virtue*, Fotinas (1990) describes the paradoxes of education and the course of education, and criticizes utilitarian education that makes us experts but takes us farther away from true knowledge. He proposes an education that is concerned with the part of the world and of ourselves that cannot be named.

The Great Education is without educations; it aspires to supreme Virtue, he says. "Supreme Virtue is without virtues; this is why it is Virtue." The Great Education emerges from the depths of the individual and the world. It's empty yet inexhaustible. That is its paradox.

As Fotinas (1990) writes, its knowledge is a non-knowledge. It manifests itself through a total silence, without desires, and is achieved through deep contemplation without action. The teacher is someone who accepts the responsibility of contributing to the education of other people who are looking for the course of their development and their destiny. He or she is the master who hands down the message of the masters of tradition. The teacher must reach deep within himself or herself, that is, within the universe of the "eternal Knowledge, thorough and inexhaustible, which is a rule and a guide for development."

Fotinas (1990) writes:

> The Teacher who has passed the Gate without a gate lets himself or herself be taught by the traditional doctrine; he or she tries to act according to the Masters of Tradition. Few are the teachers who have reached the Mystery, so that it becomes enlightenment. The Learner is someone who willingly entrusts an Educator with the responsibility for his or her development, with respect for his or her nature and improvement.

1.5 Conclusion

One can understand how spiritualistic, metaphysical or transpersonal (Fotinas), transcendental (Harman), and ecstatic (Leonard) theories of education insist on going beyond the distinctions between the individual and the universe, since these two entities constitute a whole. These educational approaches are not pedagogies of the subject or the individual, the way it is understood in humanistic, Rogerian, libertarian, or open pedagogies.

The center of this educational approach is not the individual, but rather the individual as a part of the universe. The focus is not the development of the subject, but rather the relationship of the individual as part of a larger Whole. Nor is it the existence of a truth independent from the individual.

Krishnamurti (1970) writes that you cannot depend on anyone. There is no guide, no teacher, no authority. There are only individuals in relation to others and to the world. There is not anything else.

The transcendency of the subject, the detachment from all subjectivity, is at the center of this spiritual knowledge. It is the relationship to the divine, the mystical, that is, the intuitive experiences of the unity. It is the cosmic consciousness that is at the center of the experience that some will call pure subjectivity, insofar as it has detached itself from the individual characteristics of consciousness. The self disappears into a more global experience of its relationship to the Universe.

Transcendental education consists precisely of escaping the dichotomies between object and subject, the individual and the universe, in order to reach the Unity. It includes the following operations: listening, receptivity, intuition, love, the gift of the self, and spiritual synergy.

Krishnamurti, Leonard, and Watts maintain that it leads to true joy, to a certain rapture, to a great pleasure in learning, and to ecstasy. However, as Rowan reminds us in his excellent book, *Ordinary Ecstasy* (1976), ecstasy is both an ordinary *and* an extraordinary characteristic of everyday life. One cannot always be in ecstasy.

Chapter 2

Personalist Theories

The personalist trend — also called humanistic, libertarian, or organic — is characterized by its focus on the internal dynamic of the person: needs, aspirations, desires, impulses, energy, etc.

2.1 On Becoming a Person

Student-centered education came as a reaction against training systems that placed too much emphasis on teaching subject matter using transmission methods — mostly lecturing — to large audiences. Most of those who wrote on the subject felt the need to voice their opposition to the mainstream of education. They principally objected to the low priority given to subjectivity, freedom, and the student in education.

Consequently, they tried to shift the focus of pedagogical concerns back to the *subjective dynamism* of students. Philippe Meirieu (1991) uses the expression *construction of a free person*, which perfectly sums up the general theme of all the theories of education presented in this chapter. Lucie Léveillé Ryan (1990) gives a good description of the personalist — also called humanistic — position:

> To speak of a humanistic approach is to evoke a whole trend of American psychology influenced to a large extent, since World War II, by the European philosophies of existential phenomenology. One could define a human being — child or adult — by the life projects that lead them to invent themselves as free and responsible human beings, to become embodied in their never achieved and always growing 'humanness.'
>
> Finally, one should understand creative education as an educational experience that focuses on the existential creativity of human beings and the continuous

development of their whole potential through educational activities that make sense to them, affect them, and transform them in all their personal dimensions. From an ecological and humanistic point of view, mutuality and reciprocity of the teacher-student relationship foster this continuous self-actualization through an evolving method of free and spontaneous creative expression, in which to create means to create oneself.

2.1.1 History and Problems

Three sources of inspiration are generally singled out in the evolution of the personalist theories of education. First, there were the pioneers who conducted experiments. Then came the psychologists who developed a theory on the way a person functions. Finally, there is research on how a person functions in a group. We will now examine each of these sources.

First Source: The Pioneers of the New Schools

One of the first sources of inspiration for the personalist theories of education was probably the educational work done by several pedagogues at the beginning of the twentieth century.

Among these was A.S. Neill, founder of the Summerhill School in England, who published *A Dominie's Log*. The educational theory that was to revolutionize education in the industrial world emerged from this journal. However, it is the publication of *Summerhill* in 1960 that caused a major stir and led to the creation of free schools. The impact of the book was such that Neill was asked to write another, to explain the limits of the freedom that should be given to the child. He did so in 1966 with *Freedom, Not License!*

Note that this English educational movement, centered on the autonomous development of the child, had followers in other countries, such as France, Germany, and Italy. Thus, Maria Montessori, drawing on the organic philosophy of Cesare Lombroso (Montessori, 1913), proposed an educational approach centered on the individual. Lombroso was an Italian anthropologist and a firm believer in the theories of Jean-Jacques Rousseau, who made it a matter of principle not to impose on his own children any rule, any limitation, any tradition, and to let them develop their natural tastes and dispositions without restraint (Le Hénaff, 1937).

The notion of *new school* was fashionable at the end of the 19th century as well. Adolphe Ferrière (1925) tells us that the name "new school" was chosen by Cecil Reddie, who founded the first institution of this kind in 1889 in England (Skidelsky, 1969). The sociologist Édmond Demolins imported the concept to France, where in 1889 he established the École des Roches, in Verneuil-Sur-Avre. In Germany, Hermann Lietz called these schools *Land-Erziehungsheime*, meaning "educational homes in the country." However, the most recent of these schools — at least those that have extended the practice of self-management to the entire school community — are called *Freie-Schulgemeinden* ("free school communities").

Second Source: Personalist Psychology

Personalist theories of education were also inspired by personalist psychology. This psychology came as a reaction against deterministic psychologies, which maintained that we are controlled either by our unconsciousness or by our environment.

Several psychologists tried to avoid the dichotomy between the determinism of the unconsciousness and the determinism of the environment, and then began to look for a third course. They tried to propose an interactional conception of the person, called personalist psychology.

Abraham Maslow, discussed in Chapter 1 in terms of his contributions to spiritualistic theories, was also an important figure in personalist thinking. Maslow named this movement, made up of different schools, the *third force*.

Maslow's third-force psychology dismisses both the Freudian conception of the human as a creature dominated by his or her lower instincts and the behaviorist conception of the human as an animal that responds mechanically to the stimuli of the environment. Maslow and other researchers designed a new image of the human being: one that possesses an inborn love and develops his or her potential through contributing to the good of society.

Max Pagès introduced the first personalist ideas in France. Education, says Pagès (1965), should consist of significant or experiential learning. He maintains that the traditional approach makes significant learning unlikely, even impossible. Pagès proposes an alternative that allows the individual to experience optimal psychological growth, to be a person who functions freely in the fullness of his or her organismic possibilities, to be reliable, realistic, and socialized, and to be creative and ever-evolving.

The alternative should be a program that:

- Restores and stimulates curiosity
- Encourages students to work in accordance with their interests and to set for themselves goals that appeal to them
- Provides students with all the resources — texts, laboratories, etc. — and thus feeds their interests
- Lets students make and assume responsible choices
- Lets students participate in designing the program
- Is oriented toward the future
- Provides interactive situations
- Is focused on the real problems of individuals
- Lets students evaluate themselves
- Provides students with means to solve problems creatively

Third Source: T-Group Theory
A third source of inspiration comes from the work of Kurt Lewin (1935), who was a leading influence in the United States and in Europe, with his dynamic theory of personality. In 1935, he laid down the following principle: development is based on an inner need embodied in an object, a goal, a utopia, and is then defined as an extension of the vital space of the child in accordance with certain objectives.

Lewin also determined the conditions necessary for developing an objective vision of reality. The child forms a vision of reality according to two conditions: the resistance of things to his or her own will and the experience of the concrete difficulties to be overcome in the pursuit of his or her aims. The child lives an intense experience: reality is independent of his or her desires.

Lewin was then able to bring out a fundamental principle of pedagogy: the formation of an explicit layer of objective realities and necessities — which is certainly pedagogically desirable —

presupposes the existence of a whole situation in which the child can determine his or her goals and act freely according to his or her own needs and judgment. Objectivity cannot develop amid constraints; it develops only in a situation of freedom. Lewin thus demonstrated the interdependence of the child's development and certain conditions necessary to this development.

We should also point out the influence of the National Training Laboratory (NTL), which stressed using groups. Indeed, the idea of developing the individual through the group comes to a large extent from the NTL, which created the *T-Group* (training group). This intervention strategy has been applied in several countries since the late 1960s, and a large number of teachers have become aware of its importance.

The aim of the training group (Bradford *et al.*, 1964) is to summon up the strengths of a group in order to support the growth of its members as unique individuals and as collaborators. Influences among peers are vital in this learning process. In the training group, members develop their own abilities by giving and receiving help — which is why it is a relatively unstructured group in which members act as students. The learning material does not come from outside the group; it is directly connected to the life experiences of the participants. The material consists of the relationships among members, their behaviors within the group as they struggle to organize themselves and to stimulate and support each other's learning within this micro-society.

What about individuals? They can learn to know their motivations, feelings, and strategies when they establish relationships with other people. They also learn to know the reactions they bring about in others. By confronting their intentions and their effects, they locate the barriers to their total and autonomous functioning in relationships with other people. From this, they develop new images of their possibilities and seek help from others in order to develop their potential.

In other words, the NTL offered a solution to the problem of the pedagogical organization of this approach: the group. It is the group that was going to allow the concretization of a pedagogy centered on personal development and construction of an educational environment.

2.1.2 Two Trends

All these diverse influences gave rise to different personalist trends, two of which are very important. In their book, *Personal Models of Teaching* (1978), Marsha Weil, Bruce Joyce, and Bridget Kluwin divided the "personal" teaching models in the following way:

- Pedagogies centered on developing affectivity through nondirective strategies
- Pedagogies centered on developing creativity through more interventionist strategies

This distinction is still valid now, since it allows us to clearly see the main trends in personalist theories. We will analyze two trends:

- Nondirective education, represented by Rogerian pedagogy and neo-humanistic pedagogies (Constantin Fotinas)
- Interactional pedagogy, represented primarily by organic pedagogy (Pierre Angers), open education (André Paré), and self-development pedagogy (Claude Paquette)

2.2 Nondirective Education

2.2.1 History and Problems

One cannot ignore the impact of Carl Rogers on education in anglophone and francophone countries. His influence started in the early 1950s in francophone countries. For instance, as early as 1950, Pagès is talking about nondirective psychotherapy and admits to drawing most of his inspiration from Rogers.

Rogers is an American psychologist well-known for his approach to psychotherapy, called nondirective, client-centered, or person-centered. As early as 1930, he proposed a psychology with a personalist orientation, focused on the dynamics of personality change. While working at several American universities in the 1940s and 1950s, he published such important books as *Counseling and Psychotherapy* (1942) and *Client-Centered Therapy* (1951). Rogers caused the greatest stir in the 1960s and 1970s, with such works as *On Becoming a Person* (1961), *Freedom to Learn* (1969), and *Carl Rogers on Encounter Groups* (1970).

2.2.2 Principles

Through the years, Rogers tried to explain the many parts of one fundamental principle: all individuals have a positive orientation. Thus, Rogers was led, through his various clarifications, to create a vocabulary, even a language, that was to become quite popular in psychotherapy and work relations, and that was to leave his mark on educational thinking and practice.

Rogers insists that we must be ourselves, authentic, empathic, congruent, and recognize what is real in ourselves. We should feel things, trust our experience, listen to ourselves, express what we truly feel, accept ourselves as we are, and rely on our judgment, he says (1969). We must also accept others as they are, with their good qualities and their shortcomings. Ultimately, wisdom is more in each person's inner feelings than in an intellectual overlay. "Experience is, for me," Rogers notes (1961, p.23), "the highest authority."

These attitudes, writes Rogers (1969), are the conditions for change. To change someone is to allow him or her to change. We should follow our own interpretation of our personal experience and let others live their own freedom. Rogers makes a statement in *On Becoming a Person* (1961) that sums up his whole philosophy of intervention:

> It is a very paradoxical thing — that to the degree that each one of us is willing to be himself, then he finds not only himself changing; but he finds that other people to whom he relates are also changing (p. 22).

2.2.3 Strategies

Promoting Experiential Learning
Rogers is interested in what he calls experiential learning, characterized by the following features (1969):

- It is, first of all, a personal commitment, involving the whole person.

- Learning is based on the student's initiatives.

- Learning goes deep and changes the student's behavior, attitude, and personality.

- Students evaluate their own learning.

- Humans have a natural ability to learn. They are curious and want to grow as much and as long as their experiences of the school system do not ruin this appetite.

- Significant learning occurs when students understand the relevance of the knowledge to be acquired.

- Learning that implies a change in self-organization or self-perception is regarded as a threat, which we tend to resist.

- This learning that threatens the self is more easily perceived and assimilated when external threats are reduced to a minimum.

- When the threat against the self is weak, life experience can be perceived differently and learning can occur.

- Action facilitates significant learning. We often understand and remember things better by doing them. We remain affected by learning in this way.

- Learning is made easier when students share responsibility in the learning process. In fact, learning is maximized when students define their own problems, choose their own resources, determine their own procedures, and live with the consequences of their choices.

- Self-determined instruction, in which students are entirely committed — with their feelings as much as with their intelligence — sinks in deepest and is remembered longest.

- Students acquire a greater independence of mind, more creativity, and better self-confidence when they consider self-criticism and self-evaluation fundamental, and evaluation by others secondary.

- Learning the learning processes is socially the most useful learning in our world. That also means learning to always remain open to our own experience and incorporating into ourselves the process of change. The condition for renewing our society is that people accept change.

The Role of the Teacher

Rogers notes (1969) that traditional teaching — with its program requirements, lectures, and exams — does not foster experiential learning, which is the only kind of learning that makes sense to students. In short, students should be free to teach themselves.

Then what can the teacher do? Actually, very little, according to Rogers (1961), who uses such pithy expressions as: "It seems to me that anything that can be taught to another is relatively inconsequential, and has little or no significant influence on behavior," or "I have come to feel that the only learning which significantly influences behavior is self-discovered, self-appropriated learning" (p. 276).

Rogers also lists the qualities required to provide or restore the freedom to learn, i.e., the qualities of a facilitator. In *Freedom to Learn* (1969), Rogers answers the question, "How can I transform myself to further encourage my students to be free to learn?" (pp. 164-166)

- The facilitator plays an important role in setting the initial mood in the classroom. He or she should trust the group and the individuals.

- The facilitator helps students choose and clarify their objectives and their intentions as well as those of the whole group. He or she should also accept the fact that these objectives may well be contradictory.

- The facilitator relies on the desire of each student to carry out the projects that make sense to him or her. The facilitator helps students transform their desires into motivational energy.

- The facilitator tries to organize and to make available the widest possible range of learning resources: written material, people, and audio-visual equipment.

- The facilitator considers himself or herself a resource, an advisor, or expert for the group to use as they please.

- By responding to what is said in class, the facilitator accepts both intellectual content, such as rationalizations, and emotional attitudes. He or she tries especially to accept the particular importance attached to these aspects by the person or the group, as the case may be.

- As the climate of acceptance develops in the classroom, the facilitator becomes a participant in the collective learning process. He or she is a member of the group, and as such, expresses his or her point of view.

- The facilitator takes the initiative to share with the group his or her feelings or thoughts, in an undemanding and unimposing way. This initiative is merely a sharing of the self, which students can accept or reject.

- Through the whole experience of the class, the facilitator remains attentive to expressions of deep or violent feelings and accepts tensions within the group.

- As a learning facilitator, the teacher has to acknowledge and accept his or her own limitations. To give freedom to students is a risk that the facilitator has to assume. Should the occasion arise, he or she should also express his or her worries, angers, and fears.

2.3 Neo-Humanistic Theories

2.3.1 History and Problems

There is a whole host of theories of education that fit into a personalist or humanistic perspective, that are not directly inspired by Rogers, and that are defined as neo-humanistic. One of their sources was Vienna, with Sigmund Freud and his circle.

Alfred Adler was a psychologist who worked with Freud at the beginning of the century, but who broke away from his mentor in 1911, to create the Society for Individual Psychology in 1914. In contrast to Freud, Adler proposed a psychology in which individuals are controlled neither by their instincts nor by society. The individual is a creative force that has to rely on its heredity and the influences of its environment (Ansbacher and Adler, 1964).

Adler greatly influenced the evolution of personalist psychology in Europe, and particularly in America in the 1930s, when many European intellectuals fled from Nazism. Thus, Maslow and Erich Fromm met Adler in seminars that he was teaching in New York (Goble, 1970). Adler died in 1937.

A group of psychologists then formed an association under Rudolf Dreikurs in Chicago. These psychologists (Fromm,

Maslow, and Dreikurs) had a profound influence on educational thinking, especially during the 1950s and 1960s, and directed this thinking toward pedagogies concerned with personal development. We will now see one example of a school that still uses these pedagogies.

2.3.2 Principles

Fotinas developed a neo-humanistic theory of education that tried to reconcile a systemic approach and a humanistic philosophy inspired by Adlerian psychology and, more precisely, by the Dreikurs Chicago School. This theory has evolved with time.

At first, it was a fringe psychology tested in a laboratory, called the café-school. Fotinas suggested that training programs be redirected toward personal development and the quality of personal life. We find the following statement in Fotinas and Torossian (1977):

> Human beings have been diverted from their own great projects — science, art, technology, economy, education — by their own accomplishments. They are now claiming a central place in their universe. They are now defining themselves as the project, their main project, and redefining other projects according to their well-being.

Anthropo-biological, anthropo-social, and anthropo-educational processes constitute the foundations of human existence, according to Fotinas and Torossian (1977). These authors remind us that the café-school approach is in keeping with contemporary movements in third-force psychology, called personalist or humanistic, and with the general theory of systems.

The purpose of their course, "Cinematographic Language in a Learning Situation: Production and Use of Educational Film" (Fotinas and Torossian, 1977), is to train participants in education, producers and users who will contribute to creating learning situations centered more on the person than on information or management. Specific objectives are open, since didactic methodology suggests that in learning situations, "self-learners" should set their own objectives and evaluation criteria.

In short, the exploratory experiential method offers students a didactic framework for action and thought that will allow them, with the appropriate environment and facilitators, to define their objectives, their methods, and their evaluations within the situation. The curriculum is determined from day to day according to their needs as they arise.

2.3.3 Strategies

Pedagogical Phases
This method is based on a predefined and systematized pedagogical structure. The path, however, is determined by students according to their needs.

The Fotinas neo-humanistic pedagogy includes six phases:

1. *Unrefined praxis* (exploratory action-reflection), which includes a stage for clarifying personal values, needs, and motivations, as well as a stage for entering into a situation based on problems.

2. *Conscientization* of the unrefined praxis (study and analysis), which includes a stage for clarifying the problem situation and a stage for choosing significant problems to resolve.

3. *Exchanges in full-class session* (presentation of phases 1 and 2).

4. *Conscious praxis* (systematic action-reflection), which includes a stage for collecting data through readings, consultations, and viewings, a stage for clarifying learning objectives defined in terms of abilities to be acquired, and a stage for undertaking significant experiences, such as a research film, theoretical research, etc.

5. *Evaluation of the conscious praxis* (systematic study and analysis): evaluation of learning (i.e., abilities) and an evaluation of experienced values and created attitudes.

6. *Exchanges in full-class session* (presentation of phases 4 and 5).

All in all, students are directed in their process of self-determination. The pedagogy is an open method, since it proposes a humanistic introspection. Such activities as meditation and relaxation help each student develop his or her own method and personalized curriculum.

A Personal Path

This pedagogy, applied in college, was modified as it was being used and, in 1992, resulted in an approach that was more structured, as much in its positions as in its practice. In *L'art de vivre en éducation* (1992), Fotinas and Henri wrote a series of questions in the spirit of Adlerian pedagogy:

1. Who am I as a person and as a teacher or a student?

2. How do I act as a person and as a teacher or a student?

3. Why?

4. Am I satisfied with what I am and what I do?

5. How can I get involved in what I am and what I do?

The students have to answer these questions. Their answers constitute the basis of their learning: they learn to recognize their feelings (love, anger, desire, etc.), their thoughts, their positive and negative behaviors, and their physical sensations. They learn to know their individual logic, that of their actual experience.

Thus, in a course on defense mechanisms, for example, students will have certain learning objectives. Here is an excerpt of that list (Fotinas and Henry, 1992):

1. To explore personal situations of aggression

2. To identify personal feelings, thoughts, and actions in situations of aggression

3. To identify the personalities and actions that most threaten our well-being

4. To develop the ability to accuse and attack intentionally (and not compulsively)

5. To know the different kinds of existing social or self-defense mechanisms

6. To identify and recognize our personal profile
   of social defense

The Teacher: A Facilitator

The teacher plays the role of a facilitator. He or she brings
students to live significant experiences that help them penetrate
into their experiences, their innermost heart. There are many
pedagogical techniques for doing so, which Fotinas and Henry
(1992) call endoscopy ("the exploration of the infinitely deep
and personal aspect of the individual"). To develop specific
physical consciousness in students, the teacher-facilitator can use
different types of passive and active relaxations, concentrations,
meditations, energetic gymnastics, daydreams, tai chi chuan,
archetypal dancing, minimalist dancing, free physical expression,
and improvisation.

It must be understood that this pedagogy requires a certain
ambiance not associated with lecture classes. The following is an
excerpt from a presentation Fotinas gave at the beginning of one of
his classes, a presentation that brilliantly created the appropriate
and necessary climate for personal development (Fotinas and
Henry, 1992):

> I love you. I love you; you, "my" students in this
> class. You, sitting on pillows on the floor; you, sitting
> in chairs or on tables, in the back; you, in the front
> and right next to me. I need to love you.

> When I love, I belong. You are "my" students
> because I belong to you.

> When I belong, I function and I feel the desire to
> produce. I produce objects, meaning, life. I can
> produce only with you whom I love. I produce and I
> produce myself. I develop my potential, I become and
> I grow. I need to produce to grow. I need to grow to
> live. I need to live. I love you. ...

> I love you because you have come here with the
> intention of being the way you wish to be. At every
> turn, you will be what you want to be. It is so
> beautiful to be the way you want to be: it is one of
> nature's great miracles. I need you to constantly be in
> class what you want to be, here and now.

This speech nicely illustrates what such a conception of
education means. It also shows how this pedagogy has evolved.

From a systemic approach with a strong emphasis on techniques, it is now closer to metaphysical pedagogies in which there is a certain, more reflective and personal mood.

2.4. Interactive Theories of Personal Development

2.4.1 History and Problems

Nondirective psychologies have led, actually, to interactive pedagogies. It did not take long for nondirectivity to reach its limit: soon teachers felt the need to direct students on the pedagogical path while respecting their individual characteristics.

So there was no more talk of letting students develop without direction or of using socializing approaches in order to transform society. Rather, the point was to use teamwork processes and strategies with a view to facilitating individual development. Although certain interactive pedagogies rely on the inner dynamism of the student, they do not shift the whole educational responsibility to him or her. Teachers share power with their students. Hence the idea of interactive pedagogy. There is cooperation, then, but always with the following objective: to develop the student.

The organic theory of education is a good example of this dynamic between the individual and the group. This theory was popularized in Quebec at the beginning of the 1970s, with the publication of a report by the Conseil supérieur de l'éducation, entitled *L'activité éducative* (1971).

This report presented education as an activity that originates in the inner life of the person. Education is always the result of a personal process, the center and dynamism of which are to be found in the student, in the growth and development of the personality as it learns. Education should therefore focus on the underlying resources of the individual rather than on acquisition of cultural and technical knowledge, since personal development is more important than acquisition of subject matter. Teaching should help students develop their creativity, imagination, spontaneous expression, personal autonomy, ability to evaluate, and judgment.

At the same time, a voluminous report, based on research dating back to 1968 and entitled *Opération Départ* (1971), also presented the organic conception of educational activity. The report advanced the fundamental elements of a person-centered conception of education.

This conception fit into a system designed to enhance the conditions favorable to personal development and multiply the means of self-education; to offer services accessible in time and space to anyone wanting to satisfy his or her need to love and be loved, and to know and create; to offer resources unconditionally by helping people decide for themselves how to use them; and to constantly create and modify structures promoting the emergence of the unpredictable and a favorable attitude toward it.

2.4.2 Principles

The Person: A Relational Being
The *Opération Départ* report included some remarks on the social dimension of the individual. With regard to criticism of the asociability of this conception, the authors of the report answered that, on the whole, they perceived the individual to be a rational being right from the start. To experience oneself is, at the same time, to experience others and the social element, they said. To become oneself always proceeds from an inner space filled with the diffuse presence of others and the social element. If we did not know this from experience, perceptual psychology would teach us that the more an individual develops his or her potential, the more he or she becomes social, realistic, positive, and capable of creatively modifying his or her environment and adjusting to it.

The concept of "self-learning" was actually created by this group. Learning is something that happens first and foremost within ourselves. It is an experience that originates, takes place, and ends within the person who self-learns.

An Educational Environment
The concept of "self-learner" presupposes the existence of an educational environment. The educational process is then defined as the structured and dynamic set of interactions between the self-learner and the educational environment, as it is perceived and experienced by the self-learner. This conception of the self-learner is based on a model of the person inspired by the personalist psychology of Rogers, Maslow, and Yves Saint-Arnaud.

The human organism comprises three dimensions:

1. Behavior, which is a set of observable reactions

2. Conceptual field, which is the subjective universe of the person

3. Growth dynamism, which should be understood as:

   • The energy that drives the person

   • The root of the individual's needs, desires, aspirations, and capacities

   • The structuring principle of self-image and of the whole conceptual field

   • The deep-rooted source of all behaviors

Pedagogical application allowed Pierre Angers to increase the dimension of the school environment. Indeed, the self-learner belongs in an environment that fosters his or her development. So Angers built an interactional model of educational activity. He writes (1976):

> It is through intense, prolonged, and fruitful interaction with the object studied that self-learners, using all of their creative forces, build up their proficiencies and acquire mastery in a particular domain.

The purpose of the environment, therefore, is to favor the development of inner resources and autonomous activity in the self-learner. The self-learner is a full person in this interactional field. He or she can exercise the fullness of his or her powers and faculties to know, exert will for autonomous growth and creativity, and thus become capable of taking responsibility for learning and for developing personality. In other words, self-learners freely transform and build themselves.

Knowledge: A Personal Undertaking
Knowledge is a personal undertaking, says Angers (1976). It is acquired and enhanced through interaction with the object; it results from the construction of an inner model by the consciousness of the self-learner, fed and inspired by all the events of that consciousness.

The role of the teacher is essentially to facilitate learning. The teacher plays an important role in the interactional field and has to carry out specific tasks. This type of interactional environment requires him or her to subordinate teaching activities to the learning activities of the self-learner. The teacher sets the goal of promoting interaction between the logic of the discipline and the logic of the path of the self-learner and adapts the environment accordingly, so that it stimulates the natural curiosity of the students. The other functions of the teacher will be to observe and analyze the interactions between self-learner and environment. The teacher should not interfere with this interaction.

Didactics will consist of the study of the organization of professional fields and will take the form of a systematic reflection on the activity of knowing as triggered by the school environment, on the forms of assistance that might be useful to it, and on the conditions of the environment that foster learning and those that do not.

Evaluation will then be an internal dimension of the very process of knowing, for which it will provide substance and completion. Evaluation will be the verification of the mastery acquired by the self-learner, in reference to the inner experience.

How is the relationship between the political and the educational defined? A personalist conception underlies the reflection on the political and the individual, perceived as responsible for economic and political evolution. Angers writes (1976):

> The mainspring of this political action is an act of faith in people: through the forces of their minds and through their freedom. People are capable of creating new things and transforming the established order; and they are personally responsible for that change.

2.5 Open Education

2.5.1 Problems

André Paré and Claude Paquette are two teacher-researchers who wrote a lot about the characteristics of an open education that would be the application of an interactive theory of education.

In three volumes, Paré (1977) presents an organic theory of open education. This model is based on the properties of the organism. There are always sensorial, emotional, and intellectual constituents in any kind of learning. The central factor of all learning is interaction between the self and its environment. We will now try to outline the principal characteristics of this organic theory of education.

The idea of open education is also found in the work of Paquette. His analyses are based on one idea: individuals should be the authors and the actors of their lives. The problem is to break away from one's dependency, to gradually move toward autonomy. The preferred tool is self-analysis, which permits self-reflection and a greater understanding of the inner forces that drive the person — hence the possibility for self-development.

Paquette wrote several books that explain this philosophy of education. According to this researcher and practitioner, to intervene means to influence and educate, to direct this influence. In line with Angers, Paré, and the open education movement that was taking shape in particular in several American movements, Paquette gives a good description in his books of the practical and concrete organization of the intervention that aims at personal self-development within the framework of an open education.

2.5.2 Principles

The Importance of the Person
Paré based his model on a few basic beliefs regarding the person:

- Human beings are the most important things in the world.
- Children are human beings.
- Each individual is unique.
- If an individual is diminished, the whole community is diminished.
- Children are normal when they are born.
- Throughout their lives, human beings change, and they change for the better.
- No growth is possible without a deep commitment.
- Feelings are as important as knowledge.
- The realization of human potential implies freedom.
- Any form of rejection or segregation impedes growth.
- Our task as teachers is to optimize growth.

Optimal Personal Growth

Self-actualization is a more fundamental objective than merely acquiring technical abilities. School has to produce an "actualized" person, i.e., a person who has grown in all his or her dimensions.

Paré refers to Rogers, from whom he draws the concept of *openness to experience*: contact with everything that happens, both externally and internally. We let all existing information come to us; we receive, perceive, and treat it. We become a process, i.e., a fluidity, a constant change in every movement at every moment. We understand that we are constantly changing and we enjoy getting involved in that change. We trust ourselves. Our optimal functioning becomes a guarantee of success when we take new paths. It is on the basis of this past experience that we, as organisms, feel that we are in control of ourselves.

Paquette said the same thing and also supported open education. He wrote in 1976:

> In an open and informal pedagogy, students are thought to have an inner device that allows them to undertake a process of autonomous and personal growth. This growth will happen to the extent that there is an interaction between them and the adapted environment. The teacher will play an important role with the students in adapting this environment. Learning is above all an awareness of the relations that the student will develop in the educational environment. Learning will be diverse and varied. The basic values are autonomy and freedom (to make choices and to assume them).

An Open School

Paré proposes an open school, based on the participation of those who live in it and which allows for optimization of growth. He says (1977) that school should be open and founded on the following principles:

- Focus on learning
- Acceptance of the student as a person
- Construction of a positive self-image
- Development of individuality and originality
- Teachers perceived as partners and guides

- Evaluation understood as an information tool

Paquette (1976) sets forth very clear principles regarding the nature of open education:

1. To allow for personal growth (development of aptitudes) to be individualized by respecting the pace and style of this growth

2. To allow for the personal abilities of each student to be used constantly in a rich and stimulating environment

3. To allow for students to draw meaningful learning from their interaction with the environment

Talking about teacher involvement, Paquette writes (1985):

> It stands to reason that, in open education, the teacher cannot work from a pre-established set of objectives. His or her role is first and foremost to have the students undergo enriching experiences, then help them analyze what they might have learned. Obviously, this pedagogical context leads to questioning certain key elements, such as curriculum, school timetable, and the relationship between student and teacher.

The Curriculum

Paré (1977) proposes a theory of the curriculum that is not based on the systematic and sequential organization of predetermined subject areas, but on the constant evolution of the inner structure of each individual in contact with his or her environment. The curriculum is based on the knowledge of the characteristics of the organism, on the use and mastery of different languages.

Paré (1977) considers the human organism as a data-collecting system, capable of transforming and processing these data in multiple ways (rational and irrational processes) and of generating behaviors. It is understandable, he says, that part of the growth depends on the environment, the way it is organized, the quantity of data it contains, the richness of the stimuli, and the precision and relevance of the feedback that comes from it.

2.6 Conclusion

Jacques Ardoino (1977) says that, in the United States, the schools of Lewin and Rogers have ultimately influenced pedagogical revolutions and different crises within the traditional systems more than the growth of child psychology, considerable as it may be, or research on learning.

On the other hand, Marie-Louise Poeydomenge observes, in her book *L'éducation selon Rogers* (1984), that nondirectivity is in a bad way! In the 1990s, is an obituary all that is left for this movement? The last two books by Howard Kirschenbaum and Valerie Land Henderson (1989) appear to provide a review of a movement from the past. They tell us how it used to be in the good old days of open schools ....

A strange principle can be found in open pedagogies: students should be given principles of self-management. This often leads to a certain paradox: How do we organize a learning environment, when it is the student who should be its main organizer?

This principle has often triggered a strange phenomenon in pedagogical applications: people attempt a pedagogy that is simultaneously directive and nondirective. Personalist or nondirective pedagogies have always had to face this dilemma: How can we organize a learning environment that is both directive and nondirective? How can we direct yet not direct the freedom of the individual?

A choice had to be made. Researchers and teachers turned to teamwork theories, such as cooperative teaching and more spiritualist theories. In other words, a theory centered on the autonomy and the freedom of the individual often takes noninterventionist forms: nonpedagogy (Neill), nondirectivity (Rogers), negative pedagogy (Rousseau, Georges Lapassade), open education (Paré), exploratory experiential pedagogy (Fotinas), and autobiographical histories (Lapassade). It often leads to more organized educational interventions, such as group pedagogies.

Chapter 3

Psychocognitive Theories

Psychocognitive theories are concerned with the development of cognitive processes in the student, such as reasoning, analysis, problem-solving, representations, prior conceptions, mental images, etc. The foundations of these educational theories are often found in the cognitivist psychological research that investigated diverse aspects of learning. The cognitivist theories are more interested in the internal processes of the mind.

3.1   The Construction of Knowledge

Psychology has greatly influenced research in education, and the number of studies dealing with learning processes, cognitive treatment of information, and learner characteristics keeps increasing.

This chapter is an introduction to the body of theories usually described as *constructivist*. Special emphasis will be placed on theories in which students construct knowledge. We will examine with particular attention two trends of the constructivist movement:

- Theories dealing with students' prior conceptions — which we will call "constructivist didactics"
- Theories dealing with students' pedagogical profiles

3.2   Constructivist Didactics

3.2.1   History and Problems

Two people marked the origin of research on learning: Jean Piaget and Gaston Bachelard.

Piaget's work on genetic epistemology has influenced genetic psychology and research on education. Piaget's point of view is fundamentally constructivist. Piaget (1979), who was born in 1896 and died in 1980, concluded toward the end of his life:

> Fifty years of experience have taught us that knowledge cannot be the result of the simple recording of observations without some structuring due to the activities of the individual. Nor can there be (in the human being) innate or *a priori* cognitive structures: only the functioning of intelligence is hereditary and it can generate structures only by organizing successive actions exerted on objects. Consequently, an epistemology in accordance with the fundamental ideas of psychogenesis could not be empiricist or preformist, but could consist only of constructivism, with the continuous elaboration of new operations and structures.

The work of Piaget and the Geneva school made it possible to formulate constructivist theories of education. Researchers in different countries focused their attention on two major aspects of Piagetian theory: first, interaction fields in which the individual constructs his or her knowledge and grows in a more global process of self-regulation and adaptation to his or her environment; and second, the developmental stages of the child.

Piaget's ideas were imported to North America during the 1960s by Canadian and American researchers, notably John Flavell, Edmund Sullivan, and Irving Sigel (Joyce and Weil, 1992). In the 1960s, another American researcher, Lawrence Kohlberg, drew his inspiration from Piaget to formulate a theory on the stages of moral development. Kohlberg devoted twenty years of research to prove the validity of the stages in the moral development of children. This greatly influenced research in the United States (Kohlberg, 1981; Kegan, 1982).

In Quebec, many researchers worked on the different stages described by Piaget. For instance, they researched problems revolving around the "formal operations" phase: Do college students, who are usually between the ages of 17 and 20 and who take science classes, master the formal operations required for understanding?

Bachelard, who was interested in the philosophy of scientific knowledge as early as 1934 in France, was the first researcher to reflect on *learners' prior culture* and epistemological obstacles to learning. Bachelard's remarks are very interesting, especially for science teachers. In 1940, he formulated the following paradox:

> Ignorance is a form of knowledge! Scientists do not see that ignorance is made up of positive, lasting, and interdependent errors. They do not realize that intellectual darkness has a structure and that any correct objective experience should always determine the correction of a subjective error. However, it is not easy to suppress errors one by one. They are coordinated. Scientific thinking can be developed only by suppressing nonscientific thinking. Too often, scientists rely on a fractionized pedagogy, whereas scientific thinking should aim at a total subjective reform. Any real progress in scientific thinking requires a conversion.

Bachelard proposed a constructivist philosophy that influenced many researchers. *The Philosophy of 'No'* (*La philosophie du non*, 1940) is not a negativistic book. On the contrary, it embraces the transformation of the very principles of knowledge and constructivist activity.

Scientific knowledge is an ever-evolving construction: "To properly think about what is real is to take advantage of one's ambitions to modify and alert thought." We can enrich our explanations by rejecting old experience and by opposing those explanations. One should search reality for whatever contradicts previous experiences. "To dialecticize thought," says Bachelard (1940), "is to increase the guarantee of scientifically creating complete phenomena, of regenerating all the degenerated or stifled variables that science and naive thought neglected in their first study."

This is the reason why Bachelard was so interested in Alfred Korzybski's non-Aristotelian logic (1933) and in Stéphane Lupasco's antagonistic dualism. Bachelard had access to an unpublished manuscript by Lupasco when he wrote *La philosophie du non*. This is why he asked scientists to explain their unexpressed intuitions and their dreams in which their seemingly realistic thoughts originate.

Bachelard's philosophy is, therefore, fundamentally dialectical and constructivist. We construct our knowledge through critical examination of our current knowledge and experiences. Consequently, our perception of reality evolves.

Bachelard introduced the concept of *epistemological profile*, which was taken up under different forms in subsequent research. We will now briefly summarize this notion, since it was to have an enormous influence on research in education.

Individuals have a scientific culture that evolves in certain stages. They usually go from naive realism to discursive rationalism. It would be possible, Bachelard adds (1940), to compile albums of epistemological profiles. Bachelard had already written, in *La formation de l'esprit scientifique* (1938):

> I have always been amazed by the fact that science teachers — even more than anyone else, if that is possible — cannot understand that someone does not understand. They have not considered the fact that students come to class with an empirical knowledge that is already formed. The point is not to acquire an experimental culture, but rather to change cultures, to knock down obstacles accumulated by everyday life.

Whole research programs in France, Switzerland, and Quebec later drew their inspiration from Bachelard's paradoxical approach to knowledge. Indeed, many groups of researchers in francophone countries became interested in the phenomenon of prescientific culture in the student. We need only cite the names Jean-Marc Levi-Leblond, Guy Brousseau, André Giordan, Jean-Louis Martinand, and Andrée Tiberghien in France and Switzerland, and Alain Taurisson, Jacques Bordier, Marie Larochelle, Jacques Desautels, Catherine Garnier, Nadine Bednarz, and Claude Janvier in Quebec. The Centre interdisciplinaire de recherche sur l'apprentissage et le développement en éducation (CIRADE, Interdisciplinary Center for Research on Learning and Development in Education, University of Quebec-Montreal) and the Laboratoire en épistémologie et didactique des sciences (Laboratory for Epistemology and Didactics in the Sciences, University of Geneva) are devoting much effort to this research.

3.2.2 Prior Conceptions

Bachelard wrote in *La formation de l'esprit scientifique* (1938) that teachers should remember that their students come to their science classes with empirical knowledge and that the first concern should not be to help them acquire an experimental culture, but rather to change cultures, to overcome the obstacles accumulated through their experiences. This idea was taken up by several researchers in different countries and led to varied didactic applications, especially in science classes. Teachers tried to take into account students' prior knowledge. Larochelle and Desautels (1992) sum up perfectly how this idea was applied to science teaching:

> Even though these theorizations vary, they usually overlap in accordance with the similarity of the questions that inspire them, which can be summarized as follows: How can we imagine the changeover from one conceptual structure (in this case, students' conceptions) to another conceptual structure (scientific conceptions), considering that this process presupposes that the individual performs certain intellectual operations?

Most constructivist didactics are based on the notion of *prior conceptions*. (The literature also uses the following terms: spontaneous conceptions, misconceptions, preconceptions, proto-concepts, and naive conceptions. We will use them interchangeably here, although they all convey particular theories of knowledge, each very distinct from the others for the epistemologist.)

What is the essence of this very important notion of prior conceptions? Some interesting explanations can be found in Giordan and in Larochelle and Desautels.

Larochelle and Desautels (1992) chose the expression "spontaneous conceptions." They maintain that the expressions "preconception" and "misconception" belong to research for which "a norm governs the value of a conception and makes it in a way legitimate. Consequently, a preconception will appear immature or incomplete in comparison with the established norm when, on the other hand, a misconception will be defined as an erroneous conception in comparison with the same norm." To define "spontaneous conception," Larochelle and Desautels (1992) suggest using the definition of representation formulated by Denise Jodelet (1984): "A system of input or reference that serves as the basis for transformation, integration, and appropriation of new or different informative and representative elements." They add:

Thus, on the conceptual level, spontaneous conceptions appear to be the result of interactions between the individual and his or her environment, or explanations peculiar to the individual describing some of his or her interactions with that environment.

Giordan (1990) states that prior conceptions are complex, consisting of questions, operational invariants, semantic and reference frames, and interacting signifiers — all at the same time. Furthermore, they are brought into play according to the situation at issue and adapted to it. These representations are both decoding structures, which give meaning to the collected data, and receiving structures, which make it possible to eventually unify the new data, as necessary. They play an intermediary role, then, between knowledge and the thought structures of the individual: students construct their knowledge in an interaction between their prior conceptions and the data that they are able to collect through them.

Therefore, prior conceptions are not starting points, nor do they result from the construction of knowledge. They are the very instruments of this activity. They constantly reorganize, and new knowledge has to be incorporated into students' pre-existing structures.

In connection with this, David Ausubel (1978) advances the idea of *cognitive bridges*, which Joseph Novak (1987) takes up on the pedagogical level. By analogy with biological phenomena, Piaget includes this mechanism under the idea of "assimilation." Giordan (1990) adds that this assimilation includes an operation of distorting the cognitive structures. A process of knowledge reorganization has to take place. Talking about this, Piaget used the words *accommodation* and *reflecting abstraction*: "Students integrate data from the outside world in their own cognitive organization. New information is treated according to prior acquisitions, but this information also transforms thought designs."

Hence the paradox of this cognitive undertaking: the goal of knowledge is to self-destruct in order to be more attractive! It is both a process and a result. Giordan's position is essentially that self-transformation is a form of self-destruction.

Indeed, it is essential to consider as substratum the everyday tools of thought that the student masters. Prior conceptions correspond to the only instruments students have at their disposal; it is through them that they decode reality. However, at the same time, these conceptions have to be constantly questioned, for they inevitably lead to self-evidence. The fact that an expectation based on a spontaneous model turns out to be erroneous is not enough to replace this model; the expectation is readjusted to fit experience and the explanation is adapted accordingly. More often than not, students will most certainly have to go against their initial conception, but they will be able to do so only after seeing all of its limitations.

3.2.3 Some Constructivist Didactics

Different options emerged among proponents of a didactic treatment of prior conceptions. Two of these options attracted the attention of teachers: the expression of prior conceptions and the struggle against them.

Testing these two options through pedagogical strategies made it possible to formulate criticism that led to two other, more "evolutive" and "self-organizational" constructivist theories: Giordan's allosteric model (1990) and Larochelle and Desautels' epistemological disturbance model (1992).

We will now examine all four of these options.

Expression of Prior Conceptions
The first option considers that expression of prior conceptions is the only way to know. In this context, the teacher creates a starting situation with the objective of leading students to express their conceptions of reality. Then, either through group work or with the whole class, the teacher brings out the various representations, to fit together or to clash. Discussions that result from this lead the students to adopt a detached attitude toward their own ideas, perhaps to develop them and sometimes to reorganize them.

This is a multi-faceted position, says Giordan, that was popular among constructivists in the 1970s and still has a certain appeal, in particular among humanistic or noninterventionist teachers. Clearly influenced by the humanistic movement, this method opposes lecture instruction, in that the teacher centers essentially on the student. The teacher has to be a facilitator and authentic information source.

This method avoids any form of traditional conditioning, since students remain free to function to their fullest potential toward learning whatever they deem significant. Such a pedagogy, which goes well beyond the mere therapeutic aspect, presents some advantages. In particular, it is very useful during initiation phases, with learners of all ages. It is even, says Giordan, an indispensable stage in overcoming certain inhibitions: it restores and stimulates curiosity, boosts self-confidence, develops communication, and encourages learners to choose a certain number of objectives according to their own interests.

According to Giordan (1990) and Larochelle and Desautels (1992), this first option very quickly reaches its limits, in terms of the construction of knowledge. When students are learning basic concepts, this method does not allow them to go significantly beyond their prior conceptions. This is because this pedagogy presupposes a continuity between immediate comprehension of familiar reality and the knowledge being taught, and assumes that one can go from one to the other smoothly, without a break.

Struggle against Prior Conceptions
A second option consists of working against these prior conceptions. Teaching should counter students' representations that are obstacles to learning. According to researchers who promote this hypothesis, prior conceptions are interesting because of the mistakes they reveal. These mistakes do not merely represent an obstacle along the path to knowledge, nor are they due only to what is external to knowledge, but they appear in the very action of acquiring knowledge.

In their most significant applications, these didactic methods begin, as in the previous case, with a phase in which learners express their representations and become aware of them. For what happens from then on, cognitive theorists have advocated several alternatives:

- The teacher can act alone to question initial conceptions.
- The group can play this role, through the debate it allows.
- After the students have expressed their representations, the teacher presents the material in question, then compares it against the expressed prior conceptions, to

show students the gap between what they know and scientific reality.

Such methods are somewhat effective, at certain times and for certain types of learning. However, Giordan (1990) and Larochelle and Desautels (1992) maintain that they cannot be generalized, for reasons related either to their use or to certain unfounded presuppositions. First, after the teacher has the students express their prior conceptions, he or she too often tends to introduce material incidentally, thus bypassing the true learning mechanisms. Second, he or she too often under-estimates the resistance caused by prior conceptions or considers it sufficient to present only one argument or one crucial experience to overcome the obstacles.

Yet we cannot presume to refute prior knowledge directly: it often resists very sophisticated arguments, since it is integrated in a coherent and more comprehensive structure, with its own logical operations and systems of meanings. We should also note that initial representations do not always constitute an obstacle to learning. They show the teacher the distance that remains to be covered and the difficulties that students might encounter (Giordan and Vecchi, 1987; Giordan, 1990).

Larochelle and Desautels (1992) conclude:

> Although explanation and confrontation operations help certain students develop a better understanding of scientific knowledge, that is not so for many others: they do not always perceive the discrepancy between their conceptions and those proposed to them or, if they do, they do not consider it relevant. Finally, students tend to let both conceptions coexist: one (theirs) that is useful in everyday life and the "other" for school exams!

3.2.4 Allosteric Model

The allosteric model (Giordan, 1989 and 1990; Giordan and Girault, 1992), inspired by the way proteins function, offers a didactic alternative. Indeed, total organizational modifications of certain proteins occur under the influence of an additional element. The sequence of amino acids remains the same, but new connections develop between the chains that, in the case of enzymes, significantly modify the structure and thus the intrinsic properties.

By analogy, then, we should imagine an intellectual distortion of the active sites of learners' thought structures. And just as for proteins, this distortion, in a given place, could result in a transformation of the conceptual network. The same data stay in place, but they are neither read nor sorted in the same way, since concepts are connected through relationships that give them new meaning.

Acquisition of conceptual-type knowledge comes both through continuity with the previously acquired knowledge that supplies the questioning, reference, and interpretive frame, and through discontinuity with this knowledge. Giordan tries to understand the nature of this conflictual process by comparing the functioning of the mind to the structure and functioning of an enzyme. Proteins are made up of chains of amino acids joined end to end. The same holds true analogically with knowledge, which is formed by pieces of information. In both cases, it is the various relationships among the chain parts or among the chains themselves that constitute the structure of the macro-molecule.

Giordan upholds the idea of "conceptual active sites" where new data can federate. It is the base of the usual process of data collection, the one generally at work when one reads a newspaper or watches a debate on television. A learner has all the characteristics needed to decode and accept the message directly. Unfortunately, in class, new data cannot be directly integrated into the conceptual structure in place. At best, it is superimposed; most of the time, it is disregarded or remains isolated.

It is essential, Giordan maintains, to deform the learners' thought structure. It is in cases involving deep learning that the allosteric model becomes most meaningful. For, just like the introduction of a new amino acid or oligo-element (allosteric transformation) can totally alter the structure of the protein, so can the learner's conceptual structure change radically when certain new elements are introduced and integrated into the whole.

Such a perspective leads one to stress the importance of structures that exist among concepts. It poses the problem of how these concepts are integrated into an existing structure. Certain concepts then play the role of "intersections," i.e., organizers, while others play a more minor role. Just as the protein establishes preferential functional relationships with oligo-elements or phospholipids at very definite points of its structure, so students learn not by connecting outside pieces linearly, but by bringing this data into relationship with specific sites of their conceptual network.

These sites, which make it possible to decode new information, are activated by learning situations. These sites are also brought into play and transformed in priority to allow the integration of this new data, which brings about the development of a new conceptual level. In the case of basic learning, the new data do not fit directly into prior knowledge, which would most often represent an obstacle to integrating that data.

Therefore, it seems necessary, says Giordan (1990), to go beyond pedagogies that assign a passive role to prior conceptions. Knowledge comes through both continuity and discontinuity with the previously acquired knowledge that provided the questioning frame, for at each level of comprehension, the mental structure of the individual is reorganized according to a new approach to reality.

We know based on our prior knowledge and, at the same time, we learn against this knowledge. It is this conflictual process that researchers propose to study. Indeed, any significant learning results from the activity of a learner who produces meaning based on prior conceptions brought into play and according to situations and information he or she possesses. These representations constitute the learner's decoding grid. These new data are then integrated or rejected by the learner who takes in new knowledge.

Didactic research reveals the reasons for the failure of a number of traditional pedagogical practices, as well as of certain innovations. Knowledge acquisition results from the elaboration activity of the learner bringing together new data and his or her current knowledge, to produce new meanings more apt to answer his or her inquiries. Thus, the individual's own activity is put back into the center of the knowledge process, which sorts out, analyzes, and organizes data in order to elaborate its own answer. However, this process is not the result of chance: the probability that a learner can "discover" by himself or herself all the elements that can transform questioning, formulations, multiple connections, and reformulations, in limited time, is almost zero, if he or she is not put into appropriate situations (questioning situations, multiple confrontations), with a certain number of significant elements (documents, experiments, arguments) and a certain number of limited formalisms (symbolism, graphs, schemata, models) that he or she can integrate.

It could also be stated that another level of knowledge can take the place of the old one only if learners find an interest in it and learn to make it work. Also at this level, they should then be able to be confronted with a number of appropriate situations and selected pieces of information in order to allow them a worthwhile reinvestment.

For this reason, we should abandon the idea of being able to let students develop concepts simply from observations, exercises, or classroom experiments. This does not mean that we must return to traditional lecturing. To show or explain a notion is insufficient. It is necessary, says Giordan, to induce a series of relevant conceptual disequilibria. The idea is to provoke an elaborating activity. To do so, it is useful to motivate the learners about the question to be treated or, at least, to get them to take an interest in it.

A number of authentic confrontations are indispensable (between student and reality, student and student, student and information, student and teacher). These confrontations should convince learners that their conceptions are not appropriate to the problem at hand. That is why they need a variety of slowly elaborated arguments, and not a single argument presented rapidly. Confrontations should lead learners to collect new data to enrich their experience in relation to the question at issue, to adopt a detached attitude toward their self-evidence, most often to redefine the problem and to imagine new relationships.

It is important that learners have access to some type of formalism to help them in their reflection. This formalism, which can assume very diverse forms (symbolism, schematization, modeling), should be easy to manipulate to allow students to organize new data or serve them as a base from which to produce new knowledge structures.

Often, the main difficulty students encounter is that they do not know how to connect the known to the new, they are unable to update what they know, or they cannot find a common denominator in a set of phenomena. In short, they cannot access what they have learned. It is important to use procedures that help them connect new data with what they already know and produce new meaning. What students perceive remains isolated because there are too many links to the original situation. What they conceive stays in an old organizational framework.

Introducing a new model allows for a new vision of reality. It can be used as a "hard core" around which to organize information and produce new knowledge. This premodel should be legible, comprehensible, and adapted to students' perceptions of the problem.

As a preliminary, students should have the opportunity to become familiar with manipulating this premodel — that is, they should have the chance to produce some premodels and work with them. Knowing about the elaboration activities required to learn something can allow the teacher to handle students' difficulties by directing them to apply the missing activity and helping them through appropriate didactic methods likely to help them update their prior conceptions or activities.

However, this set of necessary parameters remains insufficient for lasting acquisition if other conditions are not also in place. It is also useful to provide situations where the students can apply their new knowledge to test how it works and its limits.

Beyond this direct contribution, situations show students that new data are more easily learned when they are integrated into students' acquisition structures. Situations accustom students to connecting the new to the old, training them to move back and forth between what they know and what they are acquiring. This way, students learn to activate the necessary pieces of prior knowledge; in some cases, they can even imagine certain personal guidance procedures that will allow them to make this connection. Next, it is important that this learning be vertically integrated according to a few organizing concepts. Finally, students should be able to apply a form of knowledge about knowledge — that is, to reflect on conceptual practices in order to perceive the full significance and interest or to become aware of the "logics" underlying their approach. Many observed difficulties show that, sometimes the obstacle to learning is not directly linked to knowledge itself, but is the indirect result of the image or intuitive epistemology that learners have about their learning method or their mechanisms for producing knowledge.

It is clear that the teacher is irreplaceable, playing a role of prime importance; all the contributions and their interactions and progression cannot be specified in a syllabus. The teacher plays a supporting role, as organizer of the learning conditions. The students learn based on their own thought structures. The students, for one reason or another, should be in a position to change their conceptions. The teacher should design and create a didactic environment, which is essential for students to develop and use knowledge.

3.2.5 Epistemological Disturbance

Larochelle and Desautels (1992) propose a theory of conceptual change that they term "epistemological disturbance." In it, we can find an affirmation of their constructivist interpretation of learning:

> By bringing to light and studying the content of the conceptions *spontaneously* formed by students with regard to phenomena in their everyday life, educational specialists have rediscovered, in their own way, the relevance of one of the propositions of constructivism, that is, that no educational method can slight learners' knowledge: you have to come to terms with it!

Larochelle and Desautels then tackle the notion of cognitive conflict. They describe its pedagogical use and mention problems presented by its use — one of which would be that the strategy of cognitive conflict still embodies an empirical and realistic perspective of scientific knowledge and production.

They suggest as an alternative the use of "conceptual change models." They sum up the didactic strategy of the cognitive conflict in the following way:

> *Presentation of a phenomenon to be studied.* The students are encouraged to formulate and discuss their conceptions of the phenomenon being studied, as well as their expectations as to how it occurs. This phase may be more or less sophisticated on the pedagogical level, especially through the organization of debates ... and the formulation of intellectual requirements linked to the development of the argumentation.
>
> *Designing a disturbing incident.* The students may be confronted with a phenomenon that they find hard to explain within the framework of their conceptions or

that occurs in a way that belies their expectations. It is then postulated that these incidents will induce a cognitive conflict in the students, resulting from, among other things, the discrepancy between their expectations and the observation data.

Restructuring of ideas. This phase is characterized by the organization of various activities (discussions, presentations, lab work, etc.) aimed at helping students resolve the problem(s) associated with the disturbing incident and therefore regaining their cognitive equilibrium. It is then postulated that this resolution will lead them to change their conceptions in favor of those that are scientifically recognized.

It is important to remember that Larochelle and Desautels have a constructivist conception of science, which is reflected in the following passage (1992):

Scientific knowledge is a constructed or invented knowledge. Scientists formulate concepts, laws, and theories in order to give meaning to the phenomena they model and thus to answer their questions about these models. Scientific knowledge is a negotiated and debated knowledge. Production of scientific knowledge is an essentially collective undertaking: there is no idiosyncratic science. The proposed models and solutions are evaluated by peers, who judge their logical and experimental relevance in relation to established knowledge. Moreover, these explicit criteria are also based on unexpressed criteria, such as metaphysical beliefs, prestige of the researchers, etc.

Larochelle and Desautels make a very interesting comment. They note that scientific conception is always presented as more desirable than prior conception. Therefore, they wonder about the principle underlying such a vision of science:

It is always the advancement of scientific conceptions that is given precedence, to the detriment of those designed by learners. Moreover, while they are discursive productions, scientific conceptions would be free of what characterizes any discourse, that is, its context of meaning; such a privilege would not apply to learners' conceptions.

Having expressed these reservations, the authors note their liking for the model of conceptual change developed by Kenneth Strike and George Posner (1982) and propose a "variation" called "conceptual complexification." Indeed, they say, knowledge develops like a complex system.

Larochelle and Desautels (1992) fit, then, into the perspective for conceptual change and propose an epistemological disturbance strategy. This strategy "consists essentially of promoting critical reflection on the postulates and finalities that guide any production of knowledge, including that of scientific knowledge."

Larochelle and Desautels offer a democratic vision of knowledge:

> Our strategy aims at helping people question their representations, with the object of going beyond them (which does not presuppose the rejection of personal options, but rather their dialectization), thanks to the development of a capacity to think and question, in a critical way, the postulates that support their strategies of knowledge construction and the strategies of others. In brief, it is a matter of promoting the opportunity to exercise an "epistemological democracy" by realizing that there are different points of view, various arguments, etc., and not to provoke an epistemological disturbance in a personal way and with the intention of 'putting down' anybody on the cognitive level.

3.3 Pedagogical Profiles

We have examined the basics of constructivist didactics. We will now examine another way of dealing with the construction of knowledge: the use of pedagogical profiles that describe the cognitive characteristics of students.

3.3.1 La Garanderie's Model

For many years and in many books, Antoine de la Garanderie (1974, 1980, 1982, 1987, 1989, 1990, 1994) has helped to popularize research on students' cognitive characteristics and work methods. He believes that experience teaches us that each student has learning abilities, a work method, and a way of processing information.

La Garanderie noted, when he first taught philosophy, that students' minds are not a *tabula rasa*. They had experience, a pre-philosophy, intuitions, and a form of argumentation that constituted a pedagogical unconsciousness or preconsciousness. La Garanderie drew the notion of epistemological profile (1980) from the works of Bachelard, especially *La philosophie du non*:

> I considered that the minds of my students were not a blank slate on which nothing had been written. They had experience, a pre-philosophy that was implicit but that comprised intuitions fed by scattered and fleeting arguments; all this formed an unconsciousness — or pedagogical preconsciousness. ... It seemed to me that one could take up and expand what Bachelard says in *La philosophie du non* about the epistemological profile. If scientists are so influenced by their cultural background that they unconsciously overvalue realistic, rationalistic, positivistic, etc., ideas, why should students, who have acquired some knowledge through their reading or as a result of everyday life, not also have a profile that we could call pedagogical? ... If students are filled with philosophical ideas likely to block their comprehension when they are presented with new ideas, would they not be conditioned as well in the way they use methods of learning, understanding, and organizing?

In other words, students have habits of mental behavior that can become epistemological obstacles to any mental change that would be imposed on them. La Garanderie confirms (1980):

> We come up against *epistemological obstacles*. The habit that was formed constitutes a force that cannot be destroyed without losing all the positive things it contains. When they are pressured to change their methods, students resist through a sort of pedagogical instinct for self-preservation.

Therefore, La Garanderie took a closer look at mental habits in classrooms and in groups of teachers and bright students. He noted that students functioned with the help of mental images or representations that became general processes applicable to all the spheres of knowledge: "The fundamental pedagogical law is that, to learn and understand, we need mental images."

La Garanderie adds (1989) that our rationalistic heritage has condemned the mental image. There is no thought without images; mental images are the substance of comprehension and memorization. He also notes that the multiplicity of mental processes and evocative habits could be reduced to two major types of pedagogical families: visual and auditory.

This distinction between visual and auditory types comes from Jean-Martin Charcot, a famous French neuropsychiatrist, who had demonstrated it in the late nineteenth century in his lessons on aphasia. Visual individuals conceive and construct reality in the form of visual mental images of objects or figures. Auditory individuals narrate reality to themselves in the form of an inner language: they work in verbal or auditory mental images.

La Garanderie gives the example of two students who are learning their theorems.

> Peter knows the wording of theorems and definitions by heart. However, when he has to do exercises or solve problems, i.e., when he has to move on to application, he is lost. Paul does not learn his lessons, but he is the first one to raise his hand and go to the blackboard to do an exercise or a problem, thus demonstrating that he 'got it.' ... Peter and Paul do not use the *same mental images*. Peter uses verbal images, which is why he buries himself in terms and definitions. Paul, on the other hand, uses visual images: he visualizes figures in geometry and symbols in algebra. He *sees* how to apply them to the question. Peter could tell with words that figures or formulas should be applied, for he has a verbal intelligence, but *he does not see how to go about it.* ... We have here, with two forms of memorization, auditory and visual, two modes of comprehension.

In short, as we are born either left- or right-handed, we are born either visual or auditory!

Analyses have brought out specific forms — visual and auditory — that have major pedagogical consequences for La Garanderie. There would seem to be a relationship between evocative habit and school aptitude. La Garanderie notes that Bachelard was a visual learner and adds (1980): "Therefore, I believe that the epistemological profile of Bachelard begets the pedagogical profile, that in the latter the former finds its explanation and psycho-pedagogical foundation."

This relationship leads La Garanderie (1989, 1990, 1994) to propose a pedagogy that embodies the evocative habit. He theorized a relationship between the success of the student and the method used by the teacher, since the method is, consciously or unconsciously, either visual or auditory. Student achievement depends on certain conditions, including knowledge of the pedagogical profiles of the students and teachers.

3.3.2 Pedagogical Profiles and the Teaching of Mathematics

Other research has dealt with pedagogical profiles and the teaching of mathematics. Students who succeed or fail in mathematics make gestures that condition their successes or failures; but these gestures are invisible — they are mental gestures. Yet, if the teacher recognized the gestures of success, he or she could accurately help students having difficulties by teaching them their own ways of learning.

What are these mental gestures in mathematics? How do you determine them? What is the relationship between the nature of mental gestures and the way to solve a problem? What are the processes that students associate with arithmetical operations and what influences do these processes have on the solutions they produce? How do you help students make the mental gestures suitable for them?

Those are the questions Taurisson tried to answer in his research on teaching mathematics in elementary school. The results of his research appear in an excellent book, *Les gestes de la réussite en mathématiques à l'élémentaire* (1988). Gestures of success in mathematics are precise mental gestures. They can be described, they can be acquired — but first we have to learn to recognize them.

Everything starts with the distinction between *perception* and *evocation* established by La Garanderie in his book, *Les profils pédagogiques* (1980), and with the relationships between these evocative habits and succeeding in school. Comprehension is based on both a perception and an evocation — going back to what is perceived to draw from it a visual or auditory image.

The evocation conditions the representations that students form of mathematical language, operations, and problem-solving strategies. To concentrate on a text is to evoke it. It is an active, natural, and ever-present phase of going back to what is perceived, to construct mental images — verbal, visual, or auditory. The mental gestures that students make to manipulate these visual or auditory images, acquire new ones, and transform them can be skillful or clumsy. Although there are also mental images that are neither visual nor auditory, Taurisson confines himself to those two types, for they are the images that condition our rational lives. Therefore, Taurisson (1988) takes up La Garanderie's theory and holds that "evocation is going back to our perceptions to create auditory or visual mental images with the object of giving meaning to what is perceived."

Research on children has allowed Taurisson to stress an unusual point: evocation depends not on *the object that is evoked*, but rather *on the person who evokes it*. Visual individuals will give themselves visual representations of a reading or piece of music, while auditory individuals will remember the verbal description they gave themselves of a painting or song. In all cases, the object triggers visual or auditory images in the observer. In other words, individuals treat reality by going through mental images according to their style, or language, which La Garanderie calls a *pedagogical profile*.

The starting point for resolving any problem is the search for a representation of the problem corresponding to the evocation style of the individual trying to solve it. Visual individuals will need a spatial representation of the problem, including all the terms of the problem. No piece of information should be lost between the terms of the problem and the representation toward which the search effort is going to be directed. Auditory individuals need to give themselves a representation of the problem in which a sequence of actions will be able to unfold. They will focus more on the players involved in the problem than on the situations.

In this interpretation, Taurisson seems at odds with La Garanderie (1980), who says:

> It is an essential pedagogical law that the teacher should provide students with the perceptions of the images students do not evoke on their own. Students who form visual images of what they perceive need

teaching that provides them with auditory perceptions — and conversely.

Problem-solving strategies closely depend on the evocation style.
Beginning with an appropriate representation, problem-solving
strategies will have the following characteristics:

- For a visual individual, they rely heavily on analogy,
  spatial reorganization of the problem, and the search for
  regularities.

- For an auditory individual, they rely heavily on iterative
  processes, breaking the problem down into a series of
  simpler problems, and numerical relationships.

- Visual individuals are more interested in the situation
  than in the players. They consider all the terms of a
  problem before they begin to solve it. Thinking occurs
  in space and ignores time. If the representation is
  numerical, the solution will come from the search for
  regularities. If the representation is geometrical, the
  solution will come from a spatial reorganization.

- Auditory individuals are more interested in players than
  in the situation. They begin solving the problem by
  talking it through. They become aware of the terms
  progressively. Thinking takes place in time. Discovery
  of a time unit is a most valuable help. If the
  representation is numerical, the solution will come from
  numerical relationships. Representations are associated
  with movement.

If the teacher is to give students representations that they will be
able to use, he or she should especially give them the means to
form the representation most suitable to them. We must not
forget that the problem to be solved is the one learners represent
to themselves and not the one the teacher gave them.

To understand is not to be a passive witness; it is to construct
representations. Without mental images, there is no coherence.
Most students having difficulties in mathematics in elementary
school do not construct any representations whatsoever of the
problems they are given. For a student, whether a teacher
explains or illustrates a problem amounts to the same thing.
Whatever its form, it is not his or her explanation of the problem
that will give students the feeling they understand it, but the
transformation they make when they listen to it. In any case,

students understand as a result of the mental gestures that they make based on what the teacher gives them to perceive, and not simply because of the mere representation of the explanation or problem. Mental representation of the problem results from this effort.

The important question is: how can we lead students to make mental images of the problem they are given? Often, teachers work harder to make students understand. They explain, use even more words, do more drawings. They ask students to pay attention, to try to understand — and often the explanation that had failed once fails again.

Taurisson reminds us that teachers forget that it is not what they say that counts, but what students tell themselves or visually represent to themselves from those explanations. Consequently, in order to be understood by both auditory and visual individuals, we should not just use words and images; we should allow them to exert a different mental dynamic. To speak to auditory and visual students in the same class, it is not enough to present material in words and in pictures; we must give students the opportunity to practice the evocation that corresponds to them.

For visual students, the silence that accompanies the presentation of a schema and the instruction to associate this schema with the terms of a problem are as important as the schema itself. Visual students have the raw material of their mental gestures (images) and the intent to direct their mental work (to associate, to interpret). As a result of their evocation, they can represent to themselves the problem as a series of successive states. For auditory students, breaking down the problem into a sequence of actions is the beginning of their mental activity, but to get them to perform the process leading to the solution, it is essential to tell them that they should talk through what they are doing and take written notes on what they say.

A schema that is used as a starting point by a visual student may be the ending point for an auditory student; an auditory student may start with a series of actions that he or she is going to translate into schemata, and these schemata may be used as a starting point by a visual student.

Finally, note that more than half of all younger students try to solve a problem they invent from one word of the text or a memory. Some change the data, sometimes unconsciously, because they do not like certain numbers with which they have difficult affective relationships. Others form a partial or totally imaginary representation of the problem, and this misrepresentation becomes the problem to be solved.

In many cases, students will become more frustrated as they understand less, and will perceive the world of mathematics as incoherent! Even those who achieve some success may, if they are unaware of the gestures that lead to understanding, view their achievement as a sham: they are haunted by this feeling that everything may collapse at any time because, deep in their hearts, they are sure that they do not understand. Mathematics gives them this feeling more than any other subject. Therefore, Taurisson thinks that teachers should find means to improve the representation that students form of a problem and create sources of joy resulting from the resolution of these problems.

3.4 Conclusion

From all these considerations on the "cognitive nature" of learners, a very important general conclusion emerges: teachers should take into account their students' learning processes and knowledge. In particular, they should find out what the students know, as well as their models, their representations, their ways of processing information, and their naive or spontaneous conceptions. We should be prepared for the possibility of epistemological conflicts with scientific knowledge and help our students progress from one stage of knowledge to another, more "scientific."

On the other hand, note that the notion of epistemological conflict is not very clear and that it does not seem to have evolved since Bachelard. The appeal that this concept once had has given way to questions.

Giordan's assertions that prior ideas are an obstacle to knowledge and that taught notions are disregarded, distorted, or isolated beside familiar knowledge do not seem to be based on a complete cognitive theory and are not unanimously accepted by researchers and practitioners of constructivist pedagogy. A prior conception may sometimes be an obstacle and sometimes not. Giordan (1989, 1992) tries to prove that Piagetian theory is insufficient.

On the other hand, researchers like Desautels and Larochelle (1989, 1992) observe that constructivist pedagogical strategies have not had the expected results because they are not really based on a constructivist vision of conflict. This conflict, according to Desautels and Larochelle, is not the *cause* of a cognitive disequilibrium, but rather the *result*. Moreover, they cite J.A. Rowell and C.J. Dawson (1983) as saying that didactic strategies of cognitive conflict function only some of the time.

There could be another problem: that such notions as *epistemological obstacle* and *prior perception* are useless. Brousseau (1989) has already indicated that an epistemological obstacle can be cultural, didactic, or ontogenetic. There is the risk of misunderstanding, he says. Might not this obstacle be first and foremost cultural *and* didactic?

Anna Sierpinska (1989) accurately defines the paradoxical problem of knowledge that is an obstacle to knowledge. She rightly notes that one could assume that the notion of epistemological obstacle makes no sense, that it is not useful in teaching, and that it is at best a very useful metaphor ... for researchers!

Supporters of constructivist approaches who use the notion of pedagogical profile say that they are effective. It seems that this success depends more on the pedagogical strength of the teacher. As quoted above, La Garanderie (1980) states:

> It is an essential pedagogical law that the teacher should provide students with the perceptions of the images students do not evoke on their own. Students who form visual images of what they perceive need teaching that provides them with auditory perceptions — and conversely.

Therefore, the responsibility lies with the teacher. He or she has to perform! How should a teacher, who is either visual or auditory, teach a group of students who, like him or her, are also either visual or auditory? How should the teacher change when told that students cannot change their mental habits? Would the problem of students' pedagogical profiles lead, paradoxically, to aporia? We cannot ask teachers, as La Garanderie (1980) suggests, to abandon their mental habits, which are so deeply rooted. People do not so easily give up a pedagogical work method just because a psychopedagogical theory suggests doing so.

Chapter 4

Technological Theories

Technological theories, also called technosystemic or systemic, generally focus on improvement of the message through the use of appropriate technologies.

Most of this research is relying on the impressive capacity of computers to process information and exploring ways to improve the quality of interaction between human and computer.

4.1 Salvation through Technology

The technological upsurge of the twentieth century had as much influence on educational institutions as on any other social institution. Its impact was felt at two levels: technological developments and the idea of utopia generated by a great potential for change.

In the 1960s, technology was regarded as the savior of education. Thus, in 1968, the United States established the Commission on Instructional Technology to analyze the benefits of technology for education. The Commission's report, published in 1971 (Tickton, 1971), announced a revolution in education — through technology — and at the same time denounced the ultraconservatives who refused to believe in it. The goals of education, the report said, cannot fall within the province of cosmic principles or absolute values found in a Platonic world. They have nothing to do with metaphysical or philosophical considerations, which have never helped education to progress anyway! The important thing, concluded the Tickton report, is to improve teaching methods, and the new technology of automated and cybernetic machines can effectively contribute to achieving this objective.

The word "technology" has a broad meaning here. It includes all the resources, tools, instruments, devices, machines, processes, methods, routines, or programs resulting from the systematic application of scientific knowledge to solving practical problems.

A technological theory of education consists of a logical sequencing of "concrete" means with the intent of organizing teaching, whatever the nature of the content. Its main focus is the practical conditions of teaching and the resolution of real-life problems. It is pragmatic and organizes pedagogical communication to such an extent that some people speak of "instructional technology."

Harold Stolovitch and Gabriel La Roque (1983) offer a restrictive but illuminating definition of instructional technology:

> Instructional technology proposes to study how to organize the pedagogical environment, set out educational or instructional methods and means, and structure information, in other words, according to what design instruction should be transmitted so that individuals may assimilate new information as effectively as possible. Instructional technology is centered on the conception, or even better, on the systemic conception of instruction.

This definition surely shows a certain desire to systematize pedagogical operations. Other researchers have a broader definition. For instance, J. Lapointe (1990) writes:

> Instructional technology will be considered an approach that consists of applying scientific knowledge and rational data, processed by the left cerebral hemisphere, as well as intuitive data, processed by the right cerebral hemisphere, with the object of developing systems (methodologies, techniques, and machines) capable of solving learning, teaching, and training practices. ...Technology is a rational intervention tool that directs the intuition of the technologist toward the research, development, and application of satisfying, realistic, desirable, and workable solutions to the practical problems encountered in the real world.

A technological theory of education is revealed by the following characteristics:

- Terminology that includes such words as: process, engineering, communication, training, technology, techniques, means, computer-based environments, interactive laboratory, instructional design, hypermedia, programming, system, and individualized teaching

- Speaking of "training" and "teaching," even "instruction," rather than "education"

- Concentration on planning and organizing training processes

- Emphasis on the components of communication, like feedback in the information transmission process

- Use of communication technologies: audio-visual equipment, videodisc, compact discs, computers, etc.

- Emphasis on the need to identify *a priori* observable behaviors in students

- A desire to systematize as much as possible the different training stages (definitions of the objectives, the tasks, the assessment, etc.) in the general perspective of applied science or engineering

- Use of description and standardization of training operations and a desire to use systematic routines

- Criticism of romantic and humanistic visions of education that are not concerned with planning and organization

As Elliot Eisner emphasizes in *The Educational Imagination* (1985), instructional technology is not concerned with the nature of the ends but with organizing the means needed to achieve these ends. The proponents of this approach phrase the problem to be solved as follows: How do you operationalize educational processes to make them efficient?

Eisner's point of view is well supported by Lapointe (1990), for whom instructional technology is a "meta" approach to the relationship between theory and practice. Instructional technology is interdisciplinary, i.e., applicable in all fields of study. Its apostles maintain that it is *the* technology, *the* general way of solving practical problems. Better still, there is only one way to improve teaching! This general way of conceiving the problems of education became so particular that many critics pointed out this restrictive particularity: salvation seems to proceed from the mere definition of the objectives.

4.2 Two Main Trends

There are two main trends in the technological movement. The first one is the *system theory* of education. It consists of examining relationships among elements in accordance with the objectives. Therefore, one should try to not forget anything, to see everything, and to make complete descriptions according to three fundamental categories: objectives, processes, and elements. One should act systematically and use a certain standard method that recurs in every theory. This method is based on the analysis of objectives and students' characteristics. It also involves developing a teaching-learning system, testing the system, assessing it, and, finally, introducing the necessary modifications to close the circle.

The second trend is the *hypermedia theory*. It originated in research in cybernetics, artificial intelligence, cognitive sciences, information science, and communication theories dealing with the use of media. It consists of examining technological environments in terms of their interactivity and building more and more interactive systems — "hypermedia environments." A lot of research in this field is inspired by certain cognitive theories of information and computer engineering. However, it is characterized most by its pragmatism: in the end, people want a system that works, an effective technology rather than a great theory.

In turn, these two trends influenced one another, with each borrowing from the other. The pedagogical design approach borrowed elements of data processing from communication theories and provided computer-assisted instruction with a description of the main parts of instruction. Cybernetics supplied systematists with the notion of feedback, which soon became a component of all these theories!

In the twentieth century, it is the nature and the quality of the systematization of instruction that has changed from year to year, with the evolution of knowledge and the influence of the new information technologies. In the 1950s, there was much talk about teaching machines and operative conditioning. In debates, educators contrasted B.F. Skinner and Carl Rogers, the machine and the human being. Today, there is more talk about the impact of theories of information on the construction of "intelligent software."

It was the work of Seymour Papert on LOGO language in the early 1980s, among other things, that kicked off research into creating open and computer-based learning environments. Papert (1980) writes that he was influenced by Jean Piaget, but notes in passing that certain emulators of Piaget totally misread him! At present, cognitive theories on exploration and discovery greatly influence the construction of these learning environments.

It is also to be noted that these trends differ from one another in everyday life by the type of products they emphasize. Even though they have a lot in common, notably a desire to systematically organize teaching, they still exhibit some differences as to their preferences. The systematic trend especially emphasizes the quality of pedagogical design. The hypermedia trend emphasizes first and foremost the quality of the software and the whole multimedia system.

We will consider systems approach theories of education first, then hypermedia theories.

4.3 Systemic Trend

4.3.1 History and Problems

An important influence on technological theories is still the general systems theory and its focus on systematizing all operations, without exception. In the early 1950s, Americans tried to apply the principles of general systems theory to education. Their work continued, and now articles on systems approach models abound. It is no exaggeration to say that there are a hundred systemic theories, and certain journals, such as *Audio-Visual Instruction* and *Educational Technology*, keep advancing new versions of them.

All of these models have a common objective: to describe all the structures and to plan all the operations. The systems approach came to Quebec in the late 1960s, after 20 years of pedagogical testing in the United States. It caught on rapidly, especially in secondary institutions and postsecondary departments of educational sciences. It is still an important theory in education (Gagné *et al.*, 1988).

However, the true origin of the systemic trend dates back to the beginning of the twentieth century, in a movement that came as a reaction to the absolute power of analytical science. An

Austrian biologist, Ludvig Von Bertalanffy, was the main champion of this global approach.

Bertalanffy did not feel comfortable with the scientific trend of his time, which was characterized by a mechanistic vision of knowledge. He studied theoretical biology and very early became interested in organisms and growth problems. His first works were published in the 1920s and deal with the organic approach, i.e., a global vision of life phenomena. In 1928, Bertalanffy wrote that the fundamental characteristic of a life form is its organization and that the analysis of parts and processes isolated from one another cannot give a complete explanation of the phenomenon of life.

It was only in 1968, while teaching biology at the University of Alberta, that Bertalanffy published a major piece of work in the systems approach entitled *General System Theory*. This book provides an excellent introduction to the subject and contains a panorama of applications in various disciplines: physics, biology, social sciences, mathematics, etc. This book gives a lot of historical information, as it includes previously published articles. Bertalanffy writes that the notion of an open system appeared in 1940 and the notion of the general theory of systems in 1945.

Yves Barel, Jean-Louis Le Moigne, Joel de Rosnay, and Edgar Morin were the first to write about the systems approach in France in the early 1970s. An issue of the *Revue française de sociologie* in 1971 was devoted to systems analysis in the social sciences. In 1975, Rosnay proposed a systems approach to education. However, it is undoubtedly Morin who popularized general systems theory and cybernetics the most with several of his books, including *La nature de la nature* in 1977.

Educational systems design reached a certain maturity in the 1970s, and its basic principles have changed little since then. We can compare the first texts written in this area with those written today — *Analyse systémique de l'éducation* by Jerry Pocztar (1989), for example — and notice no change at all. *The Systematic Design of Instruction* (1990) by Walter Dick and Lou Carey takes up in a clear and competent manner, principles of systems approach that have been known for a long time. In short, systems theories are all very much alike.

What is the present status of systems theory in education? The latest writings on teaching organization (Gagné, 1987; Dick and Carey, 1990; Lapointe, 1990; Prégent, 1992 and 1993) show that the principles of systems theory have entered into the process of instructional design. Little change can be seen in systemic theories between 1970 and 1990. In other words, the rules of modeling have been well digested.

It is now possible to dissect all these theories and reveal their basic anatomy: elements, processes, functions, a finality, aims, and objectives. The basic systems model is a framework set up to organize and account for instructional input, components, processes, and results. It helps educators keep in mind the different interactions and to work toward the training goals. It can also facilitate planning of instruction by bringing out and organizing the factors that should be considered to attain maximum efficiency.

4.3.2 Instructional Design

Instructional design theories focus on describing instructional operations, with a concern for details that varies according to the models. One can refer to Dick and Carey (1990) to see all the operations required by systematic design. We should also mention A.J. Romiszowski (1986), who includes numerous charts describing the stages of the systems approach, instructional systems that use the media, levels of pedagogical design, learning models, and so forth. In short, the "systemic processor" does it all! Merely reading Romiszowski or glancing at his charts is enough to be steeped in the technological spirit and understand what it is all about!

The principal methods are as follows. The first concern of teachers is organizing the instructional process. They first try to identify the performance objectives and sort them according to the different taxonomies in use. Next, they decide upon the necessary elements (e.g., groups, texts, audio-scripto-visual devices, computers, etc.), referring to their defined objectives. They gather information on their students' characteristics (learning profiles, knowledge, motivational factors, etc.), then modify the objectives accordingly. They also analyze their possibilities and constraints. Then, they set up an operational teaching and learning system. Finally, they prepare mechanisms to allow them to assess the results and use the information from the results to modify, if need be, the organization of the system.

Instructional design is a detailed application of this basic model. It deals with organization and planning, of course, and is inspired by the systems theories explained above. However, it is more concerned with modifying students' behavior and choosing the media. In contrast with the first model, which quite often applies only to the systematic organization of the work of the teacher, this second model focuses on the description of the work students will have to do as well as on an accurate description of the media to be used to achieve the objectives set. The result will be complete packages designed to train students.

The most explicit books on instructional design are:
- *A Guide to Systematic Instructional Design* (Wong and Raulerson, 1975)
- *Instructional Design: Principles and Applications* (Briggs, 1981)
- *Principles of Instructional Design* (Gagné, Briggs, and Wager, 1988)
- *The Systematic Design of Instruction* (Dick and Carey, 1990)
- *Charting Your Course: How to Prepare to Teach More Effectively* (Prégent, 1994)

A thorough reading of these books should take care of everything!

The logic of instructional design is based on a few simple principles. Thus, Robert Gagné, Leslie Briggs, and Walter Wager (1988) base their theory on five principles:

1. Individualized instruction
2. Short- and long-term planning
3. Necessity of planning and organization
4. Use of systems theory
5. Taking into account learning conditions

Understandably, education is nothing more than instruction, instructional design is a form of instructional systems approach and systematic organization, and instruction is a set of events systematically organized to encourage the internal learning processes! These events constitute the external learning conditions (for instance, the use of audio-visual materials), as opposed to internal conditions, such as memory functions in an individual student.

Therefore, it is this combination of external events that needs to be organized, planned, and detailed in order to form an instructional system. The organization of these events should respect the following logic proposed by Gagné, Briggs, and Wager (1988):

- Attract students' attention
- Inform students about the objectives and establish the expectation level
- Remind students of previously studied material
- Present the material clearly
- Guide learning
- Ask for "proof " of learning
- Provide feedback
- Assess performance
- Encourage information transfer to other areas of application

This procedure can be compared to the procedure proposed by Bela Banathy in *Instructional Systems* (1968):

- Formulate a description of learning objectives that students should have in mind
- Create tests to assess the degree to which these objectives will be attained
- Analyze students' characteristics and abilities
- Specify what students should learn so they can achieve the behaviors described in the objectives
- Examine the different pedagogical options and conceive a pedagogical system
- Set up the pedagogical system and collect data on its efficiency
- Ensure smooth operation of the system, taking into account the data collected in the previous step

Martin Wong and John Raulerson's systemic model (1975) offers a remarkably clear and accurate description of the different operations of pedagogical design. According to these authors, the classroom is a sub-system that includes elements, processes, and a finality. The elements are the teacher, the students, the materials, newspapers, television, and anything that can be described as being part of the system. The processes describe all the operations and all the functions that allow the system to reach its goals or its end-point. Sub-systems also include three other aspects: input assessment, results assessment, and feedback. Input assessment is concerned with students and their abilities, skills, knowledge, and motivations. Results assessment also makes it possible to assess the operation of the system and, through the feedback network, modify the system.

Charting Your Course, by Richard Prégent (1994), contains a description of a systemic and universal procedure, since it deals with all disciplines. Prégent presents what he calls concrete and versatile tools, simple outlines, practical advice, and procedures. The teacher is a stage director, an information engineer who determines what needs to be learned, who plans and assesses the activities and means necessary for the students to reach the set objectives, who prepares feedback activities to correct inadequate learning, and who assumes the role of motivator in his or her group, just like the leader of a work team.

4.4 Hypermedia Trend

The potential uses of computers in education have now become familiar. A computer using complex and interactive programs skillfully developed by multidisciplinary teams can perform instructional tasks, simulate interaction with students, and present students with varied situations and react appropriately to their answers or questions. The computer can even learn from students while teaching them! It can even adapt to students' particular characteristics (learning style, rhythm, preferences, needs, etc.). The computer can also manage a media system and process numerical and analogical data. For instance, with an "intelligent" program, the computer can control a videodisc, a compact disc drive, an image and sound digitizer, and other programs — all interactively.

In short, the computer is becoming a more powerful and more "intelligent" manager of a set of diverse information sources.

Hence, the expression "hypermedia" to describe the trend of educational theories centered around the interactive use of these technological systems or packages managed by a computer.

Where did the first ideas on the subject come from?

4.4.1 Evolution of Hypermedia

Hypermedia theories originated with the use of media in education, with cybernetics, and with information and behavioral theories. These theories aroused incredible enthusiasm for communication and for understanding how the brain works, thus facilitating the birth of educational technology or educational engineering.

Communication theories were the first source of inspiration. It was undoubtedly the interest in audio-visual methods that long ago marked the birth of technological models in education. As early as the 1930s, journals were being published in the United States dedicated to this form of instruction and to many associations devoted to spreading the gospel! More specifically, there was an interest in the choice of media, their compatibility, and their usefulness in education. Certain researchers studied the different components of communication: sounds, movements, images, etc. Others worked on the relationships between the media and pedagogical objectives and proposed using audio-visual kits.

This was really an approach centered on communication. Altogether, pedagogical communication was seen as an activity to be systematized and made more efficacious. To do so, we need to start with what we know about the receiver (the student), the message (the subject matter), the medium (means of communication), and the global organization (the system).

Cybernetics was the second source of inspiration of hypermedia theories. Cybernetics, the science of control and communication in humans and machines, began in 1948, when Norbert Wiener published the first manual on cybernetics, entitled *Cybernetics, or Control and Communication in the Animal and the Machine.*

Wiener, a mathematician, and Arturo Rosenblueth, a physiologist from Harvard Medical School created this new field of knowledge, because they were interested in all problems dealing with communication, control, and statistical mechanics. Their collaboration was the result of a war project directed by Wiener and Julian Bigelow. They were trying to control the firing of an anti-aircraft battery so that it would be able to predict the behavior of an airplane and use this information through a feedback mechanism. The term "cybernetics" now means the study of communication considered as a factor of organization and control in any system (computers, humans, animals, or social organizations).

Educational cybernetics started as the scientific study of relationships between the teaching process and its effects on learning, relationships that can be transformed into mathematical ratios. Education was to be conceived of as the technology of automating teaching processes through the use of algorithms.

The creation of computerized instructional programs started in the 1960s and laid the foundation for computer-assisted teaching. At the outset, this teaching was characterized by complete control by the computer over the student. The advent of artificial intelligence modified the nature of these programs to generate "intelligent" tutoring systems. These programs can now adapt to the student. This development offers a wide range of possibilities for organizing learning, which Elizabeth Whitaker and Ronald Bonnel (1992) have classified in the following manner:

- Ad hoc frame-oriented systems, in which the entire curriculum is stored in a predefined structure, and the material is organized in frames
- Discovery learning (microworlds), where the student has complete control, as in the LOGO system, for instance
- Question and answer, a "mixed-initiative control" system in which either the student or the system asks questions and one or the other answers, in a Socratic mode of dialogue
- Reactive learning, in which the student formulates hypotheses and performs experiments and the computer does simulations and shows the effects
- Learning by doing, in which the system gives the student a problem to solve, then critiques the solution
- Learning while doing, in which the student accomplishes a task and the system tries to infer the student's goal and provides appropriate coaching

- Diagnostic tutor, in which the computer provides a diagnosis, identifying and analyzing the student's mistakes but not providing tutoring

- Learning by explanation, in which the student asks questions and the computer answers, with explanations

The third source of the hypermedia trend can be found in information and behavioral theories. The first theory to have an important influence was behaviorism. It is Skinner, with his theory of operative conditioning, who gave the impetus to establishing an approach centered on teaching machines. Skinner's theory was very simple: good learning depends first and foremost on a good teaching environment. The more efficient the environment, the better the learning.

It is believed that this theory was successful because it allowed easier assessment of learning, defined as a behavioral change that can be attributed to modifications in the teaching environment. Increased individual freedom would not be in keeping with the behaviorist understanding of behavior. Later, behaviorists often tried to describe the nature of teaching environments in terms of stimulus-response. Other education specialists — Benjamin Bloom and his colleagues (1956), Robert Mager (1962), and David Krathwohl and his colleagues (1964) — developed taxonomies of objectives that were used in most instructional technological projects.

This way of representing environments aroused interest among the first computer users, who immediately assumed that computers logically would be machines for teaching. Theorists confirmed this belief by developing algorithmic instructional structures. Lev Landa (1974) defined the algorithm as a precise and global instruction that should effect a clearly defined sequence of elementary operations. Therefore, an algorithm describes the most efficient sequence of operations to solve a problem in mathematics, chemistry, physics, linguistics, etc. At the time, the computer was perceived as a bank of specific and predetermined answers and manager of a closed environment.

This coupling of behaviorism and instructional technology appealed to a lot of people, who regarded it as a magic solution: a "bad teacher" could be replaced by a well-programmed machine. Whatever the opinions, this marriage between behaviorism and technology did not necessarily end in divorce. There were many offspring, which in turn produced many offspring. Computer-programmed courses are countless, dominating the field. This conception of instruction, very popular in the 1970s, is still making waves.

However, constructivist cognitive theories of learning paired with software development modified the conception people had of a teaching environment. In a way, the main result was to open this environment and to make it more interactive. These various influences finally created a technological vision of training and greater interest in the sophisticated control by the computer of all aspects of education.

The terminology used reveals this desire to base training in any subject area whatsoever on the "intelligent" — or not so "intelligent" — possibilities of the computer. We used to speak in terms of "computer-managed instruction" or "computer-assisted instruction" (Kearsley, 1987; Lawler, 1987; Solomon, 1987). Today, it's "hypermedia environments" and "intelligent systems of instruction."

4.4.2 Organizational Principles of Hypermedia Environments

There is a certain synergy in the evolution of pedagogical communication technologies and theories on how students process information. The result: a technological product drawing upon the latest innovations in computer science and information theory. Indeed, the hypermedia trend is as much concerned with the modeling of information processing using new programming theories as with the computer management of media.

The possibility of storing images in the computer and its peripherals (e.g., videodiscs, compact discs) makes it possible to conceive of the computer as manager of a multimedia center. The result is a video and audio environment run by a computer and an expert system. As Gilbert Paquette (1992) sums up the situation:

> The most significant and promising aspect is the ability of computers now to manipulate and transform representations, and to make inferences that produce new data from known data. Works in artificial intelligence gave rise to a host of applications: processing of natural language, pattern recognition, and data-based expert systems.

The new field of cognitive information science also makes it possible to expand the possibilities of the most prevalent computer tools — such as spreadsheet programs, databases, and text and graphics editors — by adding processes inspired by human intelligence, allowing information processing at the highest level.

These new programs make the computer tool even more interesting as an educational and cultural instrument that facilitates:

- Non-linear data exploration
- Alternative visions of a single subject area
- Diverse interactively integrated media
- Easier data access through graphical user interfaces and natural language
- Cooperative use of information
- Long-distance information communication

Educational "technologists" used to be concerned with information programming and transmission, and with preparing a great message, such as a high-quality television program. They are now trying to combine knowledge about the cognitive functioning of learners and the many audio-visual possibilities of the computer and related technologies, such as data digitalization. Thus, for example, a cognitivist may collaborate with a videodisc expert.

In the early 1980s, there was much talk about creating "intelligent" educational software. The teacher would rely on different programs that would use applications of artificial intelligence to help teach or create learning environments (Bergeron and Bordier, 1990; Li, 1992; Sandberg, Barnard, and Kamsteeg, 1992). These tutoring systems are called *closed* tutoring systems, because they generally try to totally control the instructional process. This control is based on a modeling of student-teacher interaction, the student's behavior, and successive stages for acquiring a concept in a field of knowledge.

Information about the learning process and the subject matter to be transmitted exists formally, i.e., it can be represented and codified in a data-processing system. From this point of view, learning is perceived as a set of stimuli and responses, while subject matter can be broken down into elementary propositions. Patrick Suppes (1988) provides a good example of this point of view: he produces totally computerized environments for teaching mathematics in high school and college.

The proliferation of cognitive research studies has radically changed this vision of the computer and given rise to another area of research: the creation of open environments. People have tried to answer the following question: How do we construct an educational environment that allows more for the relatively unpredictable and uncontrollable functioning of the student (Sandberg, Barnard, and Kamsteeg, 1992)?

The answers, although many and varied, were based on two common principles:

1. Begin with the *student* rather than the *subject matter*.

2. *Guide* the student in his or her discoveries, rather than *teach* him or her the subject matter.

Papert (1980) was undoubtedly at the origin of this important change. Inspired by Piaget, Papert and his colleagues at the Massachusetts Institute of Technology created a learning environment in which students converse "naturally" with computers. Thus, students master fundamental mathematical concepts — by playing with a turtle!

Five Organizational Principles
We will now consider the five fundamental organizational principles of a hypermedia environment, which constantly come up in the literature:

1. Variety of interactions

2. Open modeling

3. Domain independence

4. Cooperative instruction

5. Multimediatization of information

Variety of interactions (Augusteijn, Broome, and Kolbe, 1992; Barker, 1992; Fritz, 1992; Li, 1992).

This principle depends on communication between computer and student. The programming stresses student-system interactivity. The computer may automatically generate problems (for instruction or for assessment), analyze student errors and provide solutions, convey subject matter, give feedback, and/or ask students questions and adapt to their learning characteristics.

This interaction has become more and more open toward the student. In many projects, the student processes the information and the program reacts to his or her needs. Jane Fritz (1992) offers a nautical comparison: the student sails through knowledge and the computer provides beacons and assistance. Zhongmin Li (1992) says that instruction should be conceived of as a series of transactions or dialogues between computer and student. The computer should react, he says, to the needs of the student and adapt to his or her cognitive level.

Open modeling (Cunningham, 1991; Sandberg, Barnard, and Kamsteeg, 1992; Siviter and Brown, 1992).

How a hypermedia environment works is based on the student and not on the subject matter. It essentially relies on open modeling and functions according to the needs and wishes of the student. This modeling may include data from the student, such as his or her characteristics and preferences, history (how he or she answered the questions, the type of questions he or she asks, the type of solutions he or she gives to the problems), as well as inferences and interpretations that the system makes about the degree of knowledge of the student (his or her mistakes, level of mastery, and motivation).

Douglas Siviter and Keith Brown of South Bank Polytechnic School in London developed a hypercourseware program to build courses, using such tools as Hypercard. Siviter and Brown (1992) got away from "traditional" course programming methods because they were too "prescriptive." Their flexible and open instrument makes it possible to manage interactive and multimedia resources. Jacobin Sandberg, Yvonne Barnard, and Paul Kamsteeg (1992) express the same views. These researchers, members of the social sciences computer department at the University of Amsterdam, have worked a lot on student modeling.

The following is an example of open modeling. The student begins a course by stating that he or she would prefer summaries presented in tabular form. Then, in the middle of an interaction, he or she decides that narrative explanations would be better. The system accepts this change, but warns the student that it might create some confusion if the preferences change too often. The student answers that he or she gets the message.

Domain independence (Bergeron, 1990; Cunningham, 1991; Li and Merrill, 1991; Augusteijn, Broome, Kolbe, and Ewell, 1992; Li, 1992).

Although there has been a proliferation of intelligent tutoring systems designed for teaching a specific subject area, programmers have increasingly insisted that the construction of systems be independent of subject area. Li (1992) speaks of "transaction shells" that make it possible to reach objectives common to several subject areas. For example, several disciplines require such operations as "Name the parts of ... ." Consequently, Li states, programmers can prepare a "transaction shell" to facilitate this operation, whether for mechanics or for biology.

Marijke Augusteijn, Ronald Broome, and Raymond Kolbe (1992) have created an environment (ITS Challenger) that contains no data from any specific domain. The environment adapts to the student's knowledge level, processes problems, analyzes the student's errors, and gives feedback. Thus, many systems contain "banks of problems" that students typically do in their studies. In the second stage of developing the environment, the subject matter is incorporated.

Cooperative instruction (Beyou, 1992; Fritz, 1992; Paquette, 1992; Sandberg, Barnard, and Kamsteeg, 1992; Hooper, 1992a and 1992b).

More and more system programmers are trying to integrate cooperation into instruction. One form involves collaboration between the teacher and students; another form involves interaction among several students. Students can derive social and motivational benefits from this interaction. This means that the system needs a modeling of cooperative work (individual styles, time sharing, observation of individual behaviors, etc.).

Since hypermedia theory emphasizes the open architecture of a pedagogical system, the problem of interaction among students will inevitably have to be confronted at some time. As a matter of fact, the presence of several students has become an interesting challenge for system programmers. To solve this complicated problem and make hypermedia environments cooperative, programmers have to examine cooperative methods of work.

This does not mean that everyone wants to abandon very structured programs in favor of a contextualization, as advocated by John Brown, Allan Collins, and Paul Duguid (1989) and by William Clancey (1992). Sandberg and Bob Wielinga (1992), for example, offer two recommendations: avoid falling into an excessively sociocultural approach and avoid the cognitive learner theory proposed by Clancey, Brown, Collins, Duguid, and others.

Multimediatization of information (Nielsen, 1990; Woodhead, 1991; Barker, 1991 and 1992; Fritz, 1992; Seymour, 1993).
Hypermedia training projects generally contain a set of data in various forms: video (animated or still), audio, and text. These data are stored in memories (videodiscs, compact discs, hard drives) large enough to contain what is necessary for a course, so the student can at any moment request explanations in whatever form he or she wishes.

Not only does this information come from a variety of sources, but it is provided in a variety of forms. Hypertext programs allow access to texts in different ways. Hypermedia programs combine media to offer the same flexibility of access. In essence, the computer controls a multimedia information center.

To sum up, an important phenomenon is taking place in the evolution of the principles of educational technology: pedagogical research and experimentation are giving higher priority to interactivity and hypermedia techniques of presenting knowledge. Research on the conditions of open interactivity, hypertexts and hypermedia, educational software, student learning processes, and exploration and discovery now feeds the technology trend and gives it a more and more "interactive" flavor.

4.4.3 Examples of Open Hypermedia Environments

As stated earlier, the didactic use of computers is undergoing an important change. Computer-based learning environments are becoming increasingly open to the student and relying more and more on a combined and simultaneous use of multiple media.

There are now many interactive training projects that combine computer power with diversity of media — for instance, the multimedia program "Palenque," designed by Kathy Wilson of Bank Street College of Education in New York. Several interactive projects of science education are under way in the United States. For example, a number of elementary schools have used

"Window on Science," a complete course stored on 11 interactive videodiscs (Fischer, 1992). In the United Kingdom, the Netherlands, and France as well, there are numerous open hypermedia environment projects. We will now present three very interesting examples.

**Computer-Based Environment
for Learning and Developing Knowledge (France).**

This is an evolutive system designed by Claire Beyou (1992) of the Université du Maine (France) to solve the following problem in training repair technicians: What do we do when knowledge evolves as fast as the system that is supposed to teach it? In the professional world, skills are constantly evolving: they form, interact, change, and disappear. Any modeling of them at a given time will be outdated a few months later. This is a serious problem in training.

To manage and transfer these skill sets, we must consider how they evolve and design an environment that also evolves. Not only should such an environment make it possible to train operators on a given system, but it should also develop the knowledge stored in it, whether this knowledge relates to the technology (evolution of the components) or to the operators (new adjusting procedures and new troubleshooting rules).

The second characteristic of this project to train repair technicians is companionship learning. Beyou (1992) defines companionship learning as "action learning through activity in a professional environment under the guidance of one or more persons who assume the role of the 'master' and allow for the 'apprentice' to work more and more independently, according to his or her performance."

This form of learning, which takes place in the real world, is prevalent in certain professions that require a particular ability. Unlike vocational training, companionship learning is rarely guided by a linear pedagogical progression. The situations encountered by the apprentice depend on the context. In real life, situations do not necessarily go from the simplest to the most complex. The apprentice learns only from situations that he or she encounters in the course of working. Thus, in a troubleshooting context, the technician deals only with real breakdowns and proceeds according to his or her degree of experience; the only variable is his or her degree of autonomy, according to the task encountered. However, in a company, it is not the expert who decides if a student can handle a situation alone — it's the learner-worker who makes that decision about his or her abilities. There are still many cases in which the learner has no choice, but must solve the problem by himself or herself because there are no experienced people available to help.

Therefore, Beyou (1992) proposes an evolutive and open training system. The key function of the system is to serve as a dynamic memory of the attempts, providing for storage of the different data and skills called into play. To establish a cooperative dialogue with the technician, the system has certain specific functions, namely:

- To retrieve data, to find as quickly as possible the corresponding schema, the adjusting threshold values, etc.

- To train technicians to troubleshoot these units: the dialogue should be established in a companionship mode

- To continuously update data: each breakdown is studied and should be memorized enriching a data file of cases

- To assist in the work: calculations, generation of curves, tests

The technician should consider the training system as a companion with a more complete and older memory of systems and also as a calculating tool, a helper, and a notepad. The system software consists of the following components:

- A database organized so as to encourage free access to the data

- A functional model of electronic components

- A base of troubleshooting rules: rules, plans, procedures

- A base of breakdowns that have been corrected

A "pedagogical generator" steers these components according to the objectives of the interaction. The database contains different types of data, all factual: data on the chart and the components, technical notes, and theoretical reminders, such as calculus formulas. These data are in the form of texts or graphics. Beyou uses hypertexts, since they seem the most flexible tool to access these different data and the easiest to update.

Bubbles Project (Northern Ireland).
The Bubbles project from the Language Development & Hypermedia Research Group at the University of Ulster provides

another example of the hypermedia environment. The Bubbles tool has been used in the United Kingdom by children (aged 8 and up) and by adults. The children or the adults run the Bubbles software in pairs on a microcomputer. The goal is to construct a cartoon strip on the screen. The screen displays scenes with characters, but the dialogue balloons are empty. Students start thinking about real-life situations and use the keyboard to fill in the balloons with dialogues. They can go back to this dialogue and, in a reflexive mode, comment on what the characters are saying. Then, they exchange their views on the story they have built.

Bubbles is a Hypercard application that facilitates the construction of knowledge. The first reported uses of Bubbles can be found in such disciplines as composition, history, psychology, public relations and management, reading skills, and teacher training.

The designers of this project are opposed to the educational engineering trend and propose a more constructivist, more open, and less behaviorist alternative (Cunningham, 1991; McMahon, O'Neill, and Cunningham, 1992b). (In fact, they go so far as to say that those who used to believe in educational engineering have now lost all hope!) Instruction with Bubbles is less a process through which knowledge is transmitted to students as it is a way of feeding the processes through which students understand, construct interpretations, and evaluate different points of view. It is in this sense that it is open and domain-independent.

The EVE Project (United Kingdom and the Netherlands).
The EVE project is a hypermedia training program intended for midwives practicing in the Netherlands. This software and training program were designed by F.N. Arshad and P.S. Ward (1992) of the Information Modelling Programme in the School of Medicine at Leeds University.

This system was designed to provide for the continued training of midwives, who already have a substantial amount of initial information but need to keep up to date with the latest techniques and discoveries in obstetrics. The solution proposed by Arshad and Ward is a hypermedia training system based on open programming and the use of several media. The programming permits different types of interactions. The system adapts to the students according to a model specific to each of them. It provides them with data in different visual and audio forms. It allows them to learn about processes of learning, knowing, and communicating. It asks or answers questions; it presents information. It is flexible and accepts data input from the experts (the midwives), from the system designers, and from students. Teachers and students are able to construct individualized courses.

4.5 Minimal Training

Minimal training is what futurologists would call a "fact with prospects." Minimal training is to be distinguished from systemic theories in that it aims at minimum planning. It differs from hypermedia theories in its lesser concern for the multiplicity of media. However, it shares certain properties with these theories. We will now see what minimal training consists of, especially in the context of software use in instruction.

A new need arose during the 1980s: training in the use of software. Considering the popularity of word processors, it is easy to see that it poses a training problem. What training should be provided so that a person may be able to use a computer program as quickly as possible? Students often ask, "Will I be able to work with the program in five minutes?" This is all the more true as students do not want to spend their time reading a manual or consulting the computer help that is available. They would rather use the program to perform real tasks rather than learn about it!

This is a very interesting problem because it constitutes, in a way, an excellent instance of so many problems encountered in training: efficiency, rapidity, and relevance of the training in whatever domain. It would be hoped that the solution to this problem would inspire researchers and bring about innovations in education. Well, that is exactly what is going on!

The result is a model of training called minimal training. Since computer users seemed naturally disposed to explore, theoreticians identified diverse learning conceptions: by free or directed exploration, by doing, or by discovery (Brown, 1982; Carroll, Mack, Lewis, Grischkowsky, and Robertson, 1985; Robert, 1985 and 1989; Carroll and Aaronson, 1988; Lajoie, Egan, and Lesgold, 1988; Schmalhofer and Kühn, 1988).

John M. Carroll at IBM (United States), J.M. Robert of the École Polytechnique in Montreal, NASA, and Louise Régnier of the École Polytechnique have conducted many research studies to find the best possible way to train someone to use such computer programs as a spreadsheet, word processor, or computer-assisted design program.

We will now see an example of minimal training developed by Carroll, who has done a lot of research on knowledge acquisition in software use in instruction. This research led him to propose an approach to training based on the minimal manual.

The fundamental principle of this approach (Carroll, 1984a and 1984b; Carroll et al., 1985; Régnier and Ricci, 1988a and 1988b) is the following: the less you provide students, the greater their success. Carroll proposed another version of this paradoxical principle: the less you study a theory and the more you practice it, the better you learn it. One should, for instance, give less reading material and more tasks to perform in order to correct the usual errors that students make while learning. Indeed, students are generally totally overwhelmed when they are told how a program functions, with too many recommendations, explanations, rules, procedures, summaries, descriptions, etc.

Carroll maintains that students do not like being buried under tons of data. Students approach training with a series of objectives and interests that make them skip many important explanations that they deem irrelevant. They have no interest in reviews, summaries, and presentations. The consequences are often unfortunate, because students make serious mistakes and lose a tremendous amount of time trying to understand what is going on. This often happens when students have access to complex information on complex program operations.

Minimal training should also guide students more in their exploration of knowledge. Indeed, students are often treated as if they think things through, take the shortest path, and never make mistakes. This is not so! Students tend to make every possible mistake (Carroll et al., 1988). Those who learn to use a computer program tend to get stuck because they do not consider what is happening on the screen, do not take the time to read the manual carefully, make a lot of mistakes, want to understand everything instantly, want to do tasks right away, go back and forth a lot, go around in circles, and so on.

Students jump into action right away because they want to learn by doing things without following the steps described logically in the instruction manual. This is why Robert L. Mack, Clayton Lewis, and Carroll (1984) say that a logically designed manual, full of details, may be of little or no use, and even treated with aversion. Students often have the feeling that they are following instructions but not understanding what they are doing!

Carroll and his colleagues issued a series of recommendations for preparing a minimal manual and minimal training:

- Eliminate wordiness. For instance, Carroll prepared and then successfully used a minimal manual only twenty-five percent as long as the commercial manual designed to teach the use of a computer program; each chapter had fewer than three pages.

- Determine what information to provide as well as which procedures to execute in the most frequent cases of error.

- Anticipate every possible error — because students are going to make them all.

- Keep students from losing too much time in recovering from errors.

- Focus on real-life activities and tasks from the start.

- Provide tasks that make sense to students.

- Take advantage of students' interest in doing things.

- Encourage students to explore according to their interests and motivation; facilitate their exploration.

- Give advice that takes into account the context, rather than ask students to do repetitive exercises.

- Temporarily block access to complex operations of the program.

A key element of this training method has become the "electronic scenario" (Carroll and Kaye, 1988), i.e., a training interface in the computer that provides students with a training strategy consisting of simplified steps. The notion of electronic scenario developed by these authors tries to make the educational environment relatively simple and easy to manage, which reassures students. The options are reduced within the scenario, which allows access to only one possible way out of several to perform an operation. For instance, the computer displays "function not yet available" to direct students appropriately and gradually in their learning. In the WordPerfect electronic scenario, for example, there is only one way to erase a word, whereas in the complete program the expert can get the same result in twenty-five different ways. In short, students move step by step in exploring the program.

This minimalist philosophy of training goes against systemic thinking, where everything is cut up into multiple elements, where everything is foretold, stated, repeated, and summarized. It goes against behaviorist thinking, which stresses closely structuring the pedagogical environment. The minimalist philosophy relies on students' intuitive exploration, contrary to systemic thinking, which determines the best possible way in advance. In one case, all roads lead to Rome; in the other, there is only one way and you have to take it!

Carroll maintains (1984b) that adding further commentaries in a manual only undermines acquiring knowledge and skills, the real goal of instruction. Carroll (1988) admits to following the neo-Piagetian path opened by Robbie Case (1978) and being opposed to such approaches as those of David Ausubel, Joseph Novak, and Helen Hanesian (1978), Susan Meyer Markle (1978), and Robert Gagné, Leslie Briggs, and Walter Wager (1988), approaches that were essentially centered on hierarchical breakdown of the programs.

This open approach to training led Carroll and his colleagues to question what we call "open technology of computer-human interactivity." Carroll and Jean McKendree (1987) wondered how to design a system to give advice to students. They wondered about a theory of intervention. In training through more or less directed exploration and in case of a problem, how and when should intervention occur? What type of intervention? What level of explanation should be provided? How far should the system back up to give help effectively? What is the minimum knowledge required for troubleshooting? How can a system acquire this information? What should it know? How can it be efficient? How does one integrate the different intervention strategies? What are the most frequent errors? How does one take them into account in designing the system? Can help dialogues be built?

Those are very important questions that need to be answered if we want to provide an effective interactive environment. To leave students totally free to explore does not seem to be a solution. The structure of this guidance is at the heart of the proposed model.

4.6 Conclusion

In the end, technological theories, initially influenced by systems approach and cybernetics, are faced with a problem: the teacher loses control of the teaching process. Indeed, teachers have realized along the way that the use of technologies constitutes a transfer of their power over the act of educating to other people, namely instructional technologists, media specialists, information theorists, pedagogical advisors, systems experts, taxonomists, docimologists, cognitivists, constructivists, and so forth. An army of specialists has taken over the act of educating.

In the end, teachers are faced with what they consider a major problem: the erosion of their power. Now the important question is: who controls the educational process?

The problem of the teacher has shifted from the problem of *means* to the problem of controlling the technology. This explains in large part the return to classical techniques of pedagogical communication, those that teachers can master in their classrooms. Indeed, teachers have an unexpected reaction to this vast and grandiose technological upsurge — small is beautiful!

People go back to the simple technology that they themselves can control. The use of such simple means as transparencies is reassuring, unlike systemic organization or the use of such complex means as hypermedia. Hypermedia transfers to the student control over instruction. It will become more and more difficult to determine the objectives and to close the system while establishing an open, intelligent, diversified, and computer-run system. The teacher definitively loses control over the computer as the student gains control.

The same problem exists in the systemic organization of instruction. The teacher is caught in a method that he or she no longer controls because it is managed by other specialists. Systems theory was expected to produce a more global and human vision of education. It has changed through the years under the influence of analytical minds. The result: it has become an *analytical* hyper-methodology of educational processes that requires specialists to explain it!

Finally, there is no alternative but to note that cybernetics and systems theory, which are both control technologies, were used by teachers to better control the educational process. Paradoxically, this control has slowly shifted, like sand sifting through an hourglass, from the teacher to the specialists!

Chapter 5

Social Cognitive Theories

This trend of education stresses the cultural and social factors in the construction of knowledge. The focus is on the social and cultural interactions that form pedagogy and didactics. Numerous researchers are questioning the domination of the cognitivist trend in research. They note most particularly the problems caused by a vision of education that is overly psychological.

Social cognitive theories describe the social and cultural conditions of teaching and learning. Some theories dwell on the analysis of social interactions of cooperation in the construction of knowledge and propose a cooperative pedagogy in order to sensitize students to this way of working. Others stress the cultural foundations of education and propose that pedagogy include the necessary cultural dimension. These theories are thus opposed to the cognitive movement, which is rather individualistic and concerned with the very nature of the process of knowing.

5.1   Transactions between Individuals and their Environment

There is a whole body of theories of education that are especially concerned with the social and cultural dimensions of learning. Their emphasis is on the predominance of social interactions in learning mechanisms.

Social cognitive theories originated when teachers suddenly became aware of the need to take into account the cultural and social conditions of learning. This is why social cognitive theories are strongly influenced by social psychology. They naturally have a lot to say about the social nature of learning.

Social cognitive theories differ from the psychocognitive movement in that they stress the many facets of the sociocultural transactions between a person and his or her environment. Such is not the case with the psychocognitive movement, which is more concerned with what is going on in the brain, like the logic of problem resolution (Tardif, 1992), for instance.

It should also be noted that social cognitive theories differ from social theories (analyzed in Chapter 6). They do not advocate any social change (for instance, the suppression of social inequalities), but merely that we take into consideration the social and cultural factors affecting learning in a school environment. As we will see later, social theories are also interested in the influence of the sociocultural element on learning, but especially in the problems of society. They want to train students for social change.

We will analyze five different social cognitive approaches:

1. The theories of social learning principally championed by Albert Bandura in the United States

2. The theory of social cognitive conflict developed by several researchers in France

3. The sociohistorical theory of L.S. Vygotsky (also spelled Vygotski and Vygotskii) in Russia

4. The theories of contextualized learning proposed by researchers from the Institute for Research on Learning in the United States

5. Cooperative teaching and learning theories

These theories will be described in this order to emphasize the position of each in relation to the notion of environment. Indeed, the first three share a conception of the environment as limited to the school; they are especially concerned with school environment and social relationships within the school. Cognitive psychology has a greater influence over social cognitive theories than does sociology. On the other hand, the theory of contextualized learning is not limited to the school environment; it takes into account the effects of surrounding culture on learning.

The problems of social cognitive theories lie in the fact that teachers and researchers are aware of the need to allow for the cultural and social conditions of learning. Many analyses and observations made by educators conclude that these conditions should be taken into consideration in order to achieve learning. Second, there is more interest in the influences of the environment (surroundings, social classes, regional culture, and popular culture) on learning. There are questions about the importance of peers and efficiency of the participants (i.e.,tutors) in constructing a pedagogical situation. The notions of culture and contexts now play an important part in reflections on education.

Consider, for example, teaching French in a multiethnic country. French instruction in Quebec and Canada perfectly exemplifies the need for a social and cultural analysis of learning conditions. Indeed, allowance should be made for several social and cultural factors such as the existence of an anglophone minority in a mostly francophone province inside a mostly anglophone country. Such a cultural situation determines the shape of and gives a very different meaning to language learning.

Will students truly learn French if they do not come from a francophone family and if they are more interested in English, the language of the minority in Quebec, but of the majority in Canada? As a matter of fact, schools in Montreal are faced with this major problem: students do not really want to learn French under such circumstances.

A similar problem exists in the anglophone provinces. In 1990, a professor from the University of Ottawa investigated French instruction in Canada and established that instructional problems do not come from the programs, but from the way parents and students perceive French and from the attitudes of the teachers! In short, the nature of learning is fundamentally social and cultural, and the ties between learning and life should be taken into consideration. From now on, we should talk of "learning *in situ*": the pedagogical theories analyzed in this chapter are concrete examples of this concern regarding cultural and social effects on learning.

During the second half of the twentieth century, social cognitive pedagogy has evolved in the following manner. In the 1960s, some education theorists developed theories to prepare students for a more democratic life. Especially inspired by John Dewey

(1857-1952), these theorists emphasized the social dimension of school education and developed pedagogical theories with the aim of eventually improving democratic processes in school.

School organization was to provide experience-based learning situations and allow students to work in groups and acquire democratic social behaviors. Thus, Herbert Thelen (1960) formed a theory of group research that took into account three important elements: society, knowledge, and the individual. This theory, described by Bruce Joyce and Marsha Weil in *Models of Teaching* (first edition, 1972), served as a springboard for other cooperative theories, such as that of Yael Sharan and Shlomo Sharan (1990).

Indeed, according to Joyce, Weil, and Beverly Showers (1992), these theories were intended to promote greater democracy because they really emphasized social interaction and the democracy of interactions in the classroom. Joyce, Weil, and Showers (1992) concluded their analysis by saying that those who developed educational theories based on a vision of democracy-in-action tended to be social "constructivists."

The democratic process was defined as the construction of democratic worlds, i.e., the creation of interactions among the personal and unique worlds of individuals. Constructivists wanted to build a school reality that would promote individual and social growth. This theory should not be confused with the constructivism of psychocognitive theories. Psychocognitive theories are concerned with the *logical* construction of knowledge, whereas social cognitive theories are concerned with the *social* construction of knowledge.

In the 1970s, the democracy theme, which can also be found in social models, was replaced by the theme of cultural and social learning factors. The most recent theories rely more on research conducted in the fields of social psychology. They take into consideration the notion of culture, forgoing the concept of democracy for the "social and cultural form" of knowledge. These theories translate into such pedagogical strategies as cooperative instruction.

This meaning of the notion of culture should not be confused with the meaning it will later have in academic theories. In academic theories, culture is understood as a characteristic of an individual with considerable knowledge and an excellent general education. This is not the meaning given to culture in social cognitive theories. Culture, in this case, should be understood as a set of interconnected rules from which individuals derive conducts and behaviors in order to adapt to particular situations, the implicit and vague knowledge of the world from which individuals negotiate behaviors.

Cultural patterns and social deeds provide the framework and guiding principle of action for any human action, growth, and understanding. The human being is like a spider that weaves and hangs from a web of meaning, which is his or her culture.

5.2   Social Cognitive Theories of Social Learning

5.2.1 History and Issues

There are more and more theories about social learning. This is why we focus on the person who appears to be the mastermind of this important movement: Albert Bandura, the pioneer of thought on social learning.

As early as 1962, he was interested in the social origins of thought and undertook research on learning by imitation. He noted that we learn a lot by taking others as our models, and that the media greatly influences our behaviors. He also realized that psychological theories, such as Skinner's behaviorism, do not sufficiently allow for influences from symbolic worlds constructed by real-life environments. He observed that educational theories were derived from lab experiments, which exclude contextual variables, and he recommended getting out of the laboratories and going into real environments (Gredler, 1992). He rejected humanistic theories, based on the individual.

In *Social Learning Theory* (1971), he proposed a theory of social characteristics of learning. Later, in *Social Foundations of Thought and Action* (1986), he presented an interactional social cognitive theory that explained the relationships among the environment, action, and thought. He justified (1986) the use of the expression "social cognitive" in this way: "social" because thought and action are fundamentally social, "cognitive" because thought processes influence motivation, emotions, and action.

Bandura's research gave rise to many studies and much experimentation, and it led to the birth of a number of social cognitive theories of learning that were applied to the instruction provided in schools and businesses. In the early 1980s, the first authors to apply social cognitive theory in the domain of organizations were Robert Lord, Steven Feldman, Charles Manz, Henry Sims, Tim Davis, Dennis Gioia, Fred Luthans, Robert Kreitner, and David Deshler. The second wave included Eleanor Rosch, Nancy Cantor, Walter Mischel, Robert Wyer, Thomas Srull, Susan Fiske, Martha Cox, and Alice Isen.

Indeed, many people have noted the inefficacy of traditional methods, which are often limited to transmitting knowledge to passive and unmotivated students. As Rolland Viau (1994) states:

> Many teachers take their students to task for not being motivated and not making the necessary efforts to learn: "No matter how many times we explain this to them," they say, "students do not listen to us any more; nothing motivates them." But can you really blame students for not being motivated when, most of the time, they are simply asked to listen, memorize, and prove on exams that they remember information that they consider totally useless?

These teachers and researchers turned toward a constructivist vision of knowledge and toward social psychology to elaborate theories characterized by their appreciation of the social dimension of learning. Thus, a number of teachers and researchers, such as Barbara McCombs (1988), Dale Schunk (1989), Barry Zimmerman (1990), and Viau (1994) developed social cognitive theories that follow the path blazed by Bandura. However, they do not pursue their theories into social action.

5.2.2 Principles

It is not possible in this survey to analyze all of the principles of social cognitive theory as described by Bandura, Schunk, and others. We will now consider a few principles that are generally found in reflections and research on social cognitive learning: reciprocal influence, indirect learning, symbolic representation, perception of one's efficacy, self-regulation, and modeling.

Reciprocal Influence
Social cognitive theory is based on the notion of *reciprocal influence* of sociocultural, personal, and behavioral factors in learning and in action. This is its first characteristic. More

precisely, learning is based on the necessity for the triple interaction among these factors.

What Bandura (1986) proposes goes against unidirectional behaviorist theories in the style of Skinner, for whom human behavior solely depends on what is happening in his or her environment. It also goes against Freudian psychodynamic theories, according to which behavior is motivated by needs, impulses, and instincts particular to each individual.

According to Bandura (1986), people are not solely dependent on their needs, nor are they automatically controlled by their environment. They influence their environment, which in turn influences them. The three sets of elements influence one another in the development of knowledge and in action: events in the environment, characteristics of the individual, and behaviors. Bandura insists (1986) on the differences between his concept and the concept found in what he calls psychodynamic psychology (the personalist theory of education examined in Chapter 2), according to which human behavior results from the dynamism of inner forces and often unconscious compulsions. Bandura does not accept this theory of an unconscious inner dynamism that structures behavior. Instead, he suggests the theme of social transactional dynamism.

The following is what Bandura (1977, quoted by Viau, 1994, p. vii) means by "social learning":

> Social learning theory approaches the explanation of human behavior in terms of a continuous reciprocal interaction between cognitive, behavioral, and environmental determinants. Within the process of reciprocal determinism lies the opportunity for people to influence their destiny as well as the limits of self-direction. This conception of human functioning then neither casts people into the role of powerless objects controlled by environmental forces nor of free agents who can become whatever they choose. Both people and their environments are reciprocal determinants of each other.

Indirect Learning

A second characteristic of social cognitive theory is *indirect learning* (Bandura, 1986). The individual does not have to do things in order to learn; instead, he or she can merely observe others doing things. For instance, a person notices that some-body is always punished when he or she argues with the teacher. Therefore, he or she decides to avoid arguments! Another example: an individual develops an aversion to snakes by observing someone panicking upon seeing one. Therefore, any individual can learn by observing the results of actions of others.

Symbolic Representation

A third characteristic is *symbolic representation*. Our thoughts and actions are structured by representations we make of everything that is going on in the world. In fact, says Bandura (1986), humans have a certain "plasticity" that depends on what they are, what they do, what they want to do, and what they think they could do. They possess different abilities that make them human. They have ideas; they communicate them and act according to them. They can imagine the future, set goals for themselves, and act according to this representation of what could happen in the future (prospective capacity).

Perception of One's Efficacy

A fourth characteristic of social cognitive theory is the percep-tion that an individual has of his or her ability to succeed and the efficacy of his or her actions (Bandura, 1986 and 1990; Gredler, 1992). Incidentally, it should be stressed that this characteristic dominates in neurolinguistic programming theo-ries. One has to believe in success in order to succeed, according to the "neurolinguistic programmers." It should also be stressed that this idea — "stop being afraid and believe in success" — has been around for a long time. However, Bandura was one of the first to build a learning theory that took into consideration the important role that an individual's perceptions play with regard to the efficacy of his or her actions.

Individuals' learning and actions depend on their judgment of their abilities. Thus, their perception that they are capable of performing a given task is undeniably going to influence the results of their future behaviors. The more they believe in their success, the better their chance of succeeding. If they succeed, that result also modifies the perceptions they have of their ability to succeed.

However, if the results of their actions are judged as unsatisfac-tory by the members of their community, those consequences will influence their self-perceptions, positively or negatively. This could lead to the following paradox: an individual may know exactly what to do and yet fail in doing it because he or she feels incapable of succeeding (Bandura, 1990). Such would be the case, for instance, with a teacher who, in spite of competence and pedagogical experience, can no longer teach adequately because he or she has lost faith in his or her abilities.

Self-Regulation

A fifth characteristic of social cognitive theory is *self-regulation* (Bandura, 1977 and 1986; Gredler, 1992). The examples above show that individuals have the ability to regulate themselves. They are not at the mercy of their environment or their instincts. They can act in accordance with their needs and modify their actions according to the results achieved. They can think over what is going on; they can observe themselves, analyze themselves, and even analyze the way they think and modify their own perceptions and actions. This is what certain authors call metacognition. In a word, individuals possess a certain control over their own destiny.

Modeling

A sixth characteristic of social cognitive theory is the *use of models* (Bandura, 1986). Individuals learn through imitating others. In certain cases, they choose one person as a model and imitate some of his or her behaviors. (Consider, for example, Y. Bertrand, 1991, and Sims and Lorenzi, 1992.) The slight difference between indirect learning and learning by modeling is that, in the first case, one learns by observing the results of another individual's behavior, while in the second, one learns from the results of one's own behaviors.

A number of research studies of on-the-job training focus on modeling. Many questions remain. When does an employee learn by imitating either a colleague or a superior? How does one explain instances when he or she does not? How does a new employee learn the values and behaviors of an organizational culture?

5.2.3 Pedagogical Strategies

Bearing in mind these principles, how can we build a theory of instruction? It is not easy, considering that social cognitive theories of learning stress reciprocal interdependencies among many factors. Consequently, we cannot develop from social cognitive theories a simple and complete theory of instruction. However, many authors make judicious recommendations — some of which we will now consider.

1. Presenting Students with Models of Behavior
(Bandura, 1986; Gredler, 1992)
Students like to adopt the behaviors of people whom they regard as their models. Therefore, teachers should find models of behavior to be taught and present them to students.

For instance, teachers would like to teach responsibility. Explaining responsibility is a good thing, but it would be even better to bring to class a person whom society deems responsible (like a doctor) and encourage interactions that would influence students. A teacher who wants to show how to take notes should not simply lay down guidelines on the procedure, but rather should execute the required operations by taking notes. He or she should give a demonstration, clearly commenting on what he or she is doing.

2. Assessing and Justifying the Values of Behaviors
(Bandura, 1977)
Bandura maintains that learning a behavior depends on the value that one attributes to the result. Therefore, teachers should demonstrate the benefit of each lesson to students. Students learn better if they see how it could be useful in their lives.

3. Reinforcing Students in their Behaviors
(Bandura, 1986; Gredler, 1992)
It is very important to give positive feedback to a student who is making progress in learning. Among other things, it allows the student to build a positive self-image and to perceive himself or herself as being able to perform a task. It is just as important to curtail certain behaviors by punishment.

4. Practicing
(Bandura, 1986)
Bandura recommends linking practice to explanation. This is especially true for psychomotor learning. It is very difficult, for example, to learn to play golf without actually playing. This is also true for learning to write: people who can write well know that they had to practice, and practice, and practice again.

These are some of the strategies necessary for a social cognitive theory of education. We will now consider an educational theory proposed by Gredler (1992) in her analysis of Bandura, which we have modified to make more accessible to the reader who has not read Bandura. It should also be noted that strategies of a social cognitive theory of education are often very theoretical. They are always better understood through such examples as teaching tennis, taking notes, or studying film.

Step 1: Analyze the Behaviors to Be Modeled
(example: learning to write a poem)

- Determine the nature of the behavior: conceptual, affective, or motor.
- Determine the sequence of the behavior phases.
- Determine the critical points in the sequence, such as difficulties in observing the behavior and the areas where errors are more likely.

Step 2: Describe the Benefits of a Behavior and Selecting the Model of Behavior to Teach

- Determine the benefits or success, for the student, of the behavior to be learned. For instance, it is important to learn to write well if a future job requires writing a lot of reports.
- When a given behavior is of little value, find another model of behavior leading to success. Models include peers, the teacher, and social models connected to success.
- Determine if the model should be symbolic or real. A writer could be invited to class to meet the students.
- Determine what reinforcements are necessary for learning the behavior and include them in the model.

Step 3: Prepare a Sequence of Instruction

- Determine the verbal codes (comments, instructions, signs, explanations) to describe what is to be done and what should not be done.
- Identify the phases of the sequence that require more explanation time. Find explanations needed to facilitate learning.

Step 4: Implement the Sequence of Instruction
In the case of motor skills:

- Have the expert present the skills to be mastered.
- Give students the opportunity to practice.
- Provide visual and oral feedback.

In the case of conceptual behavior:

- Present a model with verbal support.
- In the case of a concept or rule, give students a chance to summarize the modeled behaviors.
- Allow students to model for each other, if it involves solving a problem or applying a strategy.
- Give students the possibility to generalize the learned behavior to other situations.

5.3 Social Cognitive Conflict Theory

5.3.1 History and Issues

A francophone educational research movement took up the constructivist point of view and stressed the notion of *social cognitive conflict* in learning. A social cognitive conflict accounts for logically and socially incompatible answers to a question within the framework of a social interaction (Carugati and Mugny, 1985).

Agnès Blaye (1989) writes that the neo-Piagetian trend of genetic social psychology is the origin of the concept of social cognitive conflict. Numerous researchers became interested in the social, cultural, and interactive dimensions of this disequilibrium. Monique Lefebvre-Pinard (1989) writes that, as early as 1968, the role that social cognitive conflicts played in cognitive development was the object of considerable research in psychological literature, which called it "cognitive-developmental." American studies on social cognitive conflicts can be found from 1966 on (Langer, 1969; Rest, Turiel, and Kohlberg, 1969; Turiel, 1969). The first francophone proponents of this theory were Willem Doise, Gabriel Mugny, and Anne-Nelly Perret-Clermont in the mid-1970s (Gilly, 1989).

The initial question was the social dimension of the notion of prior conception, which was very popular among constructivists. In the chapter on psychocognitive theories, we saw that this notion plays an important role in the construction of knowledge (Bednarz and Garnier, 1989; Giordan, 1990; Larochelle and Desautels, 1992). As research was being conducted on prior conceptions, the importance of the social and cultural dimension, of the construction of knowledge became apparent. Researchers wondered about the social and interactional significance of the obstacle to learning.

The first studies were most interested in relationships between cognitive equilibrium (in the mind of the individual) and social conflicts. Blaye (1989) reminds us that what characterizes this research trend is the proposition that social interaction is constructive only if it induces a confrontation among the divergent solutions of the parties. To bring about a change, therefore, requires a clear divergence and antagonistic social positions.

Michel Gilly (1989) distinguishes two trends. The first is genetic social psychology (Perret-Clermont, Doise, and Mugny), which is strictly in keeping with Piagetian structuralist thinking and focuses on the role of social interactions among peers in the development of intelligence in general. Gilly (1989) writes:

> The social cognitive conflict hypothesis, originally formulated in connection with social interactions, maintains that these exclusively intra-individual conflicts cannot be considered sufficient and that, at certain key moments in development, it is in inter-individual conflicts that we should search for the primary cause of individual progress.

In other words, a person's intelligence evolves through the resolution of successive conflict crises. The second trend — represented by Gilly, Blaye, and Jean-Paul Roux — tries to lessen the importance of the social cognitive conflict and to assign this concept a smaller part in the social construction of knowledge (Blaye, 1989; Gilly, 1989).

5.3.2 Principles

1. Interactions among Individuals

The first principle is that the construction of knowledge is necessarily social and based on a set of interactions among individuals. Doise and Mugny (1981) write that interactions are the source of personal development. This goes against the psychocognitive movement, which is hardly concerned with social interactivity.

2. Social Cognitive Conflict

The second principle of this theory is that the social cognitive conflict is at the root of learning: it stimulates thinking (Doise and Mugny, 1981). Piaget (1963) had already discussed the notion of disequilibrium in these terms:

> The development of intelligence or reasoning happens in stages, beginning with a new situation that upsets the existing field, creating a disequilibrium for which the individual has to compensate by adapting, which results in an improved restoration of equilibrium.

However, Piaget did not seem particularly enthusiastic about the social aspect of this disequilibrium (Piaget and Inhelder, 1969). On the other hand, the new Piagetian trend is more interested in the role that social interactions play in cognitive development and stresses the constructivist view of social cognitive conflict.

Social cognitive conflict plays a major role in this didactic trend. Its proponents depart from the Piagetian individualistic position on cognitive development, a position that postulates a parallel development between the social and cognitive elements (Bednarz and Garnier, 1989; Gilly, 1989).

Such is not the case with social cognitive theory, which tackles the problem of the relationships between individual cognitive dynamism and collective processes. Its proponents are trying to prove that the coordination of actions among individuals takes precedence over personal coordination in the construction of knowledge.

Clearly, Vygotsky's thesis (analyzed later in this chapter) has the advantage over Piaget's thesis and influences social cognitive conflict theory. Vygotsky maintained that it is the whole set of social interactions that allows the individual mind to progress. Nadine Bednarz and Catherine Garnier (1989) remind us that the early works dealt with the causal role of social interactions in accelerating the genesis of cognitive structures, i.e., in going from the pre-operational stage to the operational stage, by means of Piagetian conservation tests. Other researchers then became interested in the study of the social dynamism in the learning of problem resolution procedures.

Lefebvre-Pinard (1985 and 1989), inspired by Vygotsky, defines the problems of social cognitive conflict in these terms:

> When individuals — children or adults — approach a problem inappropriately, without being aware of the insufficiency of their strategies, merely providing them with corrective feedback is not usually enough to modify the rules by which they manage their behaviors. Under what conditions can one induce in these individuals ... a true state of conflict, that they experience as such, and that could be the source of a cognitive restructuring that can be transferred to other situations?

Lefebvre-Pinard believes that elaboration of pedagogical activities can be facilitated by the concept of *proximal development zone*, defined as the distance between the level of actual development, which can be determined by the way children solve problems by themselves, and the level of potential development, which can be determined by the way children solve problems when they are helped by an adult or when they collaborate with other, more advanced children. Lefebvre-Pinard (1989) maintains that it is probably to the extent that a social cognitive conflict situation brings the individual to reflect on his or her cognitive rules and strategies that he or she will eventually be able to use them systematically in an increasing number of situations where they are required.

3. Going beyond Cognitive Disequilibrium in the Individual

A third principle characterizes social cognitive conflict theory: seeking to go beyond the *inter-individual* cognitive disequilibrium causes one to go beyond *intra-individual* cognitive disequilibrium. Gilly (1989) deals with one form of social cognitive conflict in particular: social interactional conflict. This form of conflict can be summed up as follows: work in interaction reveals that in certain cases and under certain conditions, differences in the answers of the participants are based on differences in their points of view. A double disequilibrium often ensues from this: inter-individual — based on the differences in the answers — and intra-individual — because being suddenly aware of another answer tempts the individual to doubt his or her own. However, researchers maintain, this learning situation cannot be reduced to a personal cognitive problem. It is because this is a social problem, they say, that children are led to coordinate their points of view into a new system that will allow them to agree.

Doise and Mugny (1981) take up Vygotsky's thesis (1978) that the development of all higher functions is brought about by transforming an *interpersonal* process into an *intrapersonal* process. Mugny and Doise (1983) write that "children who participated in certain social coordinations later became capable of performing these coordinations by themselves," and that personal progress is an internalization of the new inter-individual coordinations brought about by the resolution of the social cognitive conflict.

5.3.3 Pedagogical Strategies

So far, social cognitive theory has been characterized by strong theoretic reflections on the necessity of confrontations among students. There are few pedagogical applications. However, we could derive some global strategies from the following remarks.

A social cognitive conflict can be effective in learning for the following reasons:

- It allows students to become aware of answers other than their own and of the diversity of viewpoints; this compels them to put themselves off center in relation to their initial answer.

- The conflict increases the probability that the student will be cognitively active, since there is a certain necessity for social regulations, even a coordination among the actions required by a given situation.

- Students learn to discover information (interesting, unexpected, known, reassuring, false, or whatever) in the answers of others, information that will help them construct their knowledge.

- Conflict can bring the student to accept a situation of change and to cooperate in solving problems.

5.4 Vygotsky's Sociohistorical Theory

5.4.1 History and Issues

The cultural diversity that characterizes our modern societies and Vygotsky's insistence on the important role that culture plays in learning explain why there is a growing interest in the reflections of this psychologist. *Modèles pour l'acte pédagogique* (1988), published in France by Christian Alvès, Joëlle Pojé-Chrétien, and Nicole Maous-Chassagny, is a concrete attempt to form a social interactive model inspired by Vygotsky. These teachers are clearly influenced by Vygotsky and his concept of a "zone of proximal development" (or "potential zone of development," "zone of potential development," or "proximal development zone"). They, too, use the notion of pedagogical drama. Pedagogical action, they say, is like a series of plot twists that bring actors to a quest for knowledge. Pedagogy is "the space-time where culture originates," "a potential zone of investment."

About the same time, a great American author, Jerome Bruner, was also making reference to Vygotsky. Bruner (1986) says that we are cultural and social actors. We play only one role in social and cultural dramas. The ego is never independent of its sociocultural existence. It develops out of the large toolbox that is its culture. It interprets the world, through negotiation *with others* (Vygotsky, 1986). In short, the ego is fundamentally transactional. These transactions define and guide the individual in his or her actions, and culture is the evolutive and synergistic set of these transactions.

But who was this Vygotsky, whose texts have been increasingly influential for educational theorists?

Vygotsky was born in 1896 in Russia and died in 1934. He had little time, therefore, to build a body of works, which remains incomplete. It was not until the 1960s that his books were translated into English and, in the 1980s, into French. From the beginning of his career, Vygotsky attacked Pavlov's reflexology and Kohler's gestalt psychology. Instead, he proposed a sociohistorical psychology.

The development of the human mind, he says, is part of a social and historical process. He also attacked academic education. A large number of studies, he writes in *Mind in Society* (1934, 1978), show that teaching discipline, classical languages and civilizations, and mathematics has little influence on the student's mental development. Taking the works of Edward Thorndike as support, Vygotsky maintains that he does not see how learning Latin grammar allows the development of general faculties such as memory, attention, power of observation, concentration, and reasoning skills. Such conclusions cannot be drawn, he says, because the mind is not a network of general capacities such as memory, judgment, attention, or observation.

5.4.2 Principles

We will now examines a few principles that are currently drawing the attention of researchers in education: the zone of proximal development, the link between growth and learning, and cultural mediation.

1. Zone of Proximal Development

In *Mind in Society*, Vygotsky suggests the concept of the zone of proximal development to describe the functions that are maturing in the student. He defines it as the distance between two levels: the level of current development — measured by the student's ability to solve problems *by himself or herself* — and the level of development measured by the student's ability to solve problems *when helped by someone*. Vygotsky adds that the current level measures past development, whereas the zone of proximal development measures potential development or the state of maturing processes.

Many researchers refer to this concept in their studies. An example will make it more clear. Take, for example, someone to whom we want to teach tennis. The zone of proximal development is the distance between what he or she knows how to do (his or her real state of knowledge) and what he or she can eventually do, i.e., the final state of development when taught how to play. Education deals with this zone of potential development. In other words, two individuals who are being taught tennis could reach, at the same age, the same level of development (they would be considered, based on their behaviors, equal in their development), but have different potentials (they would be considered unequal in their development).

The existence of this zone is based on two axioms: the possibility for development and the need for sociocultural mediation. We will now consider each of these axioms.

2. Link between Growth and Learning

Like many others, Vygotsky maintains that students possess a certain control over their development. They can grow. This growth is a function of their learning. Vygotsky takes the trouble to express his opposition to those who, like Piaget, think that growth precedes learning (e.g., one needs to reach a certain developmental stage to be able to learn formal reasoning). He also opposes those who, like William James, claim that learning is identical to growth and that both happen simultaneously. Finally, he opposes those for whom growth and development influence each other. They have not examined the nature of this influence, he says.

3. Sociocultural Mediation

The zone of proximal development has a very special characteristic: it is social and cultural. In other words, the individual who learns to play tennis will play the way the teacher has shown him or her and like the other students. He or she will learn a very specific behavior determined by the learning context. He or she will have a style that will imitate, to a certain degree, that of the teacher. The individual also imitates others. This constitutes a social and cultural learning process. The same thing applies if this individual learns to write. His or her writing, after learning, will reflect the culture of the teacher.

Other examples would also show that the zone of proximal development described by Vygotsky is a social and cultural theory that could have an important impact on education. Indeed, if learning depends on the interactions that take place in the student's zone of development, then we should pay close attention to those interactions, which are caused by others: fellow students, parents, and teachers.

5.4.3 Pedagogical Strategies

Vygotsky did not specifically write on instructional strategies. However, he discussed learning theories and their impact on theories of education. This is the reason why Bruner said that Vygotsky proposed a theory of education.

It is other researchers and teachers, like Annemarie Sullivan Palincsar and Ann Brown (1984), James Wertsch (1985a and 1985b), Luis Moll (1990), and Margaret Gredler (1992), who later built educational models applying his principles of "sociohistorical psychology."

Gredler (1992) describes an instructional strategy that follows Vygotsky's theory and works for a very small group (two to six persons). We will now see the main steps.

Step 1: Identify the Concepts or Principles to be Taught

1.1 What are the concepts or principles that characterize the world of the students (i.e., an interest in computer science)?

1.2 What are the concepts or principles that can help students master their own thinking (for instance, summarizing a text to show that they understand it)?

Step 2: Structure the Learning Activity

2.1 What is the level of common comprehension necessary to start learning?

2.2 What parts of the activity should the teacher model?

2.3 What activities should the teacher carry out first?

2.4 How should students use signs and symbols to regulate their behaviors?

2.5 What suggestions and feedback should the teacher give to facilitate learning?

Step 3: Implement and Assess

3.1 Did the teacher raise the level of difficulty appropriately as the students progressed?

3.2 Were the students able to function autonomously at the end of the course?

3.4 Did the students acquire skills that can be generalized to other situations?

5.5 Contextualized Learning Theory

5.5.1 History and Issues

The question on which these theories are based is that of learning context. The fundamental question: Can knowledge be drawn out of the real-life situations in which it is used?

It is often said that the primary objective of school consists of transmitting knowledge to students. It is proclaimed that students acquire the same knowledge whatever the place or school. The pedagogical context, i.e., learning activities and the learning and teaching context itself, is considered only secondarily. Such are the terms of the instructional problem.

Researchers John Brown, Allan Collins, Paul Duguid, William Clancey, Roy Pea, and James Greeno, working mostly with the Institute for Research on Learning in Palo Alto, California, maintain that knowledge acquisition cannot be separated from its pedagogical, cultural, and social contexts. A number of pedagogies assume this division between knowledge and the environment in which it is used. In contrast, these theorists claim that the learning context should be integrated. They also maintain that to ignore the learning context goes against the primary mission of education, which is to provide students with knowledge that is useful in real life.

Brown, Collins, and Duguid (1989 and 1993) assert that learning — as determined by present school culture — is incomplete, even unsuited to the real world. Schools have a problem: they act as if knowledge stands by itself, outside of all sociocultural context. Schools ignore the cultural context in which knowledge originates (Lave, 1988a) and are not concerned with the social context in which it will be used.

There are now several variants among theories of learning *in situ* and the field of inquiry is broadening. Researchers associated with the Institute for Research on Learning — John Seely Brown, Roy Pea, Allan Collins, Paul Duguid, William Clancey, Étienne Wenger — have continued their studies on the cultural context of learning. Jean Lave has been researching and publishing on different aspects of learning *in situ*, with Wenger and Seth Chaiklin. The research is exploring, among other things, the culture of learning, the impact of new communications technologies on the social aspect of learning (the situated nature of learning), and the different social contexts, such as active learning structures (Lave, 1988b; Lave and Wenger, 1993; Lave and Chaiklin, 1993; Resnick, Levine, and Teasley, 1991).

5.5.2 Principles

1. A Theory of Knowledge Should Be Social and Cultural
Theories of contextualized learning are based on a fundamental principle: knowledge is a tool that essentially depends on action

and culture. Lave (1991b), Brown, Collins, and Duguid (1989), and Clancey (1992) propose a theory of educational research based on this fundamental principle: action and everyday culture determine the structuring of knowledge. We must abandon the idea that concepts are autonomous and abstract entities, they say, and analyze them beginning with how they relate to everyday action.

Lave (1991b) gives the following question as an example:

> Are there differences in arithmetic procedures between situations in schools (e.g., taking a math test) and situations far removed from school scenarios (in the kitchen or supermarket)?

Knowledge is fundamentally the product of social and cultural activities; it cannot be analyzed properly if we begin with a cognitive psychological approach. Rather, we need to turn to social psychology and social anthropology as disciplines that can help us think about knowledge.

The heart of the problem is this: How can we analyze the environments where knowledge actually becomes structured? Lave (1991b) analyzes this position as follows:

> The project is a "social anthropology of cognition" rather than a "psychology" because there is reason to suspect that what we call cognition is in fact a complex social phenomenon.

2. Knowledge Acquisition Springs from Participation

Lave and Wenger (1991) assert that knowledge acquisition, thought, and knowledge are really relationships among individuals involved in an activity with and within a socially and culturally structured world. It is inconceivable for someone to acquire knowledge outside of participation in a social group. According to Lave and Wenger (1991), "Participation in social practice is the fundamental form of learning."

Whatever the nuances among theorists (Collins, Duguid, Pea, Lave, Wenger), conceptual knowledge is basically a set of tools that will be used in real-life situations. The term "tools" entails situation, history, expertise, accumulation of knowledge, experience, art, artisan, and, of course, apprentice. A tool makes sense only if there is a situation in which it can be used and if it relies on the history of its uses.

This is true for any field of knowledge, including mathematics (Lave, 1991b). Going through a mathematical proof, for example, makes sense in the end only if this proof is used in carrying out a task. Analogously, it may seem easy to understand how a computer works. It can be explained on the blackboard, different kinds can be shown, and so forth. However, it is the use of this tool that provides a true knowledge of it. In other words, one can learn to *use* a computer only in concrete situations. One also learns to benefit from the experience of other users, consult a manual, and exchange information. In short, a concept is always connected to an activity and a culture, say Brown, Collins, and Duguid (1989). To learn a concept is to learn a tool that has a history based on practical experiences.

Here is how William F. Hanks (1991) summarizes this position:

> Learning is a process that takes place in a participation framework, not in an individual mind. This means, among other things, that it is mediated by the differences of perspective among the coparticipants. It is the community, or at least those participating in the learning context, who "learn" under this definition.

3. Cultural Context Defines the Environment for Using Knowledge

The notion of "cultural context" should be understood as the characteristics of the environment in which knowledge will be given and used. This context is not necessarily in a school. Learning can happen at home, in the workplace, in a summer camp, in a sports center, or at the movies. And this learning often occurs in the presence of someone with expertise in the learning area. Thus, a learner can be considered as apprentice — "learners are apprentices" (Lave and Wenger, 1991) — in many situations that are not necessarily school situations.

Take, for example, automotive mechanics. Learning in school and learning at the corner garage are two very different things because the contexts are different. Learning automotive mechanics is one thing; it's quite another to solve the problems of a customer who comes to the garage to gripe at you about the maintenance done on his or her car. The difference between the two cases comes from the concrete insertion of knowledge, i.e., the presence of a context that, in real-life situations, considerably modifies the use of the knowledge acquired in school.

School culture almost always presents well-defined problems, whereas problems in real-life culture are poorly defined or only partially explained. Thus, in the example above, the mechanic will also have to try to understand what it means when the customer says, "My car is making weird noises!" He or she will often have to use knowledge not acquired in school, knowledge that comes from living in a certain milieu.

This example may help us understand the comment by Lave and Wenger (1991):

> In our view, learning is not merely situated in practice — as if it were some independently reifiable process that just happened to be located somewhere; learning is an integral part of generative social practice in the lived-in world.

5.5.3 Pedagogical Strategies

Consequently, Clancey (1992), just like his colleagues Brown, Collins, and Duguid, maintains that knowledge should be taken out of its school context and put back into its original context, and that the cultural characteristics of the situations from which this knowledge originates should be taught through *genuine activities*, i.e., the common practices of culture. Otherwise, students have no idea of the environment in which they will have to use this knowledge.

Instructional situations are often hybrid, a mix of school culture (what teachers and students do in school) and genuine culture (what practitioners do in real life). Students are often faced with at least two different reference levels, a very strong one (school culture) and a very weak one (the culture of practitioners). Under such conditions, students cannot properly identify signs in the genuine culture that would help them better understand what they are being taught.

It should also be noted that students who do well in school culture (they understand how to answer the teacher, how to answer exam questions, etc.) are not necessarily assured of succeeding in their professional environment. They will have to adapt to another culture, which is not that of the teacher or the school. They will have to learn to function in another environment, which is not that of schools and universities. However, as a crowning misfortune, they will not have had the necessary preparation for this adaptation unless they have been lucky enough to have had some training in a company. Understandably, Clancey, Brown, Collins, and Duguid are not very fond of the following ideas: "learning is personal and has its own structure," "school is neutral and independent from its environment," "concepts are abstract and independent from all context."

Therefore, Brown, Collins, and Duguid (1989 and 1993) suggest using the notion of "apprentice." Just like an individual who learns an art (painting, engraving, martial arts, etc.) or a trade, the student should be a "cognitive apprentice" and the teacher should be a guide or instructor.

What is meant by "cognitive apprentice"? An apprentice is someone who learns a trade. Consider these four interesting aspects of the situation of an apprentice:

- **An apprentice learns in "real" situations, those of everyday life.** His or her knowledge is inserted and contextualized; therefore, he or she acquires skills that are true conceptual tools.

- **An apprentice learns with others and shares his or her knowledge, problems, and discoveries in a collective approach.** The group context allows the apprentice to play different roles. He or she will better understand what to expect when he or she has to fit into a work team. This socialization is important. Students should get used to working together. They learn how to go from a personal microworld to a more complex and extended universe.

- **An apprentice learns in a group guided by a master.** The teacher should first and foremost make explicit the prior knowledge of each student. He or she should then help the students in their attempts to understand. The teacher creates learning situations. Finally, he or she should encourage each student to continue his or her work with a certain autonomy. The teacher is a cognitive *instructor* who works with the student in the same way as, for instance, a ski instructor or a tennis instructor.

- **An apprentice learns to overcome obstacles.** This pedagogical strategy also relies on exchanges dealing with inefficient strategies, errors, misconceptions, etc. Thus, students' prior conceptions can be detected more easily, the obstacles presented by these conceptions can be overcome, and students can become accustomed to living in ill-defined situations, with errors, wasted time, and so forth.

5.6 Cooperative Teaching and Learning Theories

5.6.1 History and Issues

Cooperative teaching and learning theories are quite popular at the moment. More and more teachers are interested in this conception of education. These theories are presently back in favor in France and the United States. Two journals, *Le Nouvel Éducateur* (France) and *Cooperative Learning* (U.S.), contain a number of very illuminating and interesting texts on the everyday reality of cooperation.

Cooperative theories have been around for a long time. France had its theorists very early. French cooperative pedagogy is mainly inspired by Célestin Freinet, who introduced his theory of education in France in 1936-37. The objectives of cooperative pedagogy inspired by Freinet can be summed up as follows (M. Bertrand, 1992):

Freinet's pedagogy is based on four main ideas:
- The right to express oneself and communicate
- Critical analysis of reality
- Taking charge of oneself
- Taking charge of the group

It is a permanent process:
- Between the individual and the group, at the level of students, teachers, and different groups of adults
- Between theory and practice, using material means (pedagogical tools) and institutional means (cooperative and correspondent)
- Between the class and the environment

It is a materialist pedagogy, in which the use of tools and work techniques — which are always perfectible — allows the students to become personally and collectively autonomous and acquire knowledge.

The thinking that underlies cooperative instruction is based on a few observations that constantly come up in writings:

- Passivity generated by traditional teaching
- Absence of direct contact among students
- Pedagogical weakness of certain active methods
- Low tolerance of cultural, economic, social, and ethnic diversity

Thus, the rather conservative teaching of the 1980s encouraged group divisions according to explicit or implicit criteria of social and cultural selection. The American expression "tracking" adequately fits the situation — especially when we realize that there are inevitably "sidings" for shunting students who seem less gifted!

It should also be noted that traditional teaching translates into pedagogical practices for transmitting knowledge. This everyday practice leaves little room for developing humanistic and personalist pedagogical methods that would allow the student greater freedom.

Finally, it may be observed that many teachers favor interactivity in the classroom but do not use the appropriate means to achieve positive results. One research study has shown that to have students participate is not as easy as it would seem, that two or three students (in a class of 40) control half of the interactions, and that four or five students are at the origin of 75% of all interactions in a class (Karp and Yoels, 1987). On the other hand, many studies and experiments (Schniedewind and David-son, 1983; Slavin, 1987, 1990a and 1990b, and 1991; Augustine, Gruber, and Hanson, 1990; Johnson and Johnson, 1990; Levin, 1990; Bennett, 1991; Joyce, Weil, and Showers, 1992; and Shor, 1992a) have shown the efficacy of cooperative learning with regard to functioning in a group, learning to think critically, and acquiring "meta-cognitive" methods of learning.

All of these problems — student passivity, difficulties of working in groups, and pedagogical conservatism — led many teachers and researchers to consider cooperative methods. Indeed, as teachers reacted against pedagogical conservatism and especially against student passivity, they sought a solution to these problems in theories of teamwork that gave a higher priority to student activities. They developed educational interventions that were characterized primarily by the active participation of students and by the integration of all students, irrespective of their ethnic, economic, social, or other origins.

5.6.2 Principles

Cooperative instruction is based on great principles that have been described a number of times, including writings from the beginning of the twentieth century. What people were saying about cooperative instruction many years ago still holds true. Any differences are due especially to this "new" social and cultural complexity created by urbanization, immigration, and mass media. These changes call for adapting the theories of yesteryear. The principles, however, remain the same.

We will now give a short description of these principles, which can be found in almost all teaching and learning cooperative theories (Houssaye, 1988a and 1992; Augustine, Gruber, and Hanson, 1990; Cooper, Prescott, Cook, Smith, Mueck, and Cuseo, 1990; Kagan, 1990a; Joyce, Weil, and Showers, 1992; and Shor, 1992b).

Partnership

Cooperative learning is based on a very simple principle: students learn more when they can work together on a common project. Consequently, instructional structures should be put into place to facilitate the synergy of students working together. Partnership should replace competition. Thus, grouping students around a common project is a strategy generally used in cooperative instruction.

Flexibility

There is an almost infinite number of ways to carry out cooperative instruction, as this theory is characterized by its great flexibility. One has to adapt according to the circumstances, the groups of students, cultures, regions, etc. No single model works in all circumstances.

Mutual Aid

Cooperative learning is based on the principle that everyone should help one another. Each participates in a collective work. The more gifted students should help the less gifted, for a chain is never stronger than its weakest link.

Dianne Augustine, Kristin Gruber, and Lynda Hanson (1990) maintain that cooperative instruction has positive effects on all students — weak, average, or strong. The weak can benefit from the support of the group and succeed where they had failed. Average students generally see their performance improve. Stronger students learn to work with others, as they have not done before, given their superior aptitude. Within cooperative work formats, they take greater pleasure in helping the group.

Cognitive Complexity
Learning situations are based on student grouping. A student is necessarily in a position to experience a cognitive, psychological, and social situation involving many variables. Therefore, he or she learns to "evolve" in a more stimulating context.

A Variety of Social Situations
Cooperative instruction relies on the acquisition of more useful social behaviors, such as tolerance. A decrease in such behaviors as racism or competitiveness can be observed. Augustine, Gruber, and Hanson (1990) noted that cooperative instruction brought about a radical change in students' perception of learning and teaching and helped them acquire such skills and social behaviors as the sharing of ideas, the acceptance of others, better psychological health and better reaction to the group, and so on.

Spencer Kagan (1990a) maintains that it is the situations that we experience that determine our competitive or cooperative behaviors. Competitiveness increases, he says, with the degree of urbanization. Students from the country are much more coopera-tive than those from the city. Moreover, in experiments con-ducted with 2,000 students in California, he observed that cooperative instruction in multi-racial teams greatly decreased racism among students.

Kagan (1990b) insists on the importance of positive interdepen-dency and suggests using class projects to make students cooperative and thwart a competitive spirit. With this method, students are not penalized if they do not know the answer to the teacher's question, since the objective is to make progress on the project as a whole.

Personal Validation
Students see their self-perception improve as they work together. They feel more valued, less alone, and better supported when

they have problems, which greatly helps their motivation. Research conducted by Shlomo Sharan (1990) of Tel-Aviv University shows that cooperative methods reach these objectives of personal validation and that students, whether weak or strong, do better in school.

5.6.3 Pedagogical Strategies

Pedagogical practices can easily be drawn from those who write about cooperative pedagogy. In suggesting strategies, proponents of cooperative learning pay great attention to experience; most of their recommendations are based on experimentation. We have grouped the strategies proposed by proponents of cooperative instruction:

1. Make Each Individual Responsible
(Johnson, Johnson, and Holubec, 1986; Cooper *et al.*, 1990; Slavin, 1990b; Kohn, 1991)

The student should feel responsible for how the group functions. Students get more involved if they know that they will be rewarded for their personal efforts. Therefore, it is necessary to:

- Reward students according to the performance of the group and give extra points to the individual student (for instance, when the team gets 90% in certain activities).

- Avoid abuse of extrinsic rewards (money, gifts, etc.).

- Evaluate each student, with assessment that is criterion-referenced, not norm-referenced.

- Insist on personal responsibility when groups consist of more than three members.

2. Form Small Heterogeneous Groups
(Johnson and Johnson, 1989; Cooper et al., 1990; Hooper, 1992a)

Most research studies insist on forming small groups that should preferably be heterogeneous. Therefore, it is necessary to:

- Form groups of four or five people; in larger groups students cannot practice enough; groups that are too small lack diversity in their interactions.

- Form heterogeneous groups to maximize the social benefits, and ensure that groups include students presenting diverse academic, social, ethnic and cultural differences.

- Promote long-term grouping (at least one semester): from four to 16 meetings are recommended per team.

- Avoid homogeneous groups for weak or very young students.

- Create new teams if any present too many functional problems.

3. Program Activities
(Cooper et al., 1990)

The role of the student should not be limited to receiving information. The student should be active and clearly understand what is expected of him or her. The teacher should:

- Structure activities for all classes.

- Specifically define the objectives and the procedures.

- Avoid ambiguous activities, as they force students to try to figure out the intentions of the teacher.

- Begin with simple activities, then proceed to more complex activities once students have learned to work as teammates.

4. Develop Social Skills
(Johnson and Johnson, 1994; Cooper et al., 1990; Hooper, 1992b)

One of the main objectives is the acquisition of social skills. Students should learn to collaborate on common tasks. Consequently, the teacher should:

- Train students to interact effectively before beginning cooperative learning.

- Give instructions to facilitate activities.

- Organize collaboration practices (collaboration is something that is learned!).

- Bring the students to reflect on the efficacy of their cooperative activities.

5. Facilitate
(Dweck and Leggett, 1988; Johnson and Johnson, 1989 and 1994; Cooper et al., 1990; Hooper, 1992a and 1992b)

The teacher does not just transmit information. He or she performs several functions in facilitating individual and group work. The teacher should

- Provide feedback to explain learning achievements or failures.
- Avoid feedback that focuses only on achievement.
- Stick with groups that experience functional problems.

We will now consider two examples of thought on organizing cooperative instruction. They have been chosen to show that cooperative instruction can be practiced in countries with rather different cultures, that one of its main objectives consists of learning to cooperate, and that sciences can be taught effectively through cooperative techniques.

Example 1: Cooperative Instruction in Multi-Ethnic Classrooms
Israel is faced with an important problem: its educational system must absorb students who come from countries with very different cultures, such as the countries of the former USSR, North Africa, and North America. A team of researchers and teachers (Sharan, Kussel, Hertz-Lazarowitz, Bejarano, Raviv, and Sharan, 1985) from several universities (Tel-Aviv University, Everyman's University, and the University of Haifa) compared cooperative and traditional ways of teaching English as a second language in classes that included students of different origins. This example is very interesting because more and more countries are faced with a major problem: cultural, ethnic, social, and religious diversity in one class.

This research, which involved about 800 high school students, establishes that organizing a class according to a cooperative theory facilitates interracial relationships among students. It encourages higher social integration. It also encourages more cooperation among students than through lecture methods. Thus, in a cooperative class, competitiveness decreases from a ratio of one competitive action for one cooperative action to a ratio of one competitive action for five cooperative actions (Sharan et al., 1985).

Example 2: McLean's Cooperative and Socio-Inductive Theory
Leslie McLean (1988) developed a cooperative pedagogical theory that applies especially to mathematics instruction. For the last twenty years, there has been a lot of talk about the

crisis of science instruction at all levels. Studies have revealed that half the students in North America cannot solve simple percentage problems by the end of eighth grade. In Ontario, for instance, it was reported that the percentage of correct answers went from forty-two percent at the beginning of the year to fifty percent at the end of the year!

This led McLean, of the Ontario Institute for Studies in Education, to do some research on the efficacy of instruction and assessment during learning and to propose a theory on mathematics instruction that is more deeply rooted in real life. McLean set as his goal to replace lecture, theoretical, and deductive instruction with inductive strategies based on having the students solve practical problems that mean something to them. It is indeed possible to successfully pair a cooperative model with inductive learning strategies. Research done by Bharati Baveja, Showers, and Joyce (1985) and by Joyce, Showers, and Murphy (1989) suggest that this pairing is quite productive.

An Inductive Teaching Strategy

To improve the quality of learning, McLean (1988) proposes cooperative and inductive teaching strategies. What does this mean?

First of all, induction is a mental operation that consists of proceeding from the facts to the rule or from specific cases to a general proposition. To be able to state that "all crows are black," for example, one must have been able to observe a crow, then another, and yet another to finally come to the conclusion that they all look alike and that they all are black.

In other respects, it should also be noted that questions about the nature of induction date back a long time. Indeed, philosophers have been trying for hundreds of years to define induction. Behavioral psychologists have invested a lot of time in operative conditioning that is based on induction. Now researchers in artificial intelligence are exploring the mechanisms of inductive thought. In short, induction is currently an important field of research, which influences educational research.

What is an inductive strategy of instruction? It is a pedagogy that brings students to infer general rules from observing specific cases. McLean may have gone in this direction to conceive his theory of instruction. However, he gave it an original touch by including processes of cooperative work, problems relevant to students, and an assessment based on the student dossiers. We will now consider each of these three elements.

Cooperative Work among Students

First, students should adopt a cooperative mode of work among themselves and with the teacher. This can be done either in pairs or in small groups. McLean refers to Robert Slavin (1987) in stating that cooperative work is the best way to use both the time available and everyone's talents. Two heads are better than one for solving problems, McLean claims, especially since students learn a way of working and living that will be useful to them in society.

Problem-Solving

Second, students learn by solving problems that are meaningful to them. Current manuals contain problems that mean nothing to students. In his works, McLean mentions numerous research studies that establish that mathematics and science instruction make no allowance for the student's context. These problems, McLean claims, should be inspired by the real life of the student. In 1984, the Science Council of Canada had already asked for a more "genuine" and less standardized instructional approach to teaching science. McLean goes further and demands that instruction be contextualized. Students are more motivated and learn more when they can verify that the knowledge they have acquired is useful.

Assessment Based on Dossiers

Third, assessment is based on dossiers assembled by students. As the school year progresses, the student must present, at regular intervals, his or her work, which constitutes a dossier or portfolio. McLean maintains that the current approach to assessment is not suitable for assessing genuine learning, i.e., learning that is meaningful to the student. McLean concludes that the existing tests do nothing but reinforce a pedagogy that is deficient and inappropriate.

McLean also took into consideration certain reforms in language instruction based on a functional approach. This approach stresses the context rather than the structural approach, which emphasizes the very structure of language. McLean claims that structuralist theories — whether in the fields of language, science, or mathematics — produce bad pedagogies. In other words, McLean wanted to attack the powerful "structuralist" clique of mathematics instruction by proposing an approach that is less formalist as well as more contextual and relevant. This approach is more concerned with the *usefulness* of acquired knowledge than with its *structure*.

The meaning of acquired knowledge cannot be abstract, says McLean. We construct the meaning of things from our experiences and according to situations. Meaning develops in a specific and real context; hence it is important that we consider context in instruction.

5.7 Conclusion

The first conclusion to be drawn from analyzing these social cognitive theories is that they have the unquestionable merit of stressing the social dimension of learning. They emphasize a great number of social factors, such as the influence of other students, the teacher's perceptions, the student's personal perceptions, and relationships with parents and society. They also examine all the possible cultural and social factors that can influence education. To be sure, they have left nothing out!

Certain studies — those by Bandura, for instance — are very complex and analyze an incredible number of interactions in learning. Others show a certain originality. Research on social cognitive conflicts reveals unexpected aspects of learning. Other research shows the extent to which relationships among students and perceptions of their own ability greatly influence the quality of their learning.

However, these theories often have the defects that go with their merits. Their heavy emphasis on the multiplicity of factors does not really facilitate getting an overall picture or putting theory into practice. Thus, social cognitive conflict theories do not seem to get away from theory and have little ground in pedagogical reality. They suffer from being vague, which does not facilitate real-life applications.

Social cognitive theories of instruction, such as Bandura's, are rather difficult to understand when they are examined macroscopically. They are very interesting when we try to understand how learning functions, but they present a number of difficulties when it comes to defining pedagogical strategies. Indeed, applying a theory of self-regulation in a classroom is not easy. The same goes for Vygotsky's sociohistorical theory. Vygotsky left us a captivating theory but little advice on implementing it.

If we analyze cooperative theories, we notice that they have characteristics that are almost the opposite of other social cognitive theories. Clearly, they are more vague about the concept of learning. They are not really grounded in theoretical details. Their aim is more concrete applications, and they are generally based on numerous experiments.

Indeed, many studies and applications have allowed an accumulation of relevant information on their feasibility. These practical experiences have established the efficacy of these theories in elementary school, high school, and college instruction. Positive results have been noticed with regard to the development of certain social aptitudes: an acceptance of others, a decrease in racism and segregation, improved self-perception, and a greater ability to work with others. McLean's research is particularly interesting in that it reveals important pedagogical principles. McLean rightly insists on the "contextualization" of the problems to be solved. It is best to construct learning situations that take into consideration what the student knows and what he or she is.

However, researchers do not all agree on the virtue of cooperation in education, since implementation can raise many concrete problems. They are not all convinced that cooperative instruction is efficient for all types of teaching and learning. It seems to work well for elementary learning, but opinions differ as to its efficacy in learning difficult tasks. Fred Newmann and Judith Thompson (1987) do not believe that the cooperative approach is generally effective in high school instruction. Slavin (1990b) also notes that research studies dealing with the first two years of college are neither sufficiently numerous nor unanimous to allow any conclusions about the efficacy of the cooperative approach.

Chapter 6

Social Theories

Social theories are based on the principle that education ought to allow us to resolve social, cultural, and environmental problems. The primary mission of education, then, is to prepare students to find solutions to these problems.

6.1 Social Theories of Education

The theories presented in this chapter are based on a social vision of the changes that need to be made in education. The main purpose of education is to reform society. As a matter of fact, it should play an important part in the reconstruction of society. According to these theories, the educational system is obsolete, since it is based on an industrial mode of social organization that is likely to disappear. We should do away with the industrial approach to organizing education.

Most of the authors analyzed in this chapter claim that our everyday life shows serious signs of a cultural, social, and ecological crisis. This is why education should take into account these components of everyday culture.

This is the point of view of such authors as Henry Giroux (1992a), C.A. Bowers (1993), and Jennifer Gore (1993). Moreover, education should provide students with a number of tools to modify these situations (Grand'Maison, 1976; Brown, Collins, and Duguid, 1989; Morin, 1989; Bowers, 1993). Students should acquire affective, intellectual, psychomotor, imaginative and other tools that will allow them to intervene in a situation and consequently transform everyday reality.

In short, education is merely one dimension of the evolution of reality. To educate, says Jacques Grand'Maison (1976), is to encourage the emergence of new tools designed to transform the reality we all experience, to give students the means to transform reality, to ensure our mutual evolution, to interpret and transform everyday life, and to live.

The educational theories described in this chapter are founded on reflections on preparing for the often radical transformation of culture and society. First, we will consider institutional and socio-critical pedagogies that influenced educational thinking in the 1960s and 1970s. Second, we will treat social pedagogies of conscientization as defined by Paulo Freire, Ira Shor, Henry Giroux, and Grand'Maison. Third, we will describe eco-social theories, which deal with the global relationship between education and the workings of our planet. The approaches taken by Joel de Rosnay, Erich Jantsch, and Alvin Toffler exemplify this global vision of our universe in all its glory and all its problems. These eco-social educational theories share a common objective: to establish new societies characterized by greater social, cultural, and ecological responsibility.

6.2 Institutional Pedagogies

Institutional pedagogy is a movement of pedagogical change that had its glory days in the 1960s and 1970s in France and Quebec. Its objectives were essentially social: to rebuild society, question capitalist society, attack social class divisions, and do away with bureaucratic institutions. This global vision of social change gave rise to institutional pedagogies that attack the weaknesses of school and social institutions and, of course, traditional pedagogies.

Institutional pedagogy pursues essentially the following goals:

- To propose a conception of institutions in terms of bottom-to-top regulation, permanent criticism of established norms, and development of instituting forces

- To expose the "conspiracy" of institutions, a conspiracy that consists of imposing a false vision of the relationship of production through material (economic or physical) and ideological constraints

- To show how the State, economy, and class struggle determine institutions

- To take the mystery out of the notions of the "autonomized group" and "autonomized organization" through the psychology of groups and the sociology of organizations

Institutional pedagogy dominated writings in French during the 1970s. However, the first steps of this movement can be traced back to the pedagogy of Célestin Freinet, a French educator, as well as to the writings of Anton Makarenko, a Soviet educator who, as early as 1917, proposed a pedagogy centered on groups for the "new socialist society." Institutional pedagogy — an eclectic trend — also has its source in the German libertarian pedagogy of the 1930s, the experiments of A.S. Neill in England, and in institutional critical experiments that were popular in psychoanalysis in the late 1950s and the early 1960s in France.

To quote Rémi Hess (1975b), the 1960-64 period is rich in "organizational" events. The notion of socio-critical pedagogy appeared in Royaumont (France) in 1962. The Groupe de Pédagogie Institutionnelle was founded in 1963. The main proponents of this institutional approach to education were Georges Lapassade, Michel Lobrot, Philippe Kaepelin, Jacques Ardoino, Jacques Guigou, Hess, René Barbier, René Lourau, Fernand Oury, and Aïda Vasquez.

It could be said that institutional pedagogy comes from two sources, which share some common aspects and which have influenced one another through an osmosis that is difficult to describe — Marxist sociology and psychosociology (Lobrot, Lapassade, and Lourau) on the one hand and, on the other, institutional psychotherapy (Oury and Vasquez), which attacks institutions.

6.2.1 Psychosociological Trend

Socio-critical pedagogy characterizes the psychosociological trend and references to sociology dominate its reflections. Texts by Lapassade and Lourau are more concerned with the transformation of institutions, whereas those by Lobrot deal with the transformation of people through Rogerian methods.

Socio-critical pedagogy seeks to abolish the instructional relationship between "teacher" and "taught" or "dominant" and "dominated," and it challenges current social and school systems by examining their weaknesses and the construction of counter-institutions. Therefore, socio-critical pedagogy does not aim at improving the pedagogical situation. Its objectives are altogether different. Socio-critical pedagogy is an instrument designed to analyze the contradictions in the school system and clarify the social and political causes of these contradictions. Since the school organization is a social system with the same characteristics as the society around it, a socio-critical movement that conducts its own institutional analysis thus helps make way for a self-managed society without a ruling class.

Besides, socio-critical pedagogy is not independent of political self-management: it depends on it. Political self-management is the essential foundation of socio-critical pedagogy or social self-management. Indeed, its goal is to suppress the division between those who lead and those who are led, and it affirms the ability of people to organize themselves collectively without social classes, bureaucracy, and state control. Lapassade (1967) defines self-management as "an organizational system of the population and social life in which the organization and management cease to be private property of a few (minority groups, castes, or ruling classes) to become collective property."

Institutional pedagogy and socio-critical pedagogy fundamentally stand out as a criticism of capitalist societies and the rules by which they function. They are pedagogical movements with a goal of social change based on a Marxist vision of society.

Proponents of this conception of education like to remind us that the earliest theorists of socialism established how the workers' movement revealed through its struggles, the faults in the capitalistic system. The movement then became the *analyzer* of nineteenth-century industrial capitalism.

The underlying aspiration of socialism at that time took the shape of a self-managed society that was to follow the destruction of the bureaucratic state apparatus in France. According to Lapassade (1967), the Commune of 1871 is an example of this realization, since the function of that revolution was to destroy the superstructure and *liberate* the creative spontaneity of the social body. The Revolution should replace institutions with the process of institutionalization. This is how socio-critical pedagogy appears as the liberation of instituting forces.

Socio-critical pedagogy should be understood as an educational system in which the instructional relationship is, in principle, abolished. The students decide what their instruction should be and they manage it.

In the beginning, socio-critical pedagogy had another goal: to challenge the system in place by exposing its weaknesses. The model of pedagogical institutional analysis cannot be limited to the educational system; it necessarily accompanies a social analysis. Lourau (1970) claims that the crisis is at three levels:

- In the classroom
- In educational institutions
- In society

In other words, the problem of the educational system is not limited to that organization only. The educational system is a place where the general crisis of society is breaking out. The function of the psychosociological theory of education is to achieve social self-management.

Lobrot (1972) reminds us that social self-management is an ideal: its goal is to solve the essential human problem, that of production or, in other terms, that of human transformation of the world. It aims at getting individuals to participate as much as possible in the production processes and to overcome their alienation.

In short, social self-management is the main objective of socio-critical pedagogy, since it makes it possible to satisfy essential human needs aimed at creation, invention, initiative, research, and human communication. According to Lobrot, the most dreadful form of people exploiting people remains bureaucracy. Social self-management is the only solution to this problem. However, it presupposes a profound modification of social institutions and, consequently, socio-critical pedagogy. Lobrot (1972) concludes by saying that, without self-management at school, without students taking charge of themselves, and without at least partial destruction of pedagogic bureaucracy, we can expect no true education, and so no change in individual mentalities. Consequently, society sinks deeper into insolvable problems.

6.2.2 Psychoanalytical Trend

Influenced by Marxism, institutional pedagogy is also marked by a form of clinical psychology intended as a critique of institutions: Oury's institutional psychotherapy. In brief, this trend claims that mental illness is more social than we might believe. Therapists who work in institutions are really the prisoners of a system, a set of organizational modalities, rules, and attitudes that globally condition how the therapist thinks and acts. Therefore, it is the environment of the patient, says Oury (1973), that needs to be treated first!

Teachers would be in an analogous situation. This conception of institutional pedagogy (Ardoino, 1980) is centered on reorganizing relationships in the classroom and in the institution by explicitly taking into account the presence of the unconscious (in the psychoanalytical sense of the word) in educational processes.

In 1966, Vasquez and Oury published *Vers la pédagogie institutionnelle?*, a good example of this trend. Institutional pedagogy has become distinct from psychotherapy, but its techniques still show traces of its origins. It is true that techniques of group intervention are widely used and that the influence of Rogers is omnipresent. However, techniques do not constitute an end in themselves. They are a means of facilitating institutional analysis and self-management. This is what Lourau claims (1970): institutional analysis, if practiced within a pedagogical activity, goes far beyond the presuppositions and finalities of group methods.

6.2.3 Institutional Pedagogy and Nondirectivity

Institutional pedagogy and Rogerian pedagogy should not be confused. Even though they often use the same methods, their goals are very different. Lapassade (1971) defines the relationship between institutional analysis and active methods in this way: self-management means exposing institutional violence, whereas nondirectivity means improving the climate or facilitating relationships.

Lapassade's remark is important because it reflects a fundamental distinction between the humanistic model of education and the model of institutional pedagogy. Marc Guiraud (1971) tried to explain this difference. The nondirective method, such as that conceived by Rogers in the United States and taken up by Lobrot in France, consists of putting an individual or group in a situation to solve certain problems by facilitating group communication. The quality of this communication will eventually encourage or prevent the resolution of the problems encountered by an individual. Since individuals have a natural need to find out about how they function and a tendency to develop, they will formulate wishes and requests that they will want to fulfill. The principle of the request constitutes, as we have seen, the core of nondirective pedagogy. The individual has the initiative and the choice. However, this choice is still determined by political, ideological, and economic conditions of the institutions.

In short, Rogers' point of view does not have this dimension of being critical of institutions and this political consciousness. Guiraud (1971) takes up Lobrot and Lapassade's criticism and states that, in the original Rogerianism, personal nondirectivity does not question structural directivity, since nondirective self-education is not based on self-management of this education. There lies its central contradiction: true nondirectivity presupposes going from the level of the group to the level of institutions.

6.2.4 Paradox of Institutional Pedagogy

One could talk in terms of a paradox of institutional pedagogy. Indeed, in the 1970s, the influence of sociology rose, and especially that of Pierre Bourdieu and Jean-Claude Passeron with regard to the notion of symbolic violence. Bourdieu and Passeron (1964) had introduced the concept of the power of symbolic violence, which manages to impose meanings and to impose them as legitimate by dissimulating the power relationships that are the foundation of its power.

What are the characteristics of this power? It is arbitrary: it is based on the terms that characterize, at a given time, the relationships among the groups or classes of a social structure. It is cultural: it marks off meanings as worthy of being imposed and reproduced to the exclusion of others. It is dissimulating: it is based on an "instituted misreading" of its inner mechanism and the power relationships.

René Barbier (1974 and 1977) maintains that any pedagogical action is an instance of symbolic violence. He bases that idea on the theory of Bourdieu and Passeron, claiming, as they do, that certain conditions are necessary for this process to take place:

- A "transmitter" (pedagogical presence) with relative autonomy
- A "receiver" (recipient) linked by an imposed line of pedagogical communication

- A pedagogical action, supported by a legitimate right of imposition (pedagogical authority), allowing the pedagogical work, the productivity of which is measured in terms of durability, transposability, and exhaustivity

- A principle that generates thought patterns, perceptions, judgments, and actions; a principle that results from structures, that produces corresponding practices and reproduces structures termed objective; a principle now called *organizational culture*

Barbier (1977) formulates a second conclusion, which further shows how thought on institutional pedagogy has evolved. Institutional pedagogy, like any pedagogical action, is an instance of symbolic violence and falls under the provisions of its own critical arguments. Paradoxically, it should be subjected to an institutional analysis. Thus, it is apparent that institutional pedagogy is somewhat arbitrary, just like all the other pedagogies! Institutional pedagogy is based on educational preconceptions and is dominant like all the others! Moreover, it is dissimulating, since it does not state its implications that:

- Self-management is the best social organization.

- There is a hierarchy of knowledge: knowledge as content, knowledge as doing, knowledge as being, and knowledge as self-positioning.

To sum up, any pedagogical action, whether institutional or not, would be an instance of symbolic violence, since an emitter imposes on a receiver a form of thinking or processing information. So it defends what it attacks! In this perspective, it is self-perpetuating and promotes the interests of those who own the right and means to explain what symbolic violence is. In other words, in order to be liberating, institutional pedagogy should paradoxically function like a boomerang. It should expose its own inner mechanism, so as to make clear how symbolic violence functions. This poses an interesting problem: how can one be the judge in one's own trial?

6.3 Conscientization Pedagogies

Conscientization pedagogies subsume theories of education that aim at making students aware of their roles as social agents. Two groups of thinkers will be analyzed here: those who follow the orientation initially described by Paulo Freire and the advocates of critical 'pedagogy'.

We will see that the "Freire movement" is positioned between cooperative education, which is very pedagogical in its descriptions, and critical pedagogy, which is more social and clearly less pedagogical. In certain cases, these are nuances. Proponents of conscientization pedagogy, such as Mara Sapon-Schevin and Nancy Schniedewind (1991), will naturally adopt cooperative work techniques. On the other hand, it would seem that there is sometimes a world of difference between the critical pedagogy of Henry Giroux and that of Ira Shor — a problem noted by William Stanley (1992).

6.3.1 Freire's Ideas

Paulo Freire was born in 1921 in Recife, Brazil. He started his career as a high school Portuguese teacher in the northeast of the country. Between the ages of 19 and 22, he became interested in theories of communication. While working with farmers and fishermen, he soon ascertained the impact of social differences on language learning and grappled with the crucial problem of adult illiteracy. He later developed instructional methods for parents and teachers, which would lead people to think about their social and cultural conditions.

His instructional methodology was widely used in the 1950s in literacy campaigns. After the military coup in 1964, the new Brazilian government put Freire in prison for a few days, then "invited" him to leave the country. He spent 16 years in exile. He finished his first book, *Educaçao como Pratica da libertade* (*Education as the Practice of Freedom*) in Chile in 1965 and had it published in Brazil in 1967. From 1965 to 1969, Freire worked in Chile, then left for the United States and Switzerland.

Freire is first of all a practitioner, who developed the notion of conscientization pedagogy from his first 15 years of experience as a teacher. He also put forward a critical conception of culture. His reflections on the subject deserve some attention, for they foreshadowed a debate that is currently very important in the world of education: the conflict of cultures in the face of problems of all kinds that must be solved if we are to have any hope for a better life on this planet, and, at the same time, the need to educate people for a critical culture.

In his work, Freire (1970 and 1973) observed that the lower class was being crushed and diminished by the ruling classes. The common people had become spectators, controlled by the power of the myths created for them by the all-powerful social forces. Studying the Brazilian society of his time, Freire called it a closed society in which the masses are alienated, reduced to silence, incapable of making decisions — a society in which human beings are domesticated and have lost their critical spirit.

Then came the time for change, for unlocking society, for fundamental democratization. However, the participation of the people was spurned "in the name of a threatened liberty" and "democracy" (Freire, 1973). Helping the common people assume an evolution toward democracy is the problem Freire (1973) wants to solve: "We needed an education to make us capable of making decisions and of social and political responsibility." As a matter of fact, his book *Education for Critical Consciousness* deals with the role of education in the process of democratization.

To solve this problem, then, Freire (1973) suggests education as a democratic practice of empowerment that is based on using an active method built around dialogue, criticism, and the formation of judgment.

Dialogue
The first element of his method is dialogue, understood as a nonhierarchical relationship among people. Dialogue encourages communication, as opposed to anti-dialogue, in which one pole dominates the other, which creates passive individuals. Freire (1973) maintains that we need a pedagogy of communication to overcome anti-dialogue, which lacks love and critical judgment. Someone who is engaged in a dialogue, he says, addresses someone else in order to exchange something. It is this "something" that should be the new content of the curriculum.

Inspired by Karl Jaspers, Freire treats dialogue as a relationship based on sympathy, in which love, hope, faith, trust, and critical judgment dominate. He writes (1973): "In an atmosphere of dialogue, human beings develop a sense of their participation in life shared with others. The action of dialogue entails social and political responsibility."

In a discussion with Shor (Shor and Freire, 1987), Freire adds that dialogue is a moment of reflection that people have about the making of reality. Then Shor offers this comment: dialogue is a democratic communication that attacks domination and affirms the empowerment of participants in the making of their culture. Freire adds, "Dialogue is a challenge to domination."

Thus, in education, the teacher commits to constructing knowledge with the student, in a permanent dialogue. The teacher cannot transfer knowledge from a dominating position in relationship to the student. Education that empowers is incompatible with a pedagogy that is a practice of domination.

Pedagogy Grounded in Reality
The second characteristic of conscientization pedagogy is its grounding in reality. "Dialogical" education is based on students' real-life experiences, whatever their academic level. It is a pedagogy "situated" in the concrete, in common sense, and in the everyday life of the students (Shor and Freire, 1987). Freire (1985) also uses the paradoxical expression "immersion in one's own life."

This also means establishing ties between scientific knowledge, which is detached from reality, and common-sense knowledge. For instance, to ask a student the question, "What is the sky to a fisherman?" will allow the student to make a connection between astronomy, which is an area of scientific knowledge, and the fisherman's knowledge, which is based on real-life experience.

Creation of One's Culture
The third characteristic is the notion of literacy proposed by Freire (1985). For Freire, this means social literacy, which is different from literacy in the usual sense of the word. To eliminate illiteracy means to make people aware of their culture and of the necessity for everybody to participate in the collective and democratic construction of culture and history. To learn to read and write is to acquire a language that is relevant to the individual learner. Therefore, the point is not to learn to repeat sentences that have no meaning with regard to the learner's social and cultural reality. Quite the opposite: the student uses words he or she knows ("generating words") in situations from his or her life. Thus, the word "favela" (slum) might be a generating word.

The role of the teacher is to find and represent (for instance, with a photo or slide) a typical situation pertaining to students' everyday life, to trigger a meaningful debate. Freire (1985) calls this operation "codification." This debate, which takes place in a cultural discussion circle ("circulo de cultura"), and the interpretation that results, are part of the "codification." To "decode" a situation means to pose it as a problem and expose the fundamental structure of the situation (which is necessarily alienation resulting from the domination of the upper classes).

The information should correspond to the concrete reality of everyone's life. The worker is therefore the agent of his or her learning. The individual becomes the object of his or her education and the learning process itself constitutes the content of this learning. The role of the teacher is to dialogue, using concrete cases, and to propose instruments with which the individual educates himself or herself and learns to talk about his or her own world.

Developing Critical Thinking
To learn to read and write is fundamentally a social and cultural conscientization process (Freire, 1987 and 1990; Freire and Faundez, 1989). This means that the student becomes aware of the problems of the society in which he or she lives. This focus on problems should be critical and should bear upon the experience of the student, for the point is ultimately to take control of one's culture and history.

This means that students should become conscious of the values that they have internalized (for instance, that their culture is not as good as that of the rich). Students should remove the mystery from the dominant ideology, liberate themselves from the values of the dominating class, and give themselves an "admiring" vision of their own culture.

Social Intervention Training
The fifth characteristic of this conscientization pedagogy is training for social involvement (Freire and Macedo, 1987; Shor and Freire, 1987). Freire denounces laissez-faire pedagogies that talk only of individual freedom. To educate means to give direction to the student. In this case, the point is to train him or her to participate in society, to free himself or herself and free others from the ascendancy of the ruling classes.

Freire also criticizes theories of education that aim at subduing the common people (Freire, 1985; Shor and Freire, 1987). These theories describe only the transfer of knowledge; they do not discuss the "hidden" values of education.

Freire (1985, 1987) proposes a theory of education that is fundamentally linked to social practice. His theory and practice are linked, he says, in one goal: to liberate people from the ascendancy of the ruling classes and give them control over their lives. This is what distinguishes Freire's pedagogy from social cognitive pedagogies examined in chapter 5. Freire talks of culture and social conditions in learning, of course, but with the expressed, clear purpose of liberation. Freire suggests an education centered on cultural revolution. We need only compare, for instance, the theories of Freire and Albert Bandura to notice the difference between a social vision and a social cognitive vision of education.

6.3.2 Pedagogies of Liberation

Freire's ideas have attracted a lot of interest in many countries. They have had a great influence in South America, Mexico, and Africa. In the early 1970s, traces of Freire's influence could be found in Europe, especially Belgium and France.

Numerous authors (Ada, Banks, Brown, Cummins, Davidson, Frankenstein, Horton, Olave, Sapon-Schevin, Schniedewind, Shor, and Sleeter) have taken up the torch initially carried by Freire and developed social pedagogies. In the United States in the 1980s and 1990s, Shor took up Freire's ideas and developed a very concrete social conscientization pedagogy of the individual.

Shor (1992b) develops a social problematic of education and asks the following questions: Can education train students as critical thinkers, skilled workers, and active citizens? Can it promote democracy and equitably serve all the students?

Shor proposes a pedagogy of liberation (or "liberatory education") that is clearly in the Freire spirit: to give students the power to change society. Shor (1992b) describes the characteristics of this pedagogy in his book, *Empowering Education: Critical Teaching for Social Change*. What Shor means by "empowering education" is a critical and democratic pedagogy centered on the individual and on social change. He maintains that individual growth is an active, cooperative, and social process. We will now summarize the characteristics of Shor's empowering education.

Participation

Participation is a dominant characteristic of this critical pedagogy. Indeed, it is continually "interactive" insofar as the individual and society create themselves reciprocally. Taking up the ideas of John Dewey (1938) and Freire (1985), Shor (1992a and 1992b) asserts that participation takes place not only in the classroom but everywhere in society. The individual cannot exist in a vacuum. Individuality is necessarily social. Consequently, the student should be active and participate in various school and extra-curricular activities, just as the teacher should create situations in which the student is active rather than passive.

Affective and Cognitive Learning

Learning is not only cognitive; it is also affective. Traditional instruction encourages students to be competitive, favors the wealthiest, and generates negative feelings in most of the people who cannot win at the game. Learning, according to Sapon-Schevin and Schniedewind (1991) and Shor (1992b), cannot be based on such negative feelings of frustration or envy. Indeed, such an environment encourages resistance, passivity, and discouragement. What is needed instead is an empowering education, centered on participation, which encourages all students to feel positive.

Students' Questions

Pedagogy should rely on the questions that students ask themselves naturally. This is how dialogue begins between students and the teacher. Questions serve to start a process of "critical deconstruction" of the information coming from the media and the educational system. Pedagogy starts with these questions and gradually becomes a research activity through which students progressively construct their knowledge and develop a more critical vision of society.

As an example, Shor (1992b) suggests a few questions that can lead to critical reflection:

- In a journalism class: What is news?
- In a literature class: What is the American dream?
- In a basic studies class: What do we know about Christopher Columbus?
- In a social sciences class: Where do the bananas that we eat come from?

This last question, which at first seems quite harmless, may rapidly lead to reflections on the exploitation of farmers in less industrialized countries.

Multicultural Instruction
Pedagogy should reflect the students' cultural and social conditions. It should take into consideration, first and foremost, their cultural, social, linguistic, and racial differences.

Dialogue
Very much inspired by Freire, Shor (1992b) claims that pedagogy should assume the form of a critical dialogue, i.e., poles apart from the traditional authoritative method characterized by a teacher doing a monologue and students taking notes. The teacher would not communicate knowledge to students, but speak with them about topics that interest them. Through dialogue, students would learn to develop a critical vision of their powers, their conditions, their language, their knowledge, and their society.

"Desocialization" of Students
Teachers should engage in democratic processes, i.e., share power with students, so that they question their socialization. The more teachers share this power, the more students participate and "desocialize" themselves, i.e., question the social experiences and behaviors, such as racism, that structure their everyday life as well as their school life. This does not mean that teachers teach counterculture, but that they engage with students in a common questioning of dominant cultural and social practices.

Democratic Instruction
In the traditional system, says Shor (1992b), students have learned to mechanically answer the questions rather than question the answers. Democratic instruction allows all students to express themselves freely, to make their intentions known, and to consequently act upon the world.

Cooperative instruction constitutes an excellent educational strategy, in opposition to current pedagogical models, which are hardly democratic (Oakes, 1985; Levin, 1990; Shor, 1992a). So do adaptations of Freire's methods (Schniedewind and Davidson, 1983 and 1987; Ada and Olave, 1986; Frankenstein, 1987; Shor and Freire, 1987). Let us remember that certain theorists with a pedagogical or didactic vision of education (whom we examined in chapter 5) consider cooperative instruction to be the best way to change schools. Other researchers, in the present chapter, regard it as the best way to train students to change society.

A Community of Researchers

The topics covered in a course should be examined in depth. Students must do serious research, for they are not there merely to receive knowledge. The class should become a community of researchers focused on their roles as agents of social transformation. Shor (1992b) cites as an example an experiment conducted in Scotland by Gerri Kirkwood and Colin Kirkwood (1989). Applying Freire's methods, these two educators integrated members of the community, such as former students, in their research groups.

Interdisciplinarity

The division of knowledge into subject areas constitutes a major obstacle, which must be overcome through interdisciplinary instruction. Shor claims that it is necessary in particular to avoid isolating language learning within a single discipline. The student should be able to learn to speak and write in all subject areas.

Social Action

Pedagogy cannot be limited to the classroom. It should lead to social interventions. That is the position taken by Shor (1992b), referring to Freire (1985) and his notion of "cultural action for freedom": to participate in negotiation teams, organize protests against social inequalities, get involved in the election process, participate in marches for the rights of minorities, and fight to protect the environment.

These are the main qualities of an empowering pedagogy. Shor (1992b) also proposes, as an example, a pedagogical strategy for a native language class. We will now outline its main stages.

Stages for a Pedagogical Strategy of Empowerment:

1. Questioning
The teacher and the students establish the initial issue, beginning with their questions.

2. Reflection on the issue

The teacher asks the students to clarify their thoughts about the issue, either by discussing it among themselves or by writing on the subject.

3. Writing an essay

Students draw up a rough draft on the subject and suggest a solution to the problem. They write down their ideas. Then, they work together to improve their essays, helping each other by comparing the essays in their discussions.

4. Presentation of a group report

Each team chooses a reporter who will present one text for the whole team. The teacher helps the reporter, asks questions, encourages the team, and makes sure that the other students have understood.

5. Synthesis and reformulation of the issue

The teacher gets involved through dialogues, discussing with students and presenting his or her point of view, to ensure that the issue and solutions become clear.

6. Second draft

Students develop a second draft, which integrates the work done and is continued by exchanges and group discussions.

7. Second dialogue with the class

Each committee delegates a reporter who reads his or her essay. This phase includes questions, reformulations, and exchanges.

8. Integration of the material

The teacher integrates other sources of information: films, videos, maps, illustrations, or texts. Students should work individually and collectively with this new material. The emphasis is on maintaining critical rigor, continuous learning, creative openness, continuing motivation, and a democratic climate.

9. Assessment

An assessment takes place in class. Each student

gives an anonymous assessment. The teacher synthesizes these assessments, then meets with the students in order to make any necessary changes.

10. **Presentation-dialogue**
    The teacher starts with the questions analyzed by the students and initiates a critical dialogue on their answers. He or she shares his or her knowledge on the matter.

11. **Students' answers**
    Students react to the presentation, formulate questions, provide a summary, and then draw up an issue that they would like to consider.

12. **Solutions and projects**
    Taking into account the age of the students, the teacher tries to bring the group to formulate solutions and prepare action projects, such as working to solve a local pollution problem.

This example of Shor's (1992b) strategy demonstrates the direction of a critical and democratic pedagogy. It is essentially a formula of collective research to train students to solve social and cultural problems. This strategy could be compared with the systemic and technological strategies examined in chapter 4. Shor's sociocultural strategy — with its freedom of expression, its repetitions and redundancy, and its search for community involvement — is almost diametrically opposed!

6.3.3 Critical Pedagogy

History
Critical pedagogy, which we will now consider, differs from the empowering pedagogies analyzed above, both by its more developed research on the foundations of a social education and by a more simplified description of the strategies necessary to reach its goals. ("Critical pedagogy" should not be confused with "critical thinking pedagogy," which will be analyzed in chapter 7. The former provides a scathing criticism of society, while the latter has no such intention — quite the contrary.)

Critical pedagogy is at the intersection of three trends: orthodox Marxism, the new sociology of education, and cultural studies. It strengthens a movement, says Stanley (1992), that springs from such different sources as feminist studies and critical theories of culture, and has attracted such authors as Elizabeth Ellsworth, Stanley Aronowitz, Landon Beyer, Michael Apple, Cleo Cherry-holmes, William Pinar, Lesley Roman, and Philip Wexler (Stanley, 1992). We will now see the influence of each of these trends on critical pedagogy and position them with regard to the work of Henry Giroux, the main theorist in critical pedagogy.

Orthodox Marxism

The social question of education has considerably evolved over the last few years. Social criticism has, for the most part, abandoned economic reproduction and expanded to include culture. It has distanced itself, says Wexler (1990), from the classic Marxist position, which is especially concerned with the economic problems of the working class.

It was Marxism that initially provided the terminology that made possible the social criticism of school functions in our society. This terminology refers to a fundamental category: the *reproduction of the dominant social and economic order*. According to this language, school is a mechanism for reproduction and selection, the function of which is to maintain the privileges of the ruling classes. North American and British theorists, such as Samuel Bowles and Herbert Gintis (1976) or Michael Apple (1979), have tried, to little avail, to convey this message, whereas French theorists (such as Pierre Bourdieu and Jean-Claude Passeron) managed to do so rather easily in the 1960s.

However, the critical pedagogy movement is continually trying to oppose this economic vision of reproduction (Stanley, 1992, Giroux, 1992a). Leading thinkers in this movement have adopted the idea of reproduction, but they mainly use it in the areas of culture. Giroux (1992a) observes that the book, *Schooling in Capitalist America: Educational Reform and the Contradictions of Economic Life* (Bowles and Gintis, 1976), tied into the theories of social reproduction, and its conception of power made no allowance for the language of resistance, which is the basis of critical pedagogy. Giroux adds that, in 1978, ten people at most stood forth as proponents of a socially critical position on education in the United States.

The New Sociology of Education

The works of British author Michael F.D. Young mark a turning point in British and North American sociology of education by providing researchers with a new path for reflection, a "new sociology of education." The concept emerged and subsided, Young (1991) acknowledges, in the 1970s. In 1971, Young published *Knowledge and Control: New Directions for the Sociology of Education*. This book deals with the new orientations of the sociology of education. In 1973, the expression "new sociology of education" (NSE) was coined by David Gorbutt. Gorbutt was interested, according to Young (1991), in the ties between "the analysis of curricula made by the new sociology of education and the role of teachers as agents of radical change." NSE reached its height in England around 1977, then was taken up in the United States by Apple. Young (1991) ascertained a sudden resurgence in the mid-1980s of commentaries and analyses among French and Canadian researchers.

The new sociology of education proposes radical criticism of the education provided by school systems. Young (1991) notes that "the most original and important contribution of NSE is to have made the processes by which teachers select and exclude knowledge in their classes the central factor of the sociology of education." Young (1991) writes that NSE had mostly been interested in the question of inequalities in the schools and the curriculum, and the hypothesis that teachers and teacher trainers be agents of change.

Young is rather critical of the NSE he created. He claims that it has not achieved its goal, which was to question society about social inequalities. He notes (1991):

> One could say that NSE tried to replace a reformist policy in the area of social inequalities with a cultural policy that is radical but does not go into much detail. It should also be added that, since the 'old' and the 'new' sociology of education both neglected the questions of sex and race (Acker, 1981), it is not surprising that they did not succeed in dealing adequately with social inequalities.

Young (1991) stresses, of course, the importance of sociological analysis of the curriculum. NSE considered the curriculum to be the main cause of the unequal distribution of schooling. He adds: "School subject compartmentalization, value hierarchies of fields of knowledge, and rejection of non-academic knowledge areas have been analyzed as means contributing to a selection of students according to their social class." In other words, the curriculum was judged to be an efficient means of ideological selection used by society.

The mistake of NSE, Young (1991) says, was to focus on this selection through the curriculum and to ignore "its cultural power and its capacity to provide real knowledge which, despite its ideological content, at least gave students enhanced control in the world in which they were to live." Caught in an ideological war, NSE could not help establish alternative programs to replace those that it deemed inadequate.

Finally, Young notes that NSE had overestimated the power of teachers:

> By emphasizing, with regard to the perpetuation of social inequalities, the exclusion that schools practiced through the curriculum rather than through external selection factors, it attributed to teachers a misleading autonomy as agents of curricular change.

Cultural Studies

Thinkers of critical pedagogy were more inspired by the *sociocultural* reflections found in such varied sources as anthropology, feminist studies, phenomenology, the Frankfurt School (Jurgen Habermas, Theodor Adorno, and Herbert Marcuse), structuralism, and postmodern texts. It took the diffusion of works by the European Neo-Marxist Left to establish a new language for education. Such expressions as "class consciousness" and "capital" were replaced by *modernity, postmodernity, cultural agent, cultural metaphor,* and *technocratic culture.*

The translation of German works from the Frankfurt School had an impact on North American thinking in the 1960s and especially the 1970s. Marcuse was undoubtedly the most popular and made possible the emergence of a Neo-Marxist critical theory in the late 1960s. Other authors fed this movement, particularly Fred Polak, Leo Lowenthal, and Erich Fromm, who had a great impact in those years. These authors inspired people who rejected capitalist society and were eager for social, economic, and political change.

However, French thinking was many years ahead of this American trend. Contrary to what was happening in America, the reflection of intellectuals had not suffered from any paralysis with regard to social criticism. For a long time in Europe, such authors as Louis Althusser, Gilles Deleuze, Felix Guattari, Jean Baudrillard, and Michel Foucault had analyzed social mechanisms in the construction of cultures. It was this critical thinking, at work in France since 1968, that later influenced American reflections on cultural institutions.

The Arrival of Giroux

When Giroux arrived on the scene in the early 1980s, it marked a turning point in the evolution of British and North American sociology of education, which had been rather cautious since 1950. In the 1970s and 1980s, the "alternative" American reflection had shown great interest in British, German, and French thought on the social dimension of culture. This allowed it to propose a social criticism of American liberalism without being formally identified with Marxism. This makes perfect sense if one remembers the impact of Sen. Joseph McCarthy's witch hunts in the United States in the early 1950s. McCarthy attacked intellectuals, movie directors, and all of those who wanted to obtain government research contracts, questioning if they had been associated in any way with the Communists.

This explains in part why critical thinking has had virtually no impact on American education. While French intellectuals had been quick to analyze the social functions of the educational system, Americans were much more cautious. Analyses of theories of education in the United States (Cuban, 1984; Goodlad, 1984; Ozmon and Craver, 1986; Sirotnik, 1989; Joyce, Weil, and Showers, 1992; Stanley, 1992) show the weaknesses of the educational current of social criticism between 1945 and 1980.

Giroux's work is very important in this American evolution because it allowed the renewal of social criticism and gave impetus to the emergence of a new, socially critical point of view on education. A critical theorist, Giroux felt the need to define more accurately his position on the new sociology of education. The position he presents is both positive and negative.

Giroux (1985) claims that NSE says the same thing as Freire: schools are social organizations, the function of which is social, economic, and cultural reproduction. Giroux (1985) insists in particular on cultural reproduction, i.e., the imposition through schools of cultural rules by the ruling classes. Giroux (1985) makes it quite clear. Governments are not unbiased when they finance education, nor are schools in their pedagogical practices. They confirm the richest in their privileges and exclude or insult the culture of minority groups — their experiences, histories, and dreams.

However, Giroux (1985) establishes the following difference: he hates the pessimism of the new sociology of education, which concludes that reproduction is inevitable. He prefers Freire's optimism. Indeed, beginning with this reproduction, Freire develops an empowering pedagogy that, he says, can apply as well in North America and Africa as in South America.

It is important to note that Giroux agreed to write an introduction to Freire's book, vindicated him, and analyzed the relationship — which he considered obvious — among the new sociology, Freire's thinking, and his own critical pedagogy. The three trends criticize social, economic, and cultural inequalities. It should be stressed that at the same time, from February 1984 to February 1986, Shor and Freire were meeting periodically to collaborate on a "dialogue-book": *A Pedagogy for Liberation*. This shows to what extent these theorists share the same vision of education. Giroux (1985) also wanted to settle accounts with the new sociology and suggested Freire as a refreshing antidote to the cynicism of leftist critics. (It might be added that Freire and Shor's pedagogical experiments constitute wonderful antidotes to the very theoretical, critical, and often inaccessible language of Giroux!)

Issues

The problem of school is its relationship with society: schools are a cultural instrument of selection and reproduction in the service of the ruling classes.

Aronowitz and Giroux (1985, p. 145) claim that the initial issue can be expressed in the following manner:

- What counts as school knowledge?

- How is school knowledge organized?

- What are the underlying codes that structure such knowledge?

- How is what counts as school knowledge transmitted?

- How is access to such knowledge determined?

- What kind of cultural system does school knowledge legitimate?
- Whose interests are served by the production and legitimation of school knowledge?

The fundamental problem is that school is in the service of the ruling classes of society. School legitimizes social and cultural inequalities and is much more than merely an aseptic transmission of knowledge. Pedagogy is one part of a vast political, cultural, and social operation conducted by the ruling classes. The real social and political problem is in the practice of democracy. Industrial societies are not as democratic as we have been led to believe (Aronowitz and Giroux, 1985). The organization of society favors certain social groups at the expense of others, such as minority ethnic groups, women, and critics.

This problem of school is tied to its socialization function. The problem, say Giroux (1992a) and Shor (1992a), is fundamentally that certain groups of people exercise power over other groups through school systems. This is a vast problem that affects all cultural enterprises through which the elite control the development of society. School is never neutral, for it is an agency of social change (Apple, 1988; Shor, 1992a). It is used to construct subjectivities, perceptions, and social relationships. It socializes the individual, transforming him or her according to the wishes of society.

The purpose of school is to produce meaning that does not conflict with social dynamism. School is historical and plays a part in the cultural dynamism of industrial societies: it serves the values of the groups that control society and thereby constitutes a political instrument. Society's discourse discredits social criticism and groups that criticize. "The oppressor," says Giroux (1992a), "plays the role of the victim." By so doing, society discourages people and prevents them from pursuing their analyses of the social problems generated by extreme industrialization.

Such cultural structures as television, radio, and schools serve as tools to divert the mind from real issues and direct it toward pseudo-issues. The mind is kept busy for life, in the hope that the groups holding power will hold it even longer. Society offers a mass culture characterized by mediocrity and utilitarianism (Giroux, 1992a). Therefore, it becomes very difficult in such a context to form a critical citizen capable, if necessary, of challenging and changing society.

Over the years, critical theory became more and more interested in the notion of an industry of culture. Instrumental rationality had transformed genuine culture into mass production, characterized by standardization, duplication, copying, mediocrity, and conformity, as well as by mystification and illusion.

These reflections became relevant in the analysis of education. The next step was easy: to interpret education as a cultural industry in the service of the dominant class and as an ideological maneuver ("ideology" in the sense of a false consciousness of social contradictions and an attempt to conceal them beneath a theory and a practice of social harmony).

This makes it possible to understand how analysis of the social question of education has led some researchers to both analyze an industry of culture and develop a critical language. We can see this evolution in such American authors as Giroux and Roger I. Simon, who believe that education should be analyzed through an interpretation of the educational system as a cultural agent of social transformation. So the educational system is analyzed as an industry of culture, like the movies, television, radio, and advertising!

Principles
We will now examine three principles of critical pedagogy: attention to social values, creation of a critical language, and sociality of knowledge.

Attention to Social Values. The first principle of critical pedagogy is to emphasize social values. Critical pedagogy often refers to social justice, equality, respect for individuals, overcoming social, cultural, or other barriers, and returning power to groups and the majority.

Giroux (1992a) stresses human dignity, liberty, equality, and social justice. He maintains that the objective of critical pedagogy is to create a political imagery that would make it possible to create new public spheres based on principles of equality, liberty, and justice. Critical pedagogy should encourage development of a sense of social responsibility. Students should learn to defend the rights of the individual and fight against social inequities.

Critical pedagogy is intended as an alternative to traditional instruction and to industrial instruction. Its main objective is democracy, i.e., to increase the power of individuals and minority groups (Aronowitz and Giroux, 1985). Democracy should be understood in this context as the genuine exercise of power by the majority and not merely as an application of seemingly democratic rules. Schooling is a social practice linked in essence to the exercise of power.

Creation of a Critical Language. The second principle is the use of a critical language. Critical pedagogy tries to fit into a "radical paradigm" (Giroux, 1992a). The relationship between social organizations and social capacities is such that an individual has the capacity to question the social organization when he or she has been educated to do so. Democracy is based on the self-developed critical sense of the individual, and this critical sense refuses the usual reductive language. It should acquire a new language. In fact, it might seem that critical pedagogy is limited to this function!

Critical pedagogy needs a language that is not merely an echo of the usual grand discourse about the numerous benefits of capitalist and industrial society. One should learn to criticize this language that permeates our culture. One should attack this usual language and shatter its monolithic hold. The language of critical pedagogy is that of "critical democracy." It stresses the knowledge, the skills, and the habits to be acquired in order to become a critical citizen.

We should try, says Giroux (1992a), to answer the following questions: What sort of citizen should public education shape for postmodern culture? What type of society do we want to establish, considering the present cultural and social evolution? How do we reconcile liberty and justice, equality and the recognition of differences?

Sociality of Knowledge. The third principle is that of the sociality of knowledge. Knowledge is not objective in itself. It is rather strongly tied to the social and cultural practices of a society. Critical pedagogy (Giroux, 1992a) is a set of textual, verbal, and visual practices through which individuals learn to understand themselves and analyze their relationships with others and the environment. According to Simon (1992) and Giroux (1992a), it is also a challenge to the dominant forms of symbolic production — if we accept the idea that symbolic representations that appear in the various cultural spheres are manifestations of power relationships that are questionable because they are unfair.

The subjectivity of the student is constructed socially and politically. The student should learn to respect differences among individuals and groups. He or she should form a multiethnic, ecological, antiracist, and antipatriarchal vision of the democratic community. Perceptions based on inequalities among races and between men and women should disappear, for a more democratic society. The student should also learn that negative judgments are maintained by the groups that dominate society, so these groups can preserve their privileged status.

Teachers are "cultural workers" (Giroux, 1992a), since the curriculum is the result of cultural politics. The concept of "cultural worker" — a term formerly reserved for such people as artists, writers, and movie directors — should be extended to other spheres, such as education. The educator should be thought of as a "transformative intellectual." As an intellectual, the teacher should analyze his or her own social and cultural history. The teacher should also question the contents of education and reveal the "hidden tensions," i.e., the "hidden curriculum" (Giroux, 1983a).

Pedagogical Strategies

Critical educators comment rather sparingly on their pedagogical strategies. We find very few answers to the question, "How does one teach critically?"

This is understandable, as they seem to consider pedagogy an object of analysis rather than an instructional strategy. Pedagogy structures messages and thus plays a decisive role in education. This point is well illustrated by a statement from an essay by Giroux and Peter McLaren in *Border Crossings* (1992): students should examine pedagogical relationships in the classroom, then in society, and expose how these relationships structure the constitution of meaning for people. This may remind us of similar ideas proposed by proponents of institutional pedagogy a long time ago!

Still, it is possible to find general thoughts on pedagogical strategies in a number of books dealing with critical pedagogy. Giroux (1992a) notes that pedagogy is always linked to power.

As a matter of fact, he says, theories of education are ideologies that are closely related to power. And learning should aim at transforming society. The teacher should play the role of a transformative intellectual of society and fight for democracy.

Critical pedagogy is interdisciplinary and critical of the foundations of disciplines. It takes on the public cause of making society more democratic. It seeks to be both theoretical and practical. It attributes great importance to the student's personal experience. The student exercises his or her critical spirit based on personal social and cultural experiences, i.e., his or her history.

6.3.4 Social Pedagogy for Self-Development

Jacques Grand'Maison is a prolific Quebecois author who has written on numerous social subjects. He has expressed his thoughts on education in such books as *Pour une pédagogie sociale d'autodéveloppement en éducation* (1976), *Le privé et le public* (1975), and *Des milieux de travail à réinventer* (1975).

Grand'Maison offers a social pedagogy that is very similar to Freire's thoughts. He criticizes conceptions of education and proposes a theory rooted in concrete experience. His theory is quite interesting, not only because of its content, but also because it prefigures current critical theories (Giroux, Shor, and others). Here are the principal elements of his theory.

1. Typology of Schools

Grand'Maison (1976) first attacks schools for their lack of social relevance. He describes the structures of the educational system as a sort of feudal place within a city thoroughly shaken by social, cultural, economic, political, and ideological forces from all directions. Education has become an industry while remaining a world of its own, wrapped up in itself.

Grand'Maison observes that schools suffer from reductionism — from an attempt to reduce school to one of these seven models:

1. **The techno-bureaucratic school.** The local and national administrative apparatus takes precedence over all else.

2. **The neo-corporate school.** School is defined by professionalism and unionism, a counter-power in the techno-bureaucratic game.

3. **The school as "drive belt" in the economic engine.** The school serves the capitalist society and ruling economic powers.

4. **The school as a politico-ideological instrument.** School functions as a center of ideological criticism, but an instrument of the ideological forces from the left and the right.

5. **The commune school.** Live and feel, do as you please.

6. **The school as an integrating center of learning.** In the aftermath of the technological revolution, emphasis is placed on technical processes and rational invention.

7. **The community school.** This is a return to basic communities, which masks a neo-conservatism (private schools, the appeal of the country, manual crafts, and old-time religions).

These seven conceptions of school are too instrumental, Grand'Maison argues. He notes that there are a lot of means, but that the goals get confused because of a "cookbook approach." We quickly abandon questions of "Why?" for questions of "How?" We seek the tool that will bring about an instant solution, even though the real questions are: "What is a more human school? What sort of person, individual or social, inner and political, is coming out of our schools?"

Grand'Maison (1976) writes:

> Because we insist on operationalizing, instrumentalizing, measuring, and testing every step in the process, we sterilize and restrict the human condition that education is trying to connect in all its dimensions and virtualities.

What we need, then, is an eighth conception — *school: a place for people.* How can this place be described? There are several possible answers and critical perspectives for analyzing this new school model. But most of these approaches are unsatisfactory.

Grand'Maison states that there are six critical approaches: personalist, utilitarian, critical ideological, administrative, pedagogical, and political. He offers the following comments:

- The *personalist* approach focuses too much on personal development and disregards the existence of social classes.

- The *utilitarian* approach is based on the principle that education is a means of getting a job, earning more money, or acquiring a better social status. It leads directly to the current social crisis.

- The *critical ideological* approach of the Left leads to never-ending discussions with no results. It is too often erratic and splintered. School quickly becomes an ideological laboratory.

- The *administrative* approach gives far too much importance to administrative rules and to orderly operation.

- The *pedagogical* approach is too centered on defining objectives and on the structures that are particularly pedagogical. School is reduced to questions of apprenticeship.

- The *political* approach is a battle in which the various parties (administrators, teachers, unions) have only one goal: power.

Grand'Maison (1976) concludes that school, like most social institutions, should reinvent its human and social basis. What we need is a social pedagogy based on one fundamental principle: a pedagogy of self-development cannot come into existence unless we "reinvent a social base that is more coherent, more dynamic, more in harmony with a culture, economy, and politics of social self-development." The one can't work without the other. In sum, according to Grand'Maison, a pedagogy succeeds when it becomes a social praxis of self-development, when it casts off the instrumental logic to take on a social logic of self-development for all.

(We should understand "praxis" as all of the activities appropriate to changing the world, social reality. Pedagogy that becomes praxis is, we might say, pedagogy through action and for action, pedagogy that transforms social reality. The opposite would be a pedagogy that leads only to reflections about the universe.)

When Grand'Maison uses the term "pedagogy of self-development," he means "a pedagogy that runs through every aspect of school processes to infuse them with a new coherence" (1976). The pedagogy of self-development is social because it should go beyond the school, to influence all other institutions. It is a pedagogy that "can be tested in the main institutions of a social milieu for a better orchestrated and finalized collective promotion" (1976). The pedagogy of self-development is also social because the responsibility of the school is to "reinvent a social base that is more coherent, more dynamic, more in harmony with a culture, economy, and politics of social self-development."

Pedagogy is a field that is linked to a certain historical economics and that expresses a basic philosophy, a way of critically thinking, acting, and living together, an operationalization of means and objectives. Consequently, the need for an historical consciousness is the best foundation for the perspectives of self-development in education, if education is to lead to a redefinition of humans, of their fundamental relationships, and of a liberating social praxis.

2. Pedagogical Strategy

There are three principal characteristics in the pedagogical strategy of this educational theory:

1. A common pedagogy

2. A pedagogy inseparable from personal experience and social reality

3. A synergy of the fundamental acts of life

First of all, we need a common pedagogical strategy that is the foundation for a description of the means and their use. This pedagogy will serve as the axis of integration for the multiplicity of subsystems, categories of players, rationalities (administrative, cultural, technical, social), and ideologies. This strategy should lead to a minimal consensus among all members of society.

Second, a pedagogy works when it changes into a social praxis of self-development — that is, when it is centered on transforming the personal experiences of the students. A social praxis, Grand'Maison (1976) writes, "is an original personal experience which has found its forms of expression, of critical understanding, of solidarity, and of transformative action."

An educational strategy, Grand'Maison tells us, should serve the population as a whole while ensuring the self-liberation of all and collective advancement. In education of the people, we must quickly focus on the raw and almost brutal personal experiences of an alienated human situation in the process of liberation — experiences with obscure dynamics and values. A social pedagogy should allow individuals to take control of their lives, their education, and their environment. A pedagogy that people take upon themselves has repercussions in all social areas.

Grand'Maison (1976) writes:

> Thus, workers who had achieved a mastery of their work experience that proved greater responsibility, freedom, solidarity, and creativity became more vigilant and active citizens. They no longer hesitated about meeting at school with the other parents. One type of participation supported another, with political consequences.

Third, a pedagogical process can begin with any of these fundamental dynamics of life (interpretation, transformation, expression, and sharing of personal experience) as long as it is synergistic. (Synergy is based on the principle that the action of a group depends on the full and entire cooperation of its members.) Social praxis is the synergy of interpretation, transformation, expression, and sharing of personal experience.

The social pedagogy of self-development should be understood as a recomposition of the fundamental acts of education into the principal, basic learning units. Pedagogy, Grand'Maison maintains, should establish a synergy of fundamental human acts, in which people learn to express, judge, share, and transform daily experience.

He offers language as an example. We cannot separate language from the real situations in which it is used. Also, we must not forget that language reflects the economic, political, and cultural dimensions of a particular setting. Consequently, teaching a language in school but disregarding its real-life contexts is pointless and inane.

We notice the relationship between Grand'Maison and Freire. Grand'Maison writes that liberation of expression, for an individual or a group, may be pointless if it does not open up into meanings, relationships, and actions connected to the situation that is expressed. That is what is meant by the idea of social praxis. This is the opposite of alienation. There is no longer any distance between what is learned and what is experienced in life, because learning allows the students to appropriate their personal experiences, to own them and become masters of their lives. Social pedagogy, Grand'Maison (1976) asserts, "puts fundamental human acts back into their daily real-life settings."

By moving in this direction, he says:

> We respect the basic pedagogical responsibility of the school, while situating it in the major task of reinventing a social base that is more coherent, more dynamic, more in harmony with a culture, economy, and politics of social self-development. We envision a pedagogy that can be tested in the main institutions of a social milieu for a better orchestrated and finalized collective promotion.

3. Grid of Basic Learning

The pedagogical strategy that we have just examined is founded on what Grand'Maison calls "the pedagogical grid of the fundamental acts of education," which is to support basic learning. This pedagogical grid is directly related, as we might expect, to real-life experience: there cannot be any distance between the two. Here are brief summaries of the categories used in this grid: knowledge for doing, knowledge for thinking, knowledge for living, knowledge for sharing, and knowledge for telling.

- **Knowledge for Doing.** We should find ways to use skills and technical learning on the job. We must do away with the dichotomy between manual work and intellectual work. We tend too much to devalue technical learning, which has a precious advantage over other sorts of learning: it is connected to reality.

- **Knowledge for Thinking.** School covers knowledge and techniques. But does it teach students how to think fairly, exactly, and wisely? That is the question that Grand'Maison raises. In fact, both teachers and students have trouble specifying what they want in a certain hierarchy of meanings, values, or human priorities. At the core of the current ethical crisis lies our failure to develop a sense of judgment. It is more and more difficult to think for oneself in a society where the media control discourse. The constant presence of radio and TV cultivates a basic dependency.

Grand'Maison argues that school should remain a privileged place for developing a sense for serious, autonomous, and demanding thought. Learning how to think can stimulate not only a taste for personal reflection but also the political volition to conquer a way of life that also alienates people from their most precious possession — their autonomous, free, and resolute sense of judgment.

- **Knowledge for Living**. Society suffers from a sickness: libertarian irresponsibility, anarchic permissiveness, and parasitic luxury. The breach between individuality and sociality is getting deeper. Grand'Maison (1976) writes:

> We can no longer find in society any meanings that help us live. The "free world," emancipated from needs, breeds people who try to find freedom outside it, while passively asking for what they need to live. Some of them even go so far as to believe that the machine can function without them, that they can take advantage of it without any serious consequences. Sometimes in these attitudes there is a curious mixture of depoliticization and collective ideologization.

Democracy is in danger and needs an education in social manners. Educating for freedom and democracy requires sustained learning and that people be rigorously educated on their responsibilities. In the art of living, individuals and society ought to constantly renew the dialectic relationships between liberties and necessities for all. Human freedom requires this concrete face-to-face of these vital elements if we are to live in the real world with its inevitable limits. Knowing how to live comes through "educating the consciousness of the combatants."

- **Knowledge for Sharing**. The mission of the school is to cultivate the quality of social relationships and human ties. The school must teach young people to go beyond personal interests to accede to interests of the community. But the teachers are not necessarily in the best position to discuss this, as Grand'Maison emphasizes:

Go develop knowledge for sharing among young people, when adults show that they are individually and collectively selfish, when everyone weighs contributions by the minute and by the dollar. Values such as doing something for nothing are ridiculed, to the great detriment of caring, generous, and cordial human relationships.

- **Knowledge for Telling.** School ought to present a culture close to the people. In fact, Grand'Maison wonders, "What is a culture that has no meaning in what people experience, in what they think, in their togetherness, in love, in their struggles?" School has no choice but to immerse "knowledge for telling" in actual experience. Otherwise, it is completely alienated from life.

4. Pedagogical Organization

The strategy that Grand'Maison proposes must now take on a concrete form. But we must not forget that school is inseparable from the individual, from the group, and from the milieu. In fact, the tools will come from social life itself. Pedagogy will borrow heavily from the milieu and thus become much more natural, closer to everyone. Pedagogy will help learners take hold of their personal experience in context, real life. Pedagogy, in sum, must be able to assume the cultural, social, economic, and political changes of society and of its various milieux.

Grand'Maison proposes a basic approach, although acknowledging that there are many others. We must work on the network of everyday contacts between an individual and his or her milieu. This network of relationships is broken into three levels (1976):

1. Spontaneous experiences, networks of people in their interrelationships, networks of special places and moments, networks of activities and of centers of interest

2. Structured experiences, networks of belonging (organisms, institutions), networks of power and leadership, networks of techniques used

3. Signified experiences (symbols, purposes, ideologies), networks of key words and expressions,

networks of everyday signs, networks of tenden-
cies (values, ideologies, politics)

In working on these networks, the students and the teacher will
gain a better knowledge of the milieu and a mastery of the
environment.

5. Modular Synergistic Pedagogy

In sum, education is, for Grand'Maison (1976,) a synergistic and
global way of treating everyday experiences, the situations in
which we live. We must rebuild the social base, starting with a
social pedagogy of self-development that would be shared by the
principal institutions of a milieu. That pedagogy ought to be the
responsibility of all institutions.

We would accomplish that by working systematically. A good
way to proceed would be to create modules that group the
"liberating forces" of a milieu. The module would be any group
organized in a field of activities that are circumscribed and
relatively homogenous, despite the diversity of the tasks and of
the group members.

The module is neither a pure community centered around the
individualistic development of the people involved, nor a task
force organized simply to work together on a project. A module
is an everyday place of action, reflection, and solidarity, all
organized and given purpose in a specific social and institutional
field. The module is a life setting that, in daily life, helps
everyone develop — which, Grand'Maison reminds us, should be
the ultimate goal of any pedagogy.

6.4 Eco-Social Theories of Education

The following paragraphs will provide a description of a third
trend in social theories. We have seen that institutional and
conscientization theories, analyzed above, are especially concerned with questions related to social change. The theories that
will be analyzed next have a broader vision of the problems.

Joël de Rosnay, Erich Jantsch, and Alvin Toffler are more
concerned with the macro-problems generated by our social,
economic, political, and cultural structures. The changes that
they advocate in the educational system are based on a global
vision of relationships among the individual, society, and the

universe. This is why we could term these theories "eco-social" visions of education.

Society is now going through a transition period that will probably mark the end of a cycle in the history of our planet: the unrestrained industrialization of societies. We must make major changes if we want to ensure a healthy evolution of society, the individual, and nature. The serious ecological problems that face us as we approach the twentyfirst century indicate to what extent we must think in ecological terms about the global organization of the Earth.

Nature is finally imposing limits on our anthropomorphic drifting (Petitjean, 1989). The solution to these problems does not merely lie in showing greater concern for the environment (Guattari, 1989), in making our schools more effective, in suppressing social classes, or in developing more efficacious technologies for pedagogical communication. The solution lies in *inventing a new vision* of the world — and the new educational institutions will have to contribute to its collective construction.

Education should not be reconsidered from an industrial perspective, but rather from a more global vision of the evolution of our planet. Education should be used to invent a new future for the planet. As Edgar Morin (1989) so rightly puts it:

> It is no longer a time for assessing the effects of ecological disasters. Nor should we delude ourselves with the thought that the rise of technologies could remedy them by itself and even less so overcome the major dysfunctions that threaten to wreck the planet and its biosphere forever. Salvation can come only from a radical transformation in our relationships with other human beings, with other forms of life, and with nature. An ecological consciousness of solidarity must take the place of the culture of competitiveness and aggression currently governing world relationships.

It should also be noted that these theories are not conservative. They do not advocate a return to classicism — quite the contrary! Instead, they tend to attack rearguard culture, say Robert Ornstein and Paul Ehrlich (1990), and all those who defend it, often calling traditionalists lunatics and blind fools.

6.4.1 Systematic Education in an Eco-Society

In *The Macroscope: A New World Scientific Vision* (originally published in 1975) and *Les chemins de la vie* (1983), Rosnay proposes a global, systemic, and ecological theory of education. This theory is based on a new vision of the world and a new approach, symbolized by the macroscope.

The evolution of biology, cybernetics, and computers had a certain influence on the genesis of such a vision of the world. To this should be added the many scientific discoveries that shatter our fragmentary vision of the nature of society and lead us to rediscover our belonging to life and to matter and recover our consciousness of the global functioning of the social organism. However, it is, above all, our ecological future that worries more and more people. The technological impact on industries and jobs provokes reactions against too rapid changes. In short, the pairing of a more global vision and the perception of this accelerating change provokes both a very profound criticism of society and the emergence of new values.

Rosnay tries to derive a plan for society, an alternative to "unrestrained capitalism" and "bureaucratic communism" (1979, p. 204). This third way is the "ecosociety": "The prefix 'eco' symbolizes here the close relationship between economy and ecology; it puts the accent on *relationships* among men and between men and what they call their 'home,' the ecosphere" (1979, p. 223). The eco-society is characterized by an "economy of equilibrium" (p. 223). Its purpose is "to serve better *at the same time* human needs, the maintenance and evolution of the social system, and the pursuit of true cooperation with nature" (p. 224).

Rosnay finds the model of conviviality proposed by Ivan Illich — "a society in which modern technologies serve politically interrelated individuals rather than managers" (p. 224) — interesting in many respects. In the service of the individual integrated into society, the eco-society is constructed from bottom to top, with management, planning, and telecommunication playing an important part. In fact, Rosnay notes, "Ecosociety is conviviality plus telecommunications!" (1979, p. 225)

Rosnay presents the values on which a new plan for society should be based, including participation, decentralization, cooperation, creative work, global logic, inventive thought, respect for others, and conviviality. The macroscope will be the tool that allows a new outlook on nature, society, and the human being, and the tool that symbolizes the systemic approach characterized by its global vision of problems and systems and its concentration on interactions among elements. To sum up, a new global vision (the systemic approach) encourages the emergence of new values and the scenario for tomorrow's education.

Principles of a Systemic Education

Rosnay (1983, 1979) suggests abandoning the linear and traditional approach for a new approach centered on interdependencies. Traditional instruction is putting a lot of effort into modernizing education, but new methods and techniques do not yet offer a new global vision based on a systemic approach. Rosnay is convinced that without a global approach, the various attempts to modernize instruction might be doomed to fail. The introduction of the computer, for example, does not necessarily lead to a "pedagogical revolution."

We should go beyond sporadic corrections and take a global approach. The multidimensional human being will be the keystone of systemic education, the major components of which will be:

- Biological (unit: the organism)
- Intellectual and behavioral (unit: the person)
- Social and relational (unit: the citizen)
- Symbolic (unit: the being) (1979, pp. 211-212)

What will be the general approach of the new education? The systemic approach will constitute the general method to be followed and will be based on five basic principles.

1. **Spiral approach.** The traditional approach is linear and sequential: it consists of going from one point to the next. It should be replaced by a spiral method, which "involves returning several times *at different levels* to whatever is to be understood and assimilated" (1979, p. 213).

2. **Multicontextuality.** A concept should be studied in consideration of the multiple contexts in which it can apply, rather than by polarizing it in a fixed definition.

3. **Complexity of systems.** Using disciplines "that integrate time and irreversibility," such as biology, ecology, and economics, makes it possible to emphasize "the importance of mutual causality, interdependence, and the dynamics of complex systems" (1979, p. 213).

4. **Vertical themes.** Rosnay recommends "themes of vertical integration, general themes that make it possible to integrate several disciplines and several levels of complexity around a central axis" (1979, p. 213). Vertical themes encourage integration of several areas of knowledge from different levels; e.g., "continental drift" (geography, geology, biology, and ecology, then geophysics, paleontology, genetics, and climatology), "blood and hemoglobin" (physics, organic chemistry, biochemistry, molecular biology, physiology, cyberneiics, and genetics), or "farm products" (microbiology, nourishment and diet, hygiene, the process of fermentation, and the prevention of illness) (1979, p. 213).

5. **Establishing relationships.** To understand a fact in itself presupposes establishing how it relates to other facts: "The acquisition of facts cannot be separated from the understanding of the relationships that exist among them" (1979, pp. 213-214).

Instructional Organization

The two basic methods of this approach to instruction are self-learning and interaction (generally through simulation). First of all, students should be allowed to acquire new facts at their own pace, using self-teaching modules and computer-assisted instructional programs. Second, emphasis must be placed on using simulation (films, games, and computer simulation) to facilitate interaction. Simulation makes it possible to build models of reality, and students can then better understand the dynamic relations among the elements of a complex system.

Rosnay states:

> The structure of systemic education would take the form of a pyramid; we would enter at the top through

what is most general, most common, even most intuitive in elementary education, then we would define in broad terms the goals of our own instruction and move toward the base of the pyramid to obtain essential knowledge. Ultimately, everything we learn would be related to action (or the simulation of action) (1979, p. 217).

On the other hand, we should devise structures for parallel education, alongside traditional methods, such as peer teaching, in which each individual is a node in a communication network, a potential source of knowledge and skills. An excellent way to achieve this objective is to establish small communities managed by the users themselves — groups of businesses, associations, and cultural clubs. Distance learning could be effective in this alternative form of instruction. Rosnay also suggests expanding free access to knowledge by establishing self-service centers, e.g., libraries, educational resources centers, and computers. Rosnay also proposes using companies, international symposiums, educational parks, training conferences, and third-age colleges, among other things. In short, systemic education should lead to a new form of equilibrium appropriate to an eco-society.

6.4.2 Experiential Education

Erich Jantsch's theory of education is globalist and complex. His most important book may well be *Design for Evolution* (1975), which deals with acquiring and using knowledge for human purposes. According to Jantsch, objective models of science (the "know-how") fit into a hierarchy under regulatory principles (the policies or "know-what") and, ultimately, under the principles that underlie the processes: the dynamics of evolution.

To really understand the dynamics of evolution, Jantsch believes, just like Rosnay and Toffler, that we must change our perspective and use the general theory of systems. And if all systems (social, physical, biological, and cultural) are in constant evolution, what is the function of knowledge? What is the role of education?

Jantsch maintains that cognitive systems evolve in the same way as human systems, i.e., through feedback, and that the processes are the same for learning and for conception. Hence, the importance of noetic evolution, according to which information and knowledge systems, if sufficiently disequilibriated, may be able to include an internal evolutionistic tendency toward new regimes of organizing knowledge. Therefore, our task would principally consist of managing and interpreting such forms of noetic self-organization as we find in the evolution of major scientific or philosophical concepts.

Basing himself on Thomas Kuhn, Ervin Laszlo, John Eccles, and Ilya Prigogine, Jantsch (1975) concludes that knowledge is an aspect of evolution that affects the mind. The organization of rational knowledge could be represented by a triangle: the top would consist of values, the intermediate levels would be normative planning and technologies (physical, natural, and social), and the base would consist of the physical, biological, and psychological sciences. This triangle of rational knowledge is characterized by interdisciplinarity, which is a mode of organization centered on the coordination of the elements of one level, based on the higher level. Transdisciplinarity expands this form of organization to the whole system.

However, says Jantsch (1975), comprehension cannot be founded on rationality alone. He uses the concept of "interexperiential organization" (p. 233), that is, the dynamic coordination of elements of human experience at a given level, based on the level immediately above. This concept includes scientific creativity and conceptualization. Thus, intuition will play as important a role as rationality in human experience.

The goals of education will then be the enrichment and "efficacy" of the individual's experience, that is, the growth of his or her consciousness. The individual will become more capable of organizing his or her total experience toward a goal, using interexperiential and transexperiential modes of inquiry.

This implies, consequently, a dynamic attitude that tends toward experience, an orientation toward a goal, and especially toward conceptualization, since the point is to prepare students to adjust to situations that can hardly be predicted at the time of instruction.

Education will be structured along three major axes (pp. 235-241):

> 1. **Design of human relations:** human experience
> in relation with the environment. This part of

education is concerned with the relationships of the individual with physical, social, and spiritual realities. It deals as much with communication and creativity as with scientific methods. Among the subjects "taught," according to Jantsch, "of particular importance are those which emphasize the dynamic, organizing, and integrating aspects of human relations with the world" (p. 237). These subjects may include: biology, psychology and psychoanalysis, the theory of creativity, principles of ecosystems, cultural anthropology, communication theory and basic notions of cybernetics, and other forms of communication (parapsychology and others) (pp. 237-238).

2. **Design of instrumentalities:** the organization of the world (natural, physical, and social environments). The central theme is the organization of individuals with their technologies, communication systems, ambitions, expectations, and goals. Education could include the following subjects: innovation processes, creative planning, political science, systems approach to planning, futurology, social indicators, and decision theory (p. 239).

3. **Design of institutions:** the cultural organization of social systems. At this level, "Learning is essentially geared to a better understanding or experiencing of the evolution of values" (p. 239). The fundamental notion is the axiological method, i.e., the systemic inquiry into the nature of the values of different institutions underlying behaviors and exploration of their implications. Students do "practical design work in system laboratories, relating the phenomenology of total dynamic behavior of systems to their spatial and temporal morphology" (p. 240). They study the anthropology of industrial and postindustrial societies, innovation processes, values and value dynamics, ethics, system theory, evolutionary concepts and trends (cosmological, physical, biological, social, and

noetic), religions and ideologies, as well as theories of the mind (p. 241).

These three levels of education are interconnected by feedback loops in a global cybernetics that is cultural, social, and human. However, interexperiential learning processes cannot be the object of a traditional instruction. Jantsch concludes in these terms:

> The interexperiential learning processes cannot be the subject of teaching in the traditional sense, nor of training in the use of methods. The learning processes in school and in real life have to become identical, they have to be experienced themselves in order to become part of human experience. Whether the instrumental form in which this can be achieved best will be called a school or a university or something else, and whether it will even faintly resemble contemporary educational instrumentalities, is of secondary importance (p. 243).

6.4.3 Curriculum for the Future

In his books *Future Shock* (1970), *Learning for Tomorrow* (1974), *The Third Wave* (1980), and *Previews and Promises* (1983), Alvin Toffler presents a very interesting reflection on the relationships among education, the culture of the future, and the present industrial society. First, he clearly rejects contemporary educational structures. Second, he advocates making the future a fundamental axis of education, in opposition to those who defend the past and traditions. Finally, he treats the future as a possibility for change, insofar as social institutions are unsuited to the needs of our times.

Indeed, not only is the future a starting point in relation to change in the individual, but it becomes his or her basic motivation, the vision of the future that guides his or her analyses of the transformations needed in social institutions. The future is also the symbol of the deep-seated aspirations underlying the struggle of minorities, who often have a pessimistic vision of their future. Moreover, the future can only provoke a revision of current disciplinary conventions and a new organization of knowledge in terms of all the changes in the contemporary world.

Thus, the future affects all those who learn and modifies all teaching and learning strategies. Educational methodology allows for games, simulations, and theater.

Finally, the future has a moral value, since we must speak of *desirable* futures, as well as a social value, since the future is of political and social consequence. Toffler writes (1974) that bringing the future into learning is necessarily tied to the underlying currents of change in the contemporary world — the struggles for women's rights, for racial equality, and for the recognition of youth in a system that keeps them out of decision-making and out of the work force for longer and longer periods of time.

In this perspective, Toffler anticipated, it is clear that an important social battle (in the 1970s and 1980s) would involve reformulating the meaning of work. The future cannot be conceived of merely as the prolongation of forms of work that brutalize the great majority of humans.

In short, the global revolution advocated by Toffler is based on an image of the future, as much in its relationship with the individual as with society, as much with school as with other social institutions. However, the special nature of this image is based on a perspective of adaptation. Indeed, the problems are apparent in individuals' maladjustment to society, which is the theme of *Future Shock* and *Learning for Tomorrow*.

A Future Different from the Present

Toffler stresses the role of images of the future to analyze the educational situation. Education has traditionally been assumed by the wise, the old, and parents based on an established principle: the future will not be that different from the present, so that teaching in terms of current situations means teaching in terms of situations to come.

This attitude still exists today. Politicians foster the myth that industrial society will continue indefinitely, and teachers hold the same views. They do not perceive the impact of changes — technology, family structures, and international relations — on a future bound to be radically different. In short, education is based on an image of the future that is totally inadequate, so all innovative projects become irrelevant. As Toffler (1974) puts it:

All education springs from some image of the future. If the image of the future held by a society is grossly inaccurate, its education system will betray its youth (p. 3).

Moreover, the main result of this image of the future is to breed maladjustment, since it includes no possibility of radical change. Toffler (1974) writes:

> I believe that the schools and universities, with their heavy emphasis on the past, not only implicitly convey a false message about the future — the idea that it will resemble the present — but also that they create millions of candidates for future shock by encouraging the divorce between the individual's self-image and his or her expectations with regard to social change. More deeply, they encourage the student to think of his or her "self" not as subject to change, growth or adaptation, but as something static.

Practical Image

Analysis of the future is fundamental to learning. If we cannot construct anticipatory images, we cannot learn. Indeed, each of us projects a moving image of the future on the screen of his or her consciousness. We juggle with short-, medium-, and long-range anticipations.

This invisible architecture of premises about the future is basic to personality and behavior, and it allows us to survive in an ever-changing environment. It is our base for adaptation. A good part of education rests in the process by which we enlarge, enrich, and improve our image of the future that we hold as individuals.

However, education is not limited to the formation of the mind. It involves the complete biochemistry of the individual and places this individual in a changing environment. The movement centered on the future is only a stage in restructuring the ties among schools, colleges, and their communities. The movement should first and foremost help the individual modify reality, face crises, and use the possibilities for change. The ultimate goal is to reinforce the practical ability of the individual to anticipate change and adjust to it, whether by invention, enlightened participation, or intelligent resistance.

All of this presupposes a constant two-way connection between theory and practice, between classroom and community, and between written information and broadcast news. We must, therefore, increasingly recognize the significance of "off-campus" work in industry, community projects, and ecological activities. In short, for older students, this action-learning should become the dominant form of education, with the classroom becoming merely a secondary support. The ties between society and school should be re-established.

In other words, Toffler claims (1974) that the current educational policy "is based on a perilously false image of the future." He explains:

> By maintaining the false distinction between work and learning, and between school and community, we not only divorce theory from practice and deprive ourselves of enormous energies that might be channeled into socially useful action, we also infantilize the young and rob them of the motivation to learn. ...

> The motive to learn is ... the desire to do something useful, productive and respected — to change the community. ... Only by recognizing the urgency of this desire to make a mark (and thereby to clarify or establish one's own identity) and by reconceptualizing the role of youth with respect to work and social needs can the education system become effective (p. 16).

Action-Learning
Toffler (1974) suggests a pedagogical strategy: to link learning to action:

> By linking learning to action ... we change the source of motivation. The motive to learn is no longer the fear of a teacher's power to grade or the displeasure of the parent, but the desire to do something useful, productive and respected — to change the community, to make a dent, even a small one, on reality (p. 16).

Students organize themselves into teams, which include individuals from different age groups, bridging the generation gap. These teams focus on a clear objective of a desirable change in society. Thus, the group develops a feeling of belonging and resolves the problems of loneliness and isolation related to individual learning.

The group generates its own social reinforcements for learning, thereby giving their studies greater social relevance. Members of a team working on changing the ecological conditions of their community, for example, will learn as much about sciences as about economics, sociology, and political science. Moreover, they will develop communication skills, learn to assess problems, imagine solutions, communicate, and make decisions. As they attempt to solve real problems and as they learn, students will become familiar with decision-making processes and understand the consequences of their decisions, that their decisions may have important consequences for society.

We can sum up Toffler's thought as follows. The radical and total change in education takes place at the intersection of imagery and action. This intersection will be experienced within an image of the future, which will not be predetermined by current structures of society or by the industrial myth. Rather, it will result from an individual and collective search for a more desirable future. The whole will assume the form of an image of the future in all of its dimensions — social, political, economic, and cultural. Pedagogically, this will translate into learning through action, i.e., learning based on attempts to resolve real-life problems encountered by the community and the society. The school structure is nothing more than a secondary support of education.

6.5 Conclusion

The theories of education analyzed in this chapter stress the fundamentally social nature of the education that has to prepare students and teachers to solve the problems of society. These problems are serious; social and environmental crises increasingly shape our everyday culture.

We do not think of our cultural evolution in terms of ensuring our survival on this planet. Our technology is evolving more rapidly than our control over its objectives. Tempted by industrial progress, we have many difficulties solving macro-problems such as the arms race, pollution, and industrial illnesses. Numerous authors, including Rosnay (1979), Jantsch (1981), Morin (1989), Ornstein and Ehrlich (1990), Toffler (1990), and Y. Bertrand and Paul Valois (1992) claim that we must become ecologically conscious of our solidarity.

The time has come, these authors maintain, to take control of our evolution and change our social, cultural, and ecological organizations. All of this requires a new theory of education, centered on a long-term vision. Humanity has become its own limitation, as we create problems for ourselves. We alone are responsible for our situation.

A change in mentality presupposes an attempt to answer the following questions. Are the new school environments death camps? Do we control our future? wonder Ornstein and Ehrlich (1990). How should we shape our minds, which can both save and destroy society, to create an adequate future? How do we form a new culture? How, for instance, do we modify the restrictive cultures of business people who only think about their businesses? How do we get intellectuals, who are proud of their classical culture and completely disconnected from the real world, to become aware of the importance of social and ecological problems?

Ornstein and Ehrlich (1990) maintain that the culture to be invented is neither in the past, which stresses classicism, nor in specialization such as it is now practiced in our educational institutions. To compartmentalize knowledge, even scientific knowledge, into segments (disciplines, departments, courses, and lessons) does not help the individual acquire a general vision of all the problems in society. It is not useful to know eternal truths in a time of increasing problems.

In other words, say Ornstein and Ehrlich, we must direct education toward the acquisition of a conscious, evolutive culture, i.e., an education that encourages genuine ecological and social consciousness. The point would no longer be just to learn, but to learn, when we acquire knowledge, to see the relevance of that knowledge with regard to solving our macro-problems. The educated individual would be one who is able to solve the problems of our society, rather than one who would display his or her knowledge of the past.

Chapter 7

Academic Theories

Academic theories — also called traditionalist, generalist, and classical — focus on the transmission of general knowledge. They generally oppose the domination of specialized education. The traditionalists want education to transmit a classical content, independent of current cultures and social structures. The generalists emphasize general education that stresses a critical mind, flexibility, an open mind, and so forth.

7.1 Quality Education: A Problem

In this last chapter, we will analyze the academic theories of education. These are essentially theories that define the characteristics of a general education that would allow students to become "well-educated."

First, we will examine the concern behind academic theories: students' lack of culture, the result of a general education that is deficient and often a result of premature specialization in the subjects taught in post-secondary instruction. Second, we will deal with two important academic trends: traditionalist and generalist theories.

7.1.1 Barbarians at Our Gates!

An Established Failure

In the twentieth century, we have been caught between a profusion of information, overturning traditional interpretations of reality, and a deficiency in terms of our understanding of the meaning of reality. People in the nineteenth century enjoyed an advantage: they had less knowledge than we do now, but more structure and meaning for reality.

However, the rapid progress of knowledge in various domains and access to diverse cultures make a global vision more and more difficult. Now specializations are taking over. This is why the Spanish philosopher José Ortega y Gasset stated that the professional, the engineer, the lawyer, and the scientist are learned barbarians without culture.

Both the media control of culture in industrial societies and the various attempts to democratize education forced classical culture to take a back seat during the 1960s. Science, technology, and the media have had serious effects on the evolution of culture and the curriculum. Michel Henry (1987) writes:

> Thus the result of the hyperdevelopment of hyperknowledge, the theoretical and practical means of which signal a complete break with the traditional knowledge of humanity, is to overturn not only this knowledge given as an illusion, but humanity itself.

The scientific explosion brought about the ruin of the human being, says Henry. By dismissing a certain type of knowledge that appeared at the time of Galileo and has since then been considered as the only knowledge, modern science "hurls our world into the abyss."

Other nostalgic theorists have taken as their mission to remind us of the eternal virtues of classical education. They have written about the need to return to traditional schemata, classical values, and a general education, in order to enlighten the "barbarian" that we are presently forming — so it would seem — in our schools (M. Adler, 1986; Henry, 1987; Lévy, 1987; Bloom, 1987 and 1990; Domenach, 1989; Morin and Brunet, 1992).

The Return of the Pendulum
In the United States, the 1980s and 1990s have seen a return of traditional, generalist, and elitist conceptions of education that were quite popular in the 1950s. In the 1950s, people wanted a return to competitiveness, excellence, and privatization (Hutchins, 1953; Gilson, 1954; M. Adler, 1982; Spady and Marx, 1984; Miller, 1988). The present situation is characterized by the same debates over the harmful effects of the democratization of education and the impoverishment of education for the best students.

The idea of a more general education and, for some, one that is more respectful of our cultural heritage, is not new. In this past century, there have been various attempts to make the content of instruction more classical.

In 1936, Robert Maynard Hutchins claimed that democracy did not require that higher education be open to all, and that access could be limited to those who had an ability in intellectual work. In 1954, the French philosopher Étienne Gilson asserted:

> Precisely because it is democratic and tends toward social equality, the duty of the modern State is to continuously ensure the recruitment of an intellectual elite. To this end, it should encourage the type of humanistic instruction that is necessary for the recruitment of this elite.

In 1959, Mark Van Doren wrote that the humanities, and especially the classics, constituted models of excellence. A classic, he used to say, cannot be killed (p. 145).

The periodically expressed wish to return to an academic education is often based on an individual's choice for excellence and quality to the detriment of democratization. It is often claimed that institutions should promote a high level of academic motivation and rigorous intellectual activities. Academic excellence is demanded and, consequently, the elite is privileged (Pratte, 1971; Bloom, 1990). Harry Broudy (1965) writes that general education should be provided only to the elite. Maurice Lebel (1966) claims that one should not confuse "education" and "instruction," and that what matters above all is the cult of quality and excellence. He attacks bottom-leveling and issues the following warning:

> Let us be careful not to make the highest instruction equally accessible to all; instead, let us make it accessible to those who are capable, i.e., those who are able and those who are willing, to the gifted and the strong-willed. They are the only ones who can devote themselves to the study of the humanities and to research. The democratization of instruction should give impetus to the rise of a powerful intellectual and moral aristocracy, without which there can be no elite and no democracy.

Declining Quality of Education

We are facing another problem: the alleged decline in the quality of the preparation of youth. This situation worries many groups of people: administrators, parents, and researchers. The level is falling dangerously, some say. We are shaping a democracy of learned ignoramuses, say others (Joly, 1982; National Commission on Excellence in Education, 1983; Bloom, 1990; Morin and Brunet, 1992). People cannot write any more. People no longer read. There are too many mediocre students taking exams. Civilization and culture are on the decline!

This notion of a decline in the quality of the preparation of youth — especially in such subjects as literature, language, and philosophy — reappears constantly (Kirkconnell, 1945; Léger, 1982). Christian Baudelot and Roger Establet (1989) show how this theme has periodically come up in France since 1820. We can notice a recurrence of this theme when certain groups of researchers (Conseil supérieur de l'éducation, 1990) try to establish that university curricula suffer from too much specialization, which has undesirable effects on education and too narrowly focuses the development of the student!

7.2 Two Trends

The educational theories analyzed in this chapter deserve some attention since they offer solutions to these problems and are of interest to people who question the orientations of education. These academic theories are attractive and greatly influence decision-makers. A lot of people stress the importance of general education as a cornerstone of postsecondary instruction. Consequently, these theories cannot be ignored. Thus, the position taken by the Ministère de l'Enseignement supérieur et de la Science du Quebec (1993), in favor of instructional reform based on a better general education, reveals a lot about the appeal of an academic vision of education.

Two important trends stand out within the body of academic educational theories — traditionalist and academic theories.

Traditionalist Theories

Traditionalist theories contend that the contents of instruction are the sum of the so-called classical and traditional knowledge. Its proponents talk of teaching about the past. They want to direct instruction toward classical culture and avoid the pitfall of scientific and technological knowledge. Culture should be understood as the humanities in a general sense. Thus, to study classical works such as those in *Great Books*, a collection of masterpieces of literature and philosophy published under the direction of Hutchins and Adler, gives access to ideas that do not vary with time.

The traditionalist trend is conservative insofar as it propounds changes that constitute a return to the past. Traditionalists are especially preoccupied with what should be taught in order to give the student a good basic education, a comprehensive view of knowledge, and a classical culture. To be more specific, they focus on the premise that education should transmit solid and indisputable knowledge, content that has stood the test of time.

Of course, the traditionalists may differ on the nature of the contents to be transmitted, but a consensus remains: we should go back, rediscover traditional values, and teach the masterpieces that have marked the different eras (Fin and Ravitch, 1987; Hirsch, 1987; Bloom, 1990; Walker, 1990; Morin and Brunet, 1992). And Antiquity would be favored.

Academic Theories

Academic theories represent a less traditionalist trend, more oriented toward contemporary knowledge. This second trend includes various theories based on an integrating concept: general education. This education is especially focused on the present. Concerned about the current problems of education, proponents of an academic general education attempt to answer the following questions: What is a good general education? Is a general education compatible with a specialized education?

We will see that the answer to these questions for generalist theorists is that education should develop curiosity and critical thinking, open the mind, and give it a liking for research, a way to solve problems in a democratic society, and versatile skills. These are the qualities that could not be acquired correctly in a curriculum specialized in any single disciplinary field.

7.3 Traditionalist Theories

7.3.1 History and Problems

The Greek and Roman Influence

Traditionalists base their theory on the ideas and values that time has polished through the centuries and that have reached a certain degree of maturity. These ideas and values have acquired a certain objectivity and constitute the essentials of the culture to be transmitted to each new generation. Hence, the expressions "classical realism," "academism," or "essentialism."

This cultural foundation is called Greco-Roman humanism. Its cultural contents have been transmitted, from age to age, to the next generation, which needed this knowledge to adapt. This common foundation draws its substance from the Ancients. Jean-Marie Domenach writes (1989) that "what is reputed classical results from successive decantations, according to a judgment already formed by the Greco-Roman corpus."

It should also be noted that references to Thomism and Aristotelianism are less frequent now than during the first half of the twentieth century. At that time, rational realism was defined, on the whole, by scholasticism and Aristotelianism. Now, traditionalism includes more references to the Greco-Roman and Renaissance humanities than to medieval scholasticism.

It is the Renaissance in particular, with Petrarch, Poggio, Valla, Erasmus, and Budé, that brought the cult of Antiquity back into fashion. At that time, people became suddenly aware of human forces, of their individual needs and values. With the years, this perception evolved into a philosophy called humanism, the foundation of classical culture and the humanities.

Inspired by humanism, classical culture has constituted the backbone of instruction for a long time in France, the United States, and Quebec (Gilson, 1954). Jean Houssaye (1987) describes how the humanities ruled in the school system in France in the seventeenth century. He shows how the Jesuits played a major role in this rule. He quotes a phrase by Henri-François D'Aguesseau, repeated countless times in classical colleges since the eighteenth century:

> You have learned the (ancient) languages which are the key to literature; you have practiced eloquence and poetry as much as the weakness of your age and the range of your knowledge have allowed you; you have tried to acquire in the study of mathematics and philosophy a sound mind, clear ideas, and good sense. (Compayre, 1885)

In short, education should be classical and humanistic.

This traditional pedagogy has changed very little over the years and was firmly established in the middle of the twentieth century in Western school institutions. Domenach writes that classical culture dominated French instruction until 1940. Gilson reminds his readers that classical studies created literature, art, and modern science and civilization. The curriculum taught in the colleges of the Society of Jesus set the tone, says Gilson (1954), and fixed for the next three centuries the type of instruction that would dominate Europe. Notwithstanding the evolution of scientific and literary contents, the instruction provided by the Jesuits in France and Canada in the seventeenth century remained the same in classical prep schools in Quebec until 1967. Classical culture has also dominated thinking in many North American school institutions in the twentieth century. Proponents of this orientation toward classical culture, such as described by Hutchins (1952) and A. Fortin (1954), were very influential in the evolution of educational thought in Quebec, especially through the Society of Jesus.

Conservative Criticism

Throughout history, critics have spoken up whenever there was talk of abandoning classical instruction for more specialized and more contemporary education. They have attacked the "degradation of values" caused by an education they judged too scientific and too specialized. The conservative theorists cling to values of the past and voice their opinions every time the cause requires it (Power, 1982; Houssaye, 1987; Bloom, 1990; D'Souza, 1992).

In 1936, Hutchins wrote that, if human nature, like truth, is the same everywhere, then there should be just one form of instruction. The intellect, he said, is neglected in favor of the formation of body and character and career training. In 1953, he said the same thing: "The function of man is the same in every age and in every society" (1953, p. 68). The goal of a school system, he says, does not vary with the times, since it consists of improving human beings. Human rationality is above everything else.

In 1939, Adler maintained that we should cultivate our intellect and our powers of rationality. He added that democracy was well served if youth were well-educated rather than led to participate in social unrest. He wrote that if the human being is an animal that is rational and constant throughout history, there should be some permanent characteristics of the curriculum that are independent of culture and era. Richard Pratte (1971) sums up this position with the following "quasi-syllogism" (p. 186):

Education implies instruction.

Instruction implies knowledge.

Knowledge is truth.

Truth is everywhere the same.

Therefore, education is everywhere the same.

These remarks are in keeping with those made at the beginning of the 1960s by Jean Guitton in *Apprendre à vivre et à penser* (1960), F. Robert in *Culture générale et enseignement européen* (1960), and Maurice Lebel in *L'éducation et l'humanisme* (1966).

General education should not be confused with the idea of strewing study with a little bit of everything, writes Robert (quoted in Lebel, 1966). Cultured individuals exist. They are characterized by an openness of mind, familiarity with the past, and their capacity to handle general ideas. Lebel (1966) agrees:

Students should be progressively brought — through reflection, work, and initiation to research — to adopt certain attitudes toward life, existence, the world, and knowledge; to adopt certain methods of approach, certain ways of working, searching, seeing, and thinking; to develop a certain slowness, wariness, and an adventurer's skepticism — in short, norms, frameworks, governing ideas, and a genuine hierarchy of the sense of values. ... Now, all this can be learned under the guidance of teachers aware that they are forming human beings and not merely specialists, researchers, and scholars. We should never lose sight of the human being.

The Decline of Classical Culture

Classical culture differs from contemporary culture in that the latter is more of a mass sub-culture created by the media. Certain critics talk about the degeneration of general education, even the rise of a barbarism, nourished by science and technology (Henry, 1987; Bloom, 1987 and 1990).

Alain Finkielkraut writes (1985):

The humanism of modern times is succeeded by a neo-tribalism, which asserts the essential division of humanity and leaves the members of different cultures no other human alternative but to study science or become aware of their individuality.

According to the foreword of the journal *Le temps de la réflexion* (1985):

> With culture undone, what we have is not so much a return to barbarism or the darkness of the Middle Ages; rather, it is excess that threatens us, the hubris of the uninformed who then attains the level of the uncultured.

Domenach (1989) notes the "degradation of the system" and claims that "only a radical change in the teaching of general culture can salvage what is worth saving in the old humanism." What we lack most, he says, is basic education. He adds that specialization and increasing career mobility make cultural differences among social classes more serious. The compartmentalization of knowledge and specialized languages increases the forms of inequalities and culture domination. We need a second Renaissance, a new general education with the same fundamental characteristics as Greco-Roman humanism.

7.3.2 Principles

Adler (1986) preaches a philosophy of education based on teaching the humanities in a general sense. He refers to Ortega y Gasset and asserts that his understanding of the humanities and his fight against the barbarism of specialization have greatly inspired the work done at the Aspen Institute for Humanistic Studies. He stresses the strangeness of our century in comparison with preceding centuries: we have a lot of knowledge, but very few global interpretative patterns.

Adler notes that we rely too much on alphabetical order to structure our knowledge, an approach that he considers "no more significant or intelligible than a purely random array" (p. 11). He uses the term "alphabetiasis" for "the intellectual defect that consists of refusing to go beyond the alphabet where going beyond it is possible" (p. 11).

The Paideia group, directed by Adler, took up the torch of classical culture in the early 1980s. Clearly in the same line as Hutchins, Adler proposes a classical model of education in four important books: *The Paideia Proposal: An Educational Manifesto*

(1982), *Paideia Problems and Possibilities* (1983), *The Paideia Program* (1984), and *A Guidebook to Learning* (1986).

According to these books, what humans have in common, i.e., their personal dignity, rights, and aspirations, is more important than their differences. Consequently, the objectives of mandatory education should be the same for all: to prepare students to develop themselves, to assume their civic duties, and to earn a living. Therefore, the Paideia group concludes (1983), a good basic, general, classical, and humanistic education is essential. Specialization will come later.

The model for this general education is the *paideia* or general education as taught in the days of Plato. This model naturally includes philosophy (which is in itself a general and synthetic approach), poetry, and ethics.

The first principle of this education lies in the notion that students' schooling is only one part of their education. Education is a long-term process: learning never stops. School only prepares students for life.

The second principle deals with uniformity of objectives. In the model school, learning objectives are the same for all. There are neither more difficult objectives for bright students nor easier objectives for less gifted students. This uniformity of objectives makes it possible to avoid any kind of discrimination.

The third principle is especially concerned with mandatory instruction, which will be general, to provide all students with a basic education rather than specialize them as early as age 13. Education will be provided in skills necessary for any form of work. Premature specializations will be avoided, as they are ultimately only paths that lead nowhere. Pedagogy will consist primarily of three main techniques: traditional teaching (lectures, texts, and manuals), supervision, and Socratic maieutics.

Roughly the same concerns can be found in France (Henry, 1987; Finkielkraut, 1988; Domenach, 1989). Domenach's analysis is enlightening. He claims that we cannot reform secondary education merely by adding two hours of biology or computer science, for instance. What we need, he says, is a reorganization of the corpus of general instruction, based on a unified and unifying perspective. What constituted the strength of the old corpus should be brought into the new one — "a rational and hierarchical organization of disciplines that should be taught in our time."

Denouncing egalitarian pedagogy, Domenach (1989) takes the following position:

> There is no culture without a hierarchy of values and tastes, no culture without transmission of a common heritage, for the future cannot be taught, even if the new instruction is to correspond to a present that has changed. This is why, in the face of the prevailing ideology, which proclaims that everything is culture, I maintain that culture is a process of initiation, with its milestones and stages, and that requires effort.

Reflections expressed in various countries about the nature of renewed classical instruction are very much alike. We will now consider some examples.

In France, Domenach (1989) offers some recommendations for reforming secondary instruction according to four perspectives:

1. Language, from the perspective of knowing and interpreting the masterpieces of the national heritage and of foreign civilizations

2. History, but from a perspective that goes beyond the usual bounds to apply to all orders of knowledge — an understanding of their development that may be called "genetic"

3. Science and technics, considered not as preparation for certain professions, but as part of a general education, from which they have been wrongly separated

4. Philosophy, which should be approached more carefully, since philosophy, even more than history, is closely related to almost all of the other domains

Pedagogy, according to Domenach (1989), should have the following characteristics:

- It goes from the simple to the more complex, through a rational progression.
- It emphasizes memorization.

- It follows a hierarchy of values.

- It promotes organized knowledge, rather than pieces of knowledge; the comprehension of a cause, rather than a display of phenomena; a hierarchy of values and forms, rather than a continual glorification of nothing and everything.

Classical pedagogy (Gilson, 1954; Lapp et al., 1975; Eisner, 1985; Vallance, 1986; Domenach, 1989) attempts to preserve the ancient ideas and transmit them from one generation to the next. Domenach (1989) writes:

> Indeed, what is humanistic pedagogy if not the praise of discourse (rhetoric) and, even more so, trust in the expression of truth through a language that comes down from the *corpus* through the teacher to the student?

Subject matter is of the utmost importance. It is especially composed primarily of information and ideas chosen for their value. The clear and logically organized objective of classical instruction consists of teaching a given content. Subject matter is presented to the student in this logical order, rather than in an order that would take into account his or her interest and involvement. The teacher is the expert and the role model. Trained in *what* to teach rather than in *how* to teach, the teacher brings content to the student and helps him or her absorb it.

Brickman writes (1958) that the teacher is the center of the educational universe. He or she should have a classical training, solid knowledge, an understanding of the student and of learning processes, and the ability to help students understand the principal facts. The teacher should be seriously devoted to his or her work. The student is both a receptacle to be filled and a mold to be shaped. Intellectual formation comes before emotional growth and social criticism.

7.3.3 Curriculum of a Classical Education

Paul-Émile Gingras (1989) conducted a study of general education in England. He states:

> Unlike America and more than in the other European countries, England believes in the importance of classical studies. Today, there is less emphasis on teaching classical languages than on the study of

Greco-Roman civilizations. ... For the English, the Athens of the fifth century B.C. and the Rome of the first century B.C. are exceptional stages in the history of humanity from the viewpoint of culture, social and political development, philosophy, and art.

He presents the classical education curriculum found in England, composed of the following eight elements:

1. **Language.** The study of the classics sensitizes students to language, its structure, and its usage.

2. **Art.** Ancient Greece offers a body of artistic masterpieces eminently suited to develop the aesthetic sense of the students.

3. **Moral Sense.** The classics are the source of human experience in the West. Whether historians, dramatists, or orators, the Ancients present the issue of morality.

4. **Socio-Political Training.** To question, with the Greeks or the Romans, democracy or the fall of the Roman Empire is relevant to concerns of our present age.

5. **Spiritual Experience.** Ancient civilizations have a deep sense of the spiritual dimension of life: consider, for example, Plato's *Republic*, Sophocles' *Oedipus Rex*, or the spread of Christianity in the Roman empire.

6. **Sciences.** Study of the classical age helps develop the scientific approach.

7. **Mathematics.** Beyond their contributions to mathematics as a discipline, the Ancients teach us to reason and think logically.

8. **Physical Expression.** Ancient arts and theater foster personal development of expression and dexterity.

7.4 Generalist Theories

General education is an approach that has been discussed from time to time since the beginning of the twentieth century.

Almost one hundred years ago, Europe and America were already wondering what a general education should be!

For example, the University of Chicago, as early as 1891, wanted to create a college "of general education." That university assumed leadership in this trend for many decades; in fact, the texts written in the 1930s and 1950s are now being reprinted. (The publication in 1992 of *The Idea and Practice of General Education*, first published in 1950, shows to what extent questions about general education are far from being new.)

Many researchers and teachers, such as Richard Paul (1992), claim that the twenty-first century will be an age of general education. This is why we should examine this educational trend more closely.

7.4.1 Problem of Quality Education

The problem may seem quite easy to describe: proponents of general education maintain that young people do not receive a general education. Entire societies, they say, complain that their young people cannot read or write and that they lack a general education, that they often know little about history beyond the last twenty years, and that they are ethically and morally weak.

The source of this problem lies, of course, in the current educational system, which, they claim, does not educate. It is characterized by extreme specialization and its corollary, a lack of transferable general education. For instance, young people receive specialized instruction in mathematics and physics that they will never use. They are merely taught to memorize without questioning the meaning of what they are learning (Paul, 1992): they do not learn to think. There is much concern about teaching, but little thought about actually providing students with an education.

7.4.2 Principles of General Education

Education should develop critical thinking; it should open the mind and promote a taste for inquiry and a certain intellectual curiosity. Someone with a good general education can reason soundly and express himself or herself orally and in writing, in a language that shows obvious intellectual abilities. These are abilities, general education proponents say, that students could not acquire in a specialized curriculum, which wrongly restricts the development of the mind to knowledge with limited applications.

Several more or less equivalent expressions are used to describe general education:

- Fundamental education
- Liberal education
- Education for critical thinking
- The "school for excellence"

We will now try to show the nuances among these expressions — not an easy task!

General Education

General education opposes specialization, which is deemed too specific, and proposes a global and integrating vision. J.-B. Pontalis (1985) claims that "what is called specialization of knowledge and competencies becomes, in terms of culture, fragmentation, multiplicity, and dispersion."

Strong pressure is being exerted on educational systems in North America to provide generalized secondary and postsecondary education. A general education includes what every educated person should know, particularly philosophy, ethics, literature, and logic. It is an education that, unlike specialized instruction, should lead to anywhere and everywhere.

There are many definitions of general education, Jacques Laliberté notes (1984). The following is a sample:

- A prerequisite to specialized study
- An antidote to extreme specialization
- A number of general courses in totally unrelated domains
- The rudiments necessary for a common discourse
- A liberal education
- Knowledge of the world around us
- Discipline and nourishment for the mind
- A body of knowledge and investigative methods
- Education that facilitates personal and moral development

- Basic knowledge and skills that everyone should possess

According to most analysts, general education includes courses in the social sciences the physical sciences, along with a set of courses defined as the humanities. The humanities are more oriented toward generally developing the mind; they encompass literature, philosophy, theater, poetry, languages, music, and the arts. Modes of interpretation such as history, philosophy, or drama are analyzed and compared, with objectives that include learning to analyze intelligently, to be critical, and to recognize the values involved (Thomas, 1992). The themes treated include the conflict between liberty and authority, for example, and conceptions of justice. To trigger discussions, such questions are asked as, "Should the quality of a literary work be evaluated based on its impact on people?"

In 1993, the Ministère de l'Enseignement supérieur et de la Science du Québec proposed an instructional reform based on a common general education. This education was defined in terms of the following conception of education and culture:

> To be well-educated and "cultured" today would then mean: to master one's own language — a mastery that cannot be dissociated from the very capacity to think; to be able to express oneself accurately and to understand from within the richness of the literary heritage; to be able to communicate in other languages, first in French and English, at a level beyond simple usage; to master the basic rules of rational thinking, discourse, and argumentation; to be capable of independent thinking and able to position oneself in relation to the main lines in the evolution of human thought; to be able to act responsibly in matters of health and physical condition; to understand the specifics of the approaches to reality that underlie the major fields of knowledge — art, science, technology, mathematics, human sciences, etc.

Fundamental Education
Definitions of fundamental education are plentiful, with subtle nuances that may be difficult to discern. Unlike general education, which refers to the ability to situate a discipline in relation to all fields of knowledge and major domains of culture, fundamental education deals with the appropriation of the

ideological, historical, and methodological foundations of a discipline.

Since 1978, one trend of thinking has been grappling with the need to reconsider education in terms of what is "fundamental." This education should remedy the problems resulting from education that is too specialized (Lorimier, 1987; Laliberté, 1988a and 1988b; Conseil Supérieur de l'Éducation, 1990).

Its proponents want postsecondary education to be fundamental. It should focus on the acquisition of knowledge, the essentials, the governing principles, the basic concepts, and the method appropriate to a given discipline (Conseil Supérieur de l'Éducation, 1975). Another report from the Conseil supérieur de l'Éducation (1984) contains the following definition of fundamental education: "The body of learning (in organized knowledge, abilities and capacities, attitudes and values) essential to continuous personal development and dynamic integration into society."

Fundamental education aims at integral development. In addition to developing their intellectual abilities, students should work to affirm their identity, to improve the quality of their interpersonal relationships, to succeed in social integration, and to broaden and strengthen their autonomy. Education must emphasize acquisition of a sense of history, precision of reasoning, and mastery of concepts and their application to new situations.

Having analyzed several definitions of fundamental education, Christiane Gohier (1990b) suggests one that perfectly summarizes the spirit of the other definitions:

> This education is concerned with precise thinking, a critical mind, a method of working, and historical awareness. It aims at the mastery of principles, of the method particular to disciplines, and of basic concepts and laws that allow the student to understand the essentials of a body of knowledge and to situate this knowledge in a culture.

Pierre Angers (1990) is another education specialist who has analyzed numerous texts dealing with fundamental education. He notes:

> Documents about fundamental education stress that the need to understand is a distinctive characteristic

of this education that always coincides with the mastery of the acquired knowledge. The words "understand," "grasp," and "integrate" come up in all the texts, which clearly aim at the operations of comprehension and the activity of intelligence.

Liberal Education

"Liberal education" is an expression intended to describe a British and American trend, also called "general education," "the humanities," or "liberal arts education." It is, in fact, a hybrid and baroque mix of traditional education, with its classical works, general education, with such content areas as mathematics and sciences, and training in methods of thinking that is now called "critical thinking." This trend dates back a long time in the history of American instruction — so long that in the mid-1930s, there was already talk of a crisis in liberal education!

"Liberal education" has greatly evolved and become multidisciplinary through the years. It now differs from traditional education in that it is less concerned with classical culture and proposes an education that is more general and more contemporary. It aims more at a broader range of knowledge and a good mixture of disciplines.

It is this very mixture, deemed too superficial and specialized, that Allan Bloom (1990) attacks in the name of classical education. We are faced with a crisis in liberal education, he says. A science student who takes a single course on medieval poetry will only have a semblance of a general education, he remarks. We have lost the sense of oneness, he adds, in trying to do away with everything that seemed traditional. Philosophy and theology have been consigned to oblivion, so we have lost sight of the major questions of life.

It should be remembered that "liberal arts" refers to the subjects and disciplines in which intellectual work predominates. The seven liberal arts, according to the dictionary, were the substance of classical instruction as taught in the Middle Ages in Faculties of Arts — grammar, rhetoric, logic, arithmetic, geometry, astronomy, and music. The master of arts was the degree that allowed a person to teach the humanities and philosophy.

Education for Critical Thinking

While fundamental education dwells on the foundations of knowledge and liberal education aims at a wide range of disciplines, education for critical thinking deals with the intellectual operations necessary to the exercise of thought. One should learn to think and, consequently, do a systematic analysis of the multiple operations of the mind.

There is a trend, very active in North America, that focuses on education for critical thinking. Presuming that students do not learn much in the school system and that what they do learn is limited to simple memorization, advocates of this approach propose that students be educated to think. Paul (1992), at the Center for Critical Thinking and Moral Critique, proposes structuring education for the twenty-first century to teach critical thinking. To educate, he claims, is simply to teach people to think.

This position makes it possible to understand the difference between critical pedagogy (chapter 6) and education for critical thinking. The latter is independent from content matter, as it deals with reasoning in its intellectual dimension. Such is not the case with critical pedagogy, the goal of which is to learn to look at our society critically and modify it. This leads to important questions: What is "thinking"? What is "reasoning"? How does one teach others to think?

We should begin with the definitions of critical thinking.

To think is to be able to reason properly. Laliberté (1992) suggests four definitions that he found in reading about the subject:

- Reasonable and reflexive thought that focuses on the decision to be made about what is to be believed or done

- The appropriate use of reflexive skepticism, to base beliefs on good reasons

- Smart and responsible thinking that facilitates good judgment because it relies on criteria, can be adjusted, and is context-sensitive

- Investigation, the goal of which is to explore a situation, a phenomenon, a question, or a problem in order to reach a hypothesis or conclusion that integrates all the available information and which can therefore be convincingly justified

Michael Scriven and Richard Paul (1993) maintain that critical thinking or reasoning is an intellectual process that consists of conceptualizing, analyzing, synthesizing, and evaluating information. These two researchers founded an institute devoted to describing and teaching the multiple aspects of critical thinking. The following is a sampling that shows the complexity of thought operations.

Reasoning comprises four aspects: elements, traits, standards, and abilities. Any critical thinking or reasoning worthy of the name includes a number of elements — a goal, a problem, a frame of reference or viewpoint, data, key concepts, premises, inferences, and consequences.

The principal traits of critical thinking are: humility, courage, responsibility, discipline, empathy, curiosity, perseverance, integrity, and independence of mind. Critical thought should meet fourteen standards of quality, being:

1. Logical
2. Complete
3. Clear
4. Precise
5. Specific
6. Plausible
7. Consistent
8. Deep
9. Broad
10. Adequate (for purpose)
11. Accurate
12. Relevant
13. Fair
14. Significant

And finally, critical thinking is based on intellectual abilities that can be grouped into seven domains:

1. Recognition
2. Comprehension
3. Application
4. Analysis
5. Synthesis
6. Evaluation
7. Creation

The "School for Excellence"

Some proponents of general education have shown great interest in the notion of the "school for excellence." This is why we are examining it here.

In 1983, a report entitled *A Nation at Risk: The Imperative for Educational Reform* was published in the United States. Drawn up by a national investigative commission, the National Commission on Excellence in Education, this report used an alarmist tone to advise abandoning the current system, which it compared to a cafeteria where all the dishes are diluted, homogenized, and indistinguishably alike. This commission described the urgent need for an educational reform centered on personal, institutional, and communal excellence.

"Excellence" meant personal achievement as much as institutional performance in relation to high objectives and a collective commitment to adapting toward this end. Students should put forth maximum energy to improve, just as schools should make every effort to ensure the success of each student. The watchwords of the school reform were:

- Uniform and higher norms of achievement
- Acquisition of cognitive skills
- Mastery of content
- Search for order
- Sound school administration
- Exemplary conduct of teachers
- Teaching of values and behavioral models
- An insistence on work and the constant quest for excellence

Subjects in the "new" basic education proposed by this commission should be English, mathematics, science, social sciences, and computer science.

In the United States, as in Quebec or France, the popularity of the idea of private education and questions about school denominationality as well as the suppression of "alternative" schools have signaled a return to normalization of the school system. Many people wonder if free, mandatory education has lowered expectations of quality in our schools. Parents worry that the decline in the quality of public education is affecting the future of students. Teachers worry about the fact that they spend more time enforcing discipline than teaching. Many teachers burn out providing remedial instruction instead of devoting themselves to high-level education.

Several years ago, for example, the University of Montreal reported (*Le Devoir*, March 27, 1990) that it would no longer admit any but the brightest students, and that it would rigorously select the best students to form the elite of the nation. If a society is to be able to compete with others, Girard Éthier (1989) writes, its schools have a duty to be excellent.

Louis Gadbois (1989) writes that, of all the ills from which Quebec's society, and especially its school system, are suffering, the worst is undoubtedly the general utilitarianism that has taken over, i.e., the lack of interest in any activity that does not have a short-term personal benefit. This attitude, he says, shows up in many young people in the form of a low motivation toward study and preparation for a potential role in society.

Concerned about renewing its culture, the business world has turned to the notion of excellence (Peters and Waterman, 1983; Ouvry-Vial, 1987; Y. Bertrand and Guillemet, 1989; Éthier, 1989). Society "suddenly" became interested in quality. Our everyday life — television, movies, media, schools, sports, and administration — was invaded by "excellence." Everyone has jumped into the quest for success. There is no more choice: to succeed in life, one must excel, i.e., be above the masses.

Two American researchers, William Spady and Gary Marx (1984), analyzed nine studies on excellence in education. Éthier (1989) summed up their analysis by distinguishing seven characteristics of excellence, in conclusions similar to those of John Mangieri (1985) and Arthur Marsolais (1987a and 1987b).

1. The objectives and priorities of the curriculum are made quite explicit and tied to quality expectations for education.

2. Standards, expectations, and requirements are specified and determine the true conditions for student achievement.

3. Both the curriculum content and the methods for transmitting knowledge are sufficiently ex-

plicit to form the most important supports for student success.

4. School organization and the delivery of instruction are such that everyone knows how, when, and where the educational process will take place. They affect students and teachers and their interactions.

5. The organization of the time devoted to instructional activities and the management of this time are decided by the schools. This applies to all other activities that are more or less connected to instruction.

6. All available human, material, and financial resources are used optimally to make school effective and efficient.

7. The roles and responsibilities of the professional staff are continuously specified and most often form the basis of their professional evaluations and rewards.

Éthier (1989) suggests the following definition of excellence:

Excellence exists when the school institution is capable of bringing each student to achieve the learning objectives of the curriculum at an appropriate and realistic level of success, but also to the limits of his or her personal abilities.

The goals, means, and domains of the "school for excellence" are:

Goals

- Acquisition of structured knowledge and cognitive skills
- Comprehension of democratic ideas and values
- Excellence
- Preparation to be competitive

Means

- Instruction
- Supervision
- Dialogue

- Courses
- Reading of important works
- Tutorials
- Exchanges
- Questions and discussions
- Lectures
- Exercises
- Socratic pedagogy

Domains

- Languages
- Literature
- Fine arts
- Mathematics
- Sciences
- History
- Geography
- Music
- Theater
- Painting

This concept of excellence gave rise to a number of educational projects.

7.4.3 Pedagogical Strategies

Whether fundamental education, liberal education, or education for critical thinking, the pedagogical strategies of general education consist mostly of reading and writing activities. The teacher explains what to do. Students do many textual analyses. They write essays. They do personal research. This instruction often involves several disciplines.

As the Conseil Supérieur de l'Éducation (1990) writes in its defense of fundamental education:

> Pedagogical activity follows the path of fundamental education when it allows the student to integrate all of what he or she has learned, i.e., to retain the

knowledge organically and transfer it to various situations. Indeed, a relevant pedagogical practice helps the student internalize his or her bodies of knowledge by connecting them together, on the one hand, and by establishing relationships between this knowledge and life, on the other. It encourages the experience of integration, for instance, around themes involving knowledge and skills that refer to several disciplines or by applying knowledge or skills to various real-life contexts or situations.

We will now see two examples that are good illustrations of the pedagogical strategies particular to this general trend of academic theories.

Example 1: Critical Thinking Instruction (Center for Critical Thinking and Moral Critique)

The education for critical thinking provided in this center is based on the following activities: reading, writing, listening, speaking, Socratic questioning, role play, and group work. All of these educational strategies aim at the acquisition of critical thinking, regardless of the subject taught. This can take place as much in biology as in philosophy, for critical thinking is, according to this center, independent of the discipline.

The following is a suggested example of critical thinking instruction in a high school history course. First, the teacher should have clearly in mind the characteristics of good intellectual reasoning, as listed by the Center for Critical Thinking and Moral Critique. The teacher explains these characteristics to the students, so that they know on what criteria their work will be judged. He or she should then adopt instructional strategies such as the following:

- Clarify the domain targeted (e.g. I want my students to think rationally about civil wars from a historical perspective.).

- Determine the issue or topic of discussion (e.g. How do civil wars begin?).

- Find real-life examples to help the students think (e.g. Find in a newspaper current examples of struggles that are leading to a civil war.).

- Begin with a group discussion in a Socratic mode (Students may try to play roles.).

- Go on to small group discussions (three or four students) and give groups specific tasks (e.g. Determine the points of view of two groups opposed in a civil war.).

- Direct the efforts toward individual written works (e.g. Write a five-page essay based on the group discussions and your personal research, and explain the premises underlying the viewpoints of the adversaries.).

Example 2: Fundamental Education in Elementary and Secondary Schools (Lavallée)

Micheline Lavallée (1992) offers a reflection on fundamental education for students in elementary and secondary schools. She states:

> To be truly educational, the mission of school is to develop the humanity of the student, his or her ability to produce sense and to understand the world, the will to have a history, a sense of responsibility, courage, and an aptitude for compassion. It is a civilizing mission very much rooted in the present, concerned with the future, and for which the teacher should maintain a living contact with the student.

Lavallée lists seven axioms that should constitute the foundation of education. The following is a summary of her propositions:

1. Through school, the student should be put into contact with the beauty of human creations.

2. Through school, the student should have access to instruction that gives him or her a key to interpret himself or herself and a framework for understanding life.

3. Through school, the student should be put into contact with the community of people who have discovered the world.

4. Through school, the student should learn such fundamental skills as analysis and synthesis and the experimental approach.

5. Through school, the student should get a taste of the history of humanity. He or she should have keys to understanding life and development.

6. Through school, the student should discover "taste," the "meaning of things."

7. Through school, the student should feel alive, develop, feel competent, and become capable of adapting to life situations.

7.5 Conclusion

The theories of education examined in this chapter mostly propose analyses of the contents of instruction. They generally attack pedagogies that bottom-level education and reject a hierarchy of values. A good education should go beyond present culture by returning to a more solid instruction, either of traditional, classical, and humanistic content or of more general and transdisciplinary content. They often propose a return to Greco-Roman humanism and analysis of the works that have stood the test of time.

Wanting to necessarily promote the oneness and organicity of culture and education in the form of general education, people often allude to the imbrication of pedagogy and education known as *paideia* by the ancient Athenians. An American think-tank on education called itself the *Paideia Group* to show its allegiance to classical culture.

The idea of forming elites is popular. The comments by Gilson (1954) and Lebel (1966) on the need to form elites do not differ substantially from those by Domenach (1989). Gilson (1954) claimed that no type of instruction had ever given talent or genius to those who had not received these gifts from nature. Lebel (1966) wrote that there is no true civilization without a tradition, a hierarchy, an elite, and a religion:

> Instruction will always be aristocratic, based on the master-student relationship, in spite of all the flashy and demagogic statements about democratization that we have heard *ad nauseam*. The most ingenious theories on joint management, camaraderie, parity,

and equality will in no way change the order of things. We must respect nature and time.

This is why academic theories are easily accused of being traditionalist or elitist, or of indoctrinating students into the values of the ruling classes. The descriptions of traditional pedagogy provided by Georges Snyders (1971) and Jean Houssaye (1987) follow the same lines as the comments cited above. Houssaye stresses the relationship between the so-called neutrality of traditional pedagogy and the transmission of a "free" culture, the general education of the human soul. Houssaye writes (1987): "Separation from the world and free culture are the two complementary aspects of a single educational intent finalized by religion." Traditional education, he says, is centered on the transmission of knowledge; it tends to have its own requirements and becomes a sort of microcosm of society. That means, in practical terms, that the best students will win and will always be the best by definition!

Although the academic movement may appear elitist by its choice of classical culture, it is probably less so by its stress on the study of basic subjects. The American "Back to Basics" movement is not new: it derives its theses from the American "essentialist" movement of the 1950s (Koerner, 1959; Brodinsky, 1977; Power, 1982). On the other hand, proponents of these approaches do not tolerate any disregard for culture, excellence, and merit under the "fallacious" pretexts of social equality. They refuse to let schools indulge in "soft" pedagogies that gamble on the freedom of the student. Students are there to learn, they argue, and not to manage their freedom as they please.

They insist that teachers should be well-prepared. Indeed, how could a teacher without a classical education transmit the essential of Culture to his or her students? They oppose the movement toward social renewal because it disturbs the established order. Hence, this paradoxical attitude on the part of proponents of academic approaches: they advocate transmission of a single culture to all students, without distinction, but they refuse egalitarianism in education. Lowering the level of the transmission of knowledge to please the apostles of social equality, they say, is out of the question.

Chapter 8

General Conclusion

8.1 Questions about Education

The neo-conservative movement presented in chapter 7, which grew out of the questioning of education that arose in the mid-1970s, brought back the question of the foundations of education. Various national investigative commissions on education have analyzed the weaknesses of school systems and suggested radical changes in curricula. Such was the case in the United States, Canada, England, France, and Japan.

These questions about education are part of great concerns about the evolution of industrial and non-industrial societies. Western countries are facing serious social, political, economic, and ecological problems: unemployment, drugs, social tensions, violence, mediatization of violence, religious extremism, and sectarian nationalism.

Finally, we are facing a rather surprising social paradox. Worldwide communications, exportation of Western models of technological progress and free enterprise, the industrialization of most countries, the opening of economic markets, and the expansion of relations among countries have resulted in an increasing intransigence. It is curious that, as progress opens up our world, we are becoming more closed — socially, culturally, and ethnically! Each entity — nation, ethnic group, or religious community — devotes much energy to protecting its social, economic, religious, and cultural identity. For instance, all the talk on freetrade is accompanied by stricter immigration laws. In other words, "social networking" is building, formed of links among entities that are fighting among themselves in a spirit of competition that is ever increasing.

It is in this context of social evolution that we should question the role of education in our society. And it is this context that sheds new light on the various theories of education. Do these theories contain elements of solutions to our problems? Is one theory better than the others? Is there a theory that would make it possible to solve at least most, if not all, of these problems?

8.2 The Best Theory

I have tried in this book to do justice to all of the theories that propose changes in education. There is no doubt that each theory of education deserves to be analyzed in depth. Moreover, I obviously have a preference, which is based on the following observation: Society is plagued by serious social problems to which none of us can remain indifferent.

We should ask our various institutions to contribute to resolving these problems. Our educational system cannot afford to play dead or to play around with pedagogy to create the illusion of change. In this context, then, what is the "best" theory that would help solve these serious social problems?

Academic Theories

We currently have numerous academic propositions for change (chapter 7). Some are most conservative and recommend a return to traditional values. Other theories suggest educational changes that are more in keeping with the present social and economic organization of industrial societies.

Now, there are clearly more serious problems to solve than those of Greco-Roman antiquity or of increasing industrial productivity. It seems obvious that a number of reforms proposed by educators take on the problem of adapting schools to society. Since economic progress in most highly industrialized countries is based on employing more specialized workers, economic strength should improve if we more "efficaciously" produce qualified workers for a society based on free enterprise.

However, Michael Apple, Stanley Aronowitz, Paulo Freire, Henry Giroux, and Ira Shor generally reproach conservative theorists for believing that preserving the economic order of the free market should be a priority in education. I agree with these educators: I do not see how a general or traditional education can solve the many ecological, social, and other problems that affect our universe.

Consider only the question of social differences: Jonathan Kozol recently stated (Scherer, 1993) that *equality* — not *excellence* — is the greatest problem for education.

Personalist and Spiritualist Theories

In the 1960s and 1970s, many people wrote about personalist education; some of these reflections were analyzed in chapter 2. At that time, several "alternative" schools were created, in which the student ruled. The most famous school remains Summerhill in England. The most important thinker is still Carl Rogers.

Personalist theories of education are very interesting, for they focus great attention on the individual. This is undeniable. Reading such a great author as Rogers can only be beneficial (Bertrand and Valois, 1993a).

However, a major problem arises, as these personalist theories encourage, in everyday life, development of the individual more than development of social consciousness. In my opinion, they are caught in a dilemma: How do we make anyone free? This is virtually impossible, as Jean Houssaye (1992) sums it up:

> To radically introduce freedom into education presupposes that we reject any idea of an outside goal for others, that we express our trust in a certain human nature (more or less original), and that we end up with an attitude of educational abstention.

Spiritualist theories have great merit: they remind us that there are other things on this planet besides production and consumption. Wisdom cannot necessarily be measured by the amount of money that one has! We should benefit from the thinking of spiritualist theorists, yet avoid the obvious pitfalls of dogmatism or submission to any form of transcendency.

In *École et sociétés* (1992), Yves Bertrand and Paul Valois present a theory of education that combines a spiritualist position with an eco-social position. Robert Pirsig, in *Zen and the Art of Motorcycle Maintenance*, had perfectly expressed this point of view in a pithy sentence that said it all: "If you meet Buddha in the street, kill him!"

Psychocognitive, Technological, and Social Cognitive Theories

Numerous thinkers and researchers have developed theories that are particularly centered on appropriate pedagogical strategies. Such is especially the case for technologists, psychocognitivists, and social cognitivists. These theorists are bent on solving real learning and teaching problems. Hence, their interest in learner characteristics, structures of learning, the knowledge process, communication techniques, computers, media, and social characteristics of learning.

It seems that, as we near the end of the twentieth century, research in psychology and pedagogy is increasing at an incredible pace. But can we conclude from this that we are making progress in education? That the studies are influencing real life?

Quite the opposite, it would seem. The latest surveys suggest that experiments with computers are still at an experimental level. Projects of hypermedia environment are very interesting, although they are often confined to research laboratories. The number of computers in schools has not increased as much as expected. Technology is evolving at a dizzying pace, but not its use in schools. Educational technology theorists are much more interested in problems of teaching and learning than in social, economic, and political problems. They believe that this dimension does not concern them specifically.

Social cognitive theories show to what degree instruction should allow for multiple social and cultural variables. They have expanded educational research and shown that learning is something other than problem-solving. On the other hand, research on social and cultural characteristics seems too confined to discussions among researchers, with no benefit for teachers.

Yet it is clear that cooperative theories are being applied more and more widely. They interest teachers because they are based both on research conducted in schools and on quite practical experiments.

Should we do away, then, with all of the educational theories that are essentially concerned with pedagogy? No, not at all. Ideas abound, and the time will come when we have to accept technological educational environments that will have integrated what we know about knowledge and cooperative strategies.

Social Theories

A number of social theories of education seem to me the most suited to solving the problems we are currently facing, because they are the only theories to confront them head on. We no longer have any choice: any proposition for educational change should be contextualized within the framework of reflection about the relationships between school and society. Indeed, any proposition for pedagogical change solves only the pedagogical aspect of the educational problem, while at the same time concealing its impact on society. Bertrand and Valois (1992) present a full account of the problems of society and of the proposals for the concept of education needed to solve them.

Critical pedagogy, analyzed in chapter 6, shows many advantages — and many disadvantages! It proposes to educate the student according to a culture other than the dominant culture. This alternative culture is based on such values as social justice, equality, and respect for differences. It is a protest culture with a neo-Marxist perspective.

Felix Guattari (1989) perfectly sums up, in his own way, the viewpoint of critical thinking:

> We are crushed by the weight of mass media, images of the powers that be, manipulation of the imaginary in the service of an oppressive social order, fabrication of a majority consensus at any cost, methods that consist of scaring people about nothing and everything and infantilizing them so that they no longer ask themselves any questions.

This theory is essentially characterized by critical commentaries on the problems of current education and the proposition of a new language of education. This is why there are more theoretical reflections than concrete pedagogical propositions among the proponents of this trend.

Reflections on classroom pedagogy are also too theoretical. Proponents take care to define the categories and to specify what critical pedagogy should be. For instance, they define a theory of curriculum as "a form of representation and a set of social practices tied to social and cultural forms, as well as ideologies" (Aronowitz and Giroux, 1985). This definition shows how much attention is paid to the language used to discuss education.

Finally, it is a pedagogy that, having defined well the current social problems of education, is in search of a language allowing presentation of a critical position without slipping into traditional Marxism, while at the same time taking into account the "new" critical reflections on culture, feminism, racial divisions, modernity, postmodernity, and mass culture.

On the other hand, it should be noted that certain social theories get lost in ideological quarrels among sub-groups. As William Stanley (1992) rightly points out in his analysis of critical pedagogy, it seems to be pedagogical in name alone. The strength of its social criticism is not matched by its pedagogical strategies, which seem neglected.

8.3 For a New Eco-Social Competence

Under these circumstances, the "best" educational theory is the one that encourages students to acquire a competence based on an understanding of ecological, social, and cultural problems. Such was the position we defended in *École et sociétés* (1992).

Today's students will have the task of transforming society according to values other than competition, segregation, racism, and so on. To do so, they will need an education that allows them to solve the social, ecological, cultural, and political problems that they inherit. This is what I call "eco-social competence."

My position is clear: the education that we need should be based on "new" educational strategies that are more appropriate to a global solution to the problems of our planet. In my opinion, a theory of education should include in its curriculum studies of multicultural relationships, the positive and negative effects of economic development, ecology, and the principles of democracy. It should also include cooperative educational strategies that rely on teamwork and on cooperation with those who are affected by the problems to be solved. Cooperative strategies are very effective for training students in work methods that take into account social, cultural, and religious differences. However, one cannot practice cooperation just for the sake of cooperation. These strategies should be used to learn to solve the problems of our society.

This is why I favor social theories of education, especially the theory advocated by Shor (1992b), which proposes that the ultimate goal of education should be social, ecological, and cultural changes. As I wrote in chapter 6, education should not be reconsidered from an industrial perspective, but rather from a more global vision of evolution. Education should serve to invent a new future for our planet.

Contemporary Theories and Practice in Education Matrix

Theories	Values and structural elements	Authors	Sources
(1) Spiritualistic	Spiritual values inscribed in the individual, metaphysics, Tao, God, intuition, spiritual dimension of the cosmos, cosmic consciousness, perennial philosophy	Richard Bucke, Fritjof Capra, Mircea Éliade, Ralph Waldo Emerson, Marilyn Ferguson, Constantin Fotinas, Willis Harman, Hazel Henderson, Carl Jung, Lao-Tzu, George Leonard, Abraham Maslow, Daisetz Teitaro Suzuki, Henry David Thoreau	Religions, metaphysics, Eastern philosophies, mysticism, Taoism, Buddhism, perennial philosophy, cosmic consciousness
(2) Personalist	Growth of the individual, unconscious, affectivity, desires, impulses, interests, the ego	Alfred Adler, Pierre Angers, Constantin Fotinas, Sigmund Freud, Kurt Lewin, Abraham Maslow, A.S. Neill, Claude Paquette, André Paré, Carl Rogers	Humanistic psychology, personalism, hermeneutics, psychoanalysis, open education, romantic humanism, naturalism, non-deterministic free school
(3) Psychocognitive	Learning process, prior knowledge, spontaneous representations, cognitive conflicts, pedagogical profiles, prescientific culture	Gaston Bachelard, Nadine Bednarz, Antoine de la Garanderie, André Giordan, Marie Larochelle and Jacques Desautels, Jean Piaget, Alain Taurisson	Piagetian psychology, cognitive psychology, constructivist epistemology, developmental psychology, cognitive development

Contemporary Theories and Practice in Education Matrix

Theories	Values and structural elements	Authors	Sources
(4) Technological	Information, communication technologies, computer science, computer-assisted instruction, artificial intelligence, instructional design, media, hypercourseware, intelligent learning environment, systemic approach to teaching, construction of knowledge, minimal training, competency training	Bela H. Banathy, Ludwig von Bertalanffy, Jacques Bordier, Leslie Briggs, John Carroll, Donald Cunningham, Walter Dick and Lou Carey, Robert Gagné, Robert Glaser, Lev Nakhmanovich Landa, Robert Mager, Harry McMahon, Bill O'Neill, Gilbert Paquette, Richard Prégent, B.F. Skinner, Harold Stolovitch	Cybernetics, systemics, communication theory, behaviorism, cognitive psychology, systems theory, artificial intelligence
(5) Social Cognitive	Culture, social environment, milieu, social determinants of knowledge, social interactions, cooperative learning, cooperative teaching	Albert Bandura, John Seely Brown, Jerome Bruner, William Clancey, Allan Collins, James Cooper, Willem Doise, Paul Duguid, Michel Gilly, Margaret E. Gredler, Jean Houssaye, David W. Johnson and Roger T. Johnson, Bruce Joyce, Spencer Kagan, Jean Lave, Monique Lefebvre-Pinard, Leslie McLean, Gabriel Mugny, Annemarie Palincsar, Roy Pea, Shlomo Sharan, Henry Sims, Robert Slavin, Elliot Turiel, Rolland Viau, L.S. Vygotsky	Sociology, anthropology, psychosociology

Contemporary Theories and Practice in Education

Theories	Values and structural elements	Authors	Sources
(6) Social	Social classes, social determinisms of human nature, environmental and social problems, power, liberation, social changes, empowering education, liberatory education, critical teaching, multicultural democracy, progressive education	Michael Apple, Stanley Aronowitz, Pierre Bourdieu, John Dewey, Jean-Claude Forquin, Paolo Freire, Henry Giroux, Jacques Grand'Maison, Ivan Illich, Erich Jantsch, Georges Lapassade, Peter McLaren, Jean-Claude Passeron, Joël de Rosnay, Ira Shor, Christine Sleeter, William Stanley, Alvin Toffler, Michael Young	Sociology, Marxism, political science, critical theory, ecology, feminist studies, environmental sciences
(7) Academic	Content, subject matter, disciplines, logic, reasoning, intellect, Western culture, traditions, Greco-Roman humanism, classical works, essentialism, liberal arts, critical spirit, basics, general education, critical thinking	Mortimer Adler, Allan Bloom, Jean-Marie Domenach, Girard Éthier, Louis Gadbois, Étienne Gilson, Michel Henry, Jacques Laliberté, Micheline Lavallée, Arthur Marsolais, Richard Paul, Michael Scriven	Classical literature, classical realism, philosophy, general education, culture, liberal arts, humanities, critical thinking

BIBLIOGRAPHY

Acker, Sandra. 1981. "No-Woman's-Land: British Sociology of Education 1960-1979." *Sociological Review*, 29:1 (February), pp. 77-104.

Ada, Alma Flor, and Maria del Pilar de Olave. 1986. *Hagamos Caminos: A Bilingual Reading and Language Development Series.* Reading MA: Addison-Wesley.

Adler, Alfred. 1982. *The Pattern of Life.* W. Beran Wolfe, ed. 2nd ed. Chicago: Alfred Adler Institute of Chicago.

Adler, Mortimer J. 1939. "The Crisis in Contemporary Education." *The Social Frontier*, 5 (February).

Adler, Mortimer J. 1977. *Reforming Education: The Schooling of the People and Their Education Beyond Schooling.* Boulder CO: Westview Press.

Adler, Mortimer J. 1982. *The Paideia Proposal: An Educational Manifesto.* New York: Macmillan.

Adler, Mortimer J. 1983. *Paideia Problems and Possibilities.* New York: Macmillan.

Adler, Mortimer J. 1984. *The Paideia Program.* New York: Macmillan.

Adler, Mortimer J. 1986. *A Guidebook to Learning.* New York: Macmillan.

Adler, Mortimer J., and Milton Mayer. 1958. *The Revolution in Education.* Chicago: University of Chicago Press.

Adorno, Theodor. 1974. *Minima Moralia: Reflections from a Damaged Life. (Minima Moralia.)* E.F.N. Jephcott, trans. London: New Left Books.

Allport, Gordon W. *Pattern and Growth in Personality.* New York: Holt, Rinehart and Winston.

Althusser, Louis. 1969. *For Marx. (Pour Marx.)* Ben Brewster, trans. New York: Pantheon.

Alvès, Christian, Joëlle Pojé-Chrétien, and Nicole Maous-Chassagny. 1988. *Modèles pour l'acte pédagogique.* Paris: Éditions Sociales Françaises.

Anderson, John R. 1983. *The Architecture of Cognition*. Cambridge: Harvard University Press.

Andrew, Caroline, and Steen B. Esbensen. 1989. *Who's Afraid of Liberal Education?* Proceedings of the National Conference organized by the Social Science Federation of Canada, Ottawa, Sept. 30-Oct. 1, 1988. Ottawa: Actexpress.

Andrini, Beth. 1989. *Cooperative Learning and Mathematics: A Multi-Structural Approach*. San Juan Capistrano, CA: Resources for Teachers.

Angers, Pierre. 1976. *Les modèles de l'institution scolaire: contribution à l'analyse institutionnelle*. Trois-Rivières, PQ: Centre de Développement en Environnement Scolaire.

Angers, Pierre. 1990. "Les fondements de la formation." In Christiane Gohier, ed., *La formation fondamentale: Actes du XIe Colloque Interdisciplinaire de la Société de philosophie du Québec*. Montreal: Éditions Logiques.

Angers, Pierre, and Colette Bouchard. 1978. *École et innovation*. Laval: Éditions NHP.

Ansbacher, Heinz L., and Rowena R. Ansbacher, eds. 1964. *The Individual Psychology of Alfred Adler: A Systematic Presentation in Selections From His Writings*. New York: Basic Books.

Apple, Michael W. 1979. *Ideology and Curriculum*. London: Routledge and Kegan Paul.

Apple, Michael W. 1988a. *Teachers and Texts*. London: Routledge and Kegan Paul.

Apple, Michael W. 1988b. "Redefining Equality: Authoritarian Populism and the Conservative Restoration." *Teachers College Record*, 90:2, pp. 167-184.

Apple, Michael W. 1992. "Computers in Schools: Salvation or Social Disaster?" *The Education Digest*, 57:6 (February), pp. 47-52. (Condensed from *Computers in the School*, 8 [1991], pp. 59-81.)

Apple, Michael W., ed. 1982. *Cultural and Economic Reproduction in Education*. London: Routledge and Kegan Paul.

Ardoino, Jacques. 1974. In Commission 12, VIe Congrès International des Sciences de l'Éducation, *Psychologie sociale et nouvelles approches pédagogiques*. Paris: Éditions de l'Épi.

Ardoino, Jacques. 1977. *Éducation et politique: Pour un projet d'éducation dans une perspective socialiste*. Paris: Gauthier-Villars.

Ardoino, Jacques. 1980. "Les pédagogies institutionnelles." In Gaston Mialaret and Jean Vial, eds., *Histoire mondiale de l'éducation*. Paris: Presses Universitaires de France, Vol. 4, pp. 129-150.

Ardoino, Jacques, G. Berger, *et al.* 1980. *Éducation et relations: Introduction à une analyse plurielle des situations éducatives.* Paris: Gauthier-Villars.

Arnold, Rick, Bev Burke, C. James, D. Martin, and B. Thomas. 1991. *Educating for a Change.* Toronto: Between the Lines and Doris Marshall Institute for Education.

Aronowitz, Stanley, and Henry Giroux. 1985. *Education Under Siege: The Conservative, Liberal, and Radical Debate Over Schooling.* South Hadley, MA: Bergin and Garvey.

Arshad, F.N., and P.S. Ward. 1992. "An Object-Oriented Information and Learning System for Midwifery: A Case Study." *Proceedings of the Seventh Canadian Symposium on Instructional Technology,* May 6-9, Montreal (electronic proceedings).

Astolfi, J.-P. 1992. *L'école, c'est pour apprendre.* Paris: Éditions Sociales Françaises.

Augusteijn, Marijke R., Ronald W. Broome, and Raymond W. Kolbe. 1992. "ITS — Challenger: A Domain-Independent Environment for the Development of Intelligent Training Systems." *Journal of Artificial Intelligence in Education,* 3:2, pp. 183-207.

Augustine, Dianne K., Kristin D. Gruber, and Lynda R. Hanson. 1990. "Cooperation Works!" *Educational Leadership,* 47:4 (January), pp. 4-7.

Ausubel, David Paul, Joseph D. Novak, and Helen Hanesian. 1978. *Educational Psychology: A Cognitive View.* 2nd ed. New York: Holt, Rinehart and Winston.

Avanzini, Guy. 1975. *La Pédagogie au XXe siècle.* Toulouse: Privat.

Bachelard, Gaston. 1934. *Le nouvel esprit scientifique.* Paris: Presses Universitaires de France. Translated as *The New Scientific Spirit.* Arthur Goldhammer, trans. Boston: Beacon Press, 1984.

Bachelard, Gaston. 1938. *La formation de l'esprit scientifique.* Paris: Vrin.

Bachelard, Gaston. 1940. *La philosophie du non: Essai d'une philosophie du nouvel esprit scientifique.* Paris: Presses Universitaires de France.

Bachelard, Gaston. 1949. *Le rationalisme appliqué.* Paris: Presses Universitaires de France.

Banathy, Bela H. 1968. *Instructional Systems.* Belmont, CA: Fearon Publications.

Bandura, Albert. 1977. *Social Learning Theory.* Englewood Cliffs, NJ: Prentice-Hall.

Bandura, Albert. 1978. "The Self System in Reciprocal Determinism." *American Psychologist,* 33, pp. 344-358.

Bandura, Albert. 1986. *Social Foundations of Thought and Action: A Social Cognitive Theory.* Englewood Cliffs, NJ: Prentice-Hall.

Bandura, Albert. 1990. "Reflections on Nonability Determinants of Competence." In Robert J. Sternberg and John Kolligian, Jr., eds., *Competence Considered.* New Haven, CT: Yale University Press. pp. 315-363.

Banks, James A. 1991. "A Curriculum for Empowerment, Action, and Change." In Christine E. Sleeter, ed., *Empowerment Through Multicultural Education.* Albany, NY: State University of New York Press. pp. 125-141.

Barbier, René. 1974. "Violence symbolique et pédagogie institutionnelle." In Commission 12, VIe Congrès International des Sciences de l'Éducation, *Psychologie sociale et nouvelles approches pédagogiques.* Paris: Éditions de l'Épi.

Barbier, René. 1977. *La recherche-action dans l'institution éducative.* Paris: Gauthier-Villars.

Barel, Yves. 1989. *Le paradoxe et le système: Essai sur le fantastique social.* (2nd ed.) Grenoble: Presses Universitaires de Grenoble.

Barel, Yves. 1984. *La société du vide.* Paris: Éditions du Seuil.

Barker, Philip. 1991. "Interactive Electronic Books." *Interactive Multimedia*, 2:1, pp. 11-18.

Barker, Philip. 1992. "Hypermedia Electronic Books." *Proceedings of the Seventh Canadian Symposium on Instructional Technology*, May 6-9, Montreal (electronic proceedings).

Barzun, Jacques. 1989. *The Culture We Deserve.* Middletown, CT: Wesleyan University Press.

Baudelot, Christian, and Roger Establet. 1989. *Le niveau monte.* Paris: Éditions du Seuil.

Baudrillard, Jean. 1990. *Fatal Strategies.* (*Les stratégies fatales.*) Philip Beitchman and W.G.J. Niesluchowski, trs. Jim Fleming, ed. New York: Semiotext(e).

Baudrillard, Jean. 1990. *Seduction.* (*De la séduction.*) Brian Singer, trans. New York: St. Martin's Press.

Baveja, Bharati, Beverly Showers, and Bruce R. Joyce. 1985. *An Experiment in Conceptually Based Teaching Strategies.* Eugene, OR: Booksend Laboratories.

Bednarz, Nadine, and Catherine Garnier, eds. 1989. *Construction des savoirs: Obstacles et conflits.* Montreal: Éditions Agence d'Arc et CIRADE (Centre interdisciplinaire de recherche sur l'apprentissage et le développement en éducation).

Bell, Daniel. 1966. *The Reforming of General Education: The Columbia College Experience in Its National Setting.* New York: Columbia University Press.

Bennett, Kathleen. 1991. "Doing School in an Urban Appalachian First Grade." In Christine E. Sleeter, ed., *Empowerment Through Multicultural Education.* Albany: State University of New York Press. pp. 27-47.

Berger, Peter L., and Thomas Luckmann. 1966. *Social Construction of Reality: A Treatise in the Sociology of Knowledge.* Garden City NY: Doubleday. Reprint, New York: Irvington Publishers, 1980.

Bergeron, Anne, and Jacques Bordier. 1990. "An Intelligent Discovery Environment for Probability and Statistics." *International Conference on Advanced Research on Computers in Education,* Tokyo. Amsterdam: Elsevier, pp. 191-198.

Bergeron, Anne. 1990. *Intelligence assistée et environnements d'apprentissage.* Unpublished doctoral thesis. Montreal: Université de Montréal.

Bergson, Henri. 1946. *The Creative Mind.* (*La pensée et le mouvant.*) Mabelle L. Andison, trans. New York: Philosophical Library.

Bertalanffy, Ludwig von. 1968. *General System Theory: Foundations, Development, Applications.* New York: G. Braziller.

Bertrand, Michel. 1992. "Un collège en recherche depuis 25 ans." *Le Nouvel Éducateur,* No. 41 (September), pp. 18-20.

Bertrand, Yves. 1979. *Les modèles éducationnels.* Montreal: Université de Montréal.

Bertrand, Yves. 1991. *Culture organisationnelle.* Quebec City: Presses de l'Université du Québec.

Bertrand, Yves, and Patrick Guillemet. 1989. *Les organisations: Une approche systémique.* Montreal: Éditions Agence d'Arc; Paris: Éditions Chotard; Quebec City: Télé-université.

Bertrand, Yves, and Paul Valois. 1992. *École et sociétés.* Montreal: Éditions Agence d'Arc.

Bertrand, Yves, and Paul Valois. 1993a. "Carl Rogers." In Jean Houssaye, ed., *Les grands pédagogues pour aujourd'hui.* Paris: Collin. pp. 242-253.

Bertrand, Yves, and Paul Valois. 1993b. "John Dewey." In Jean Houssaye, ed., *Les grands pédagogues pour aujourd'hui.* Paris: Collin. pp. 124-135.

Beyer, Landon E., and Michael W. Apple, eds. 1989. *The Curriculum: Problems, Politics, and Possibilities.* Albany, NY: State University of New York Press.

Beyou, Claire. 1992. "Vers un système d'enseignement du dépannage intégrant des connaissances évolutives." *Proceedings of the Seventh*

Canadian Symposium on Instructional Technology, May 6-9, Montreal (electronic proceedings).

Bissonnette, Lise. 1989. "La formation fondamentale: Au-delà des clichés." In Caroline Andrew and Steen B. Esbensen, eds. *Who's Afraid of Liberal Education?* Ottawa: University of Ottawa Press, pp. 21-33.

Black, John B., John M. Carroll, and Stuart M. McGuigan. 1987. "What Kind of Minimal Instruction Manual Is the Most Effective?" In *CHI + GI Conference Proceedings: Human Factors in Computing Systems and Graphic Interfaces.* New York: ACM, Inc., pp. 159-162.

Blaye, Agnès. 1989. "Interactions sociales et constructions cognitives: présentation critique de la thèse du conflit socio-cognitif." In Nadine Bednarz and Catherine Garnier, eds., *Construction des savoirs: Obstacles et conflits.* Montreal: Éditions Agence d'Arc et CIRADE (Centre interdisciplinaire de recherche sur l'apprentissage et le développement en éducation), pp. 183-194.

Bloom, Allan. 1987. *The Closing of the American Mind: How Higher Education Has Failed Democracy and Impoverished the Souls of Today's Students.* New York: Simon and Schuster.

Bloom, Allan. 1990. *Giants and Dwarfs: Essays, 1960-1990.* New York: Simon and Schuster.

Bloom, Benjamin Samuel, Max D. Engelhart, Edward J. Furst, W.H. Hill, and David R. Krathwohl, eds. 1956. *Taxonomy of Educational Objectives: The Classification of Educational Goals. Handbook I, Cognitive Domain.* New York: Longman.

Bordier, Jacques. 1990. *Un modèle didactique utilisant la simulation sur ordinateur pour l'enseignement de la probabilité.* Unpublished thesis. University of Paris VII.

Borning, Alan. 1981. "The Programming Language Aspects of Thinklab, a Constraint-Oriented Simulation Laboratory." *ACM Transactions on Programming Languages & Systems* [Association for Computing Machinery], No. 3. pp, 353-387.

Bourdieu, Pierre, and Jean-Claude Passeron. 1964. *Les héritiers: Les étudiants et la culture.* Translated as *The Inheritors: French Students and Their Relationship to Culture.* Richard Nice, trans. Chicago: University of Chicago Press, 1979.

Bourdieu, Pierre, and Jean-Claude Passeron. 1970. *La reproduction: Éléments pour une théorie du système d'enseignement.* Paris: Éditions de Minuit. Translated as *Reproduction in Education, Society and Culture.* Richard Nice, trans. London, Beverly Hills: Sage Publications, 1977; London, Newbury Park, CA: Sage Publications, 1990.

Bourdieu, Pierre, and Jean-Claude Passeron. 1982. *La leçon sur la leçon.* Paris: Éditions de Minuit.

Bower, Gordon H., and Ernest R. Hilgard. 1981. *Theories of Learning.* 5th ed. Englewood Cliffs, NJ: Prentice-Hall.

Bowers, C.A. 1984. *The Promise of Theory: An Essay on Education and the Politics of Cultural Change.* London: Longman.

Bowers, C.A. 1991. "Some Questions About the Anachronistic Elements in the Giroux-McLaren Theory of Critical Pedagogy." *Curriculum Inquiry,* 21:2, pp. 239-252.

Bowers, C.A. 1993. *Education, Cultural Myths, and the Ecological Crisis: Toward Deep Changes.* Albany, NY: State University of New York Press.

Bowles, Samuel, and Herbert Gintis. 1976. *Schooling in Capitalist America: Educational Reform and the Contradictions of Economic Life.* New York: Basic Books.

Boyer, Ernest L. 1983. *High School: A Report on Secondary Education in America.* New York: Harper & Row.

Boyer, Ernest L. 1985. "In the Aftermath of Excellence." *Educational Leadership,* 42:6 (March), pp. 10-13.

Bradford, Leland Powers, Jack R. Gibb, and Kenneth D. Benne. 1964. *T-Group Theory and Laboratory Method: Innovation in Re-education.* New York: John Wiley.

Brandt, Ronald S. 1990. "On Cooperative Learning: A Conversation With Spencer Kagan." *Educational Leadership,* 47:4 (January), pp. 8-11.

Brell, Carl D. 1990. "Critical Thinking as Transfer: The Reconstructive Integration of Otherwise Discrete Interpretations of Experience." *Educational Theory,* 40:1 (Winter), pp. 53-68.

Brickman, William W. 1958. "The Essentialist Spririt in Education." *School and Society,* 86:2138 (Oct. 11), p. 364.

Briggs, Leslie J., ed. 1977. *Instructional Design: Principles and Applications.* Englewood Cliffs, NJ: Prentice-Hall.

Briggs, Leslie J., and Walter W. Wager. 1981. *Handbook of Procedures for the Design of Instruction.* Englewood Cliffs, NJ: Educational Technology Publications.

Brodinsky, Ben. 1977. "Back to the Basics: The Movement and Its Meaning." *Phi Delta Kappan,* 58:7 (March), pp. 522-527.

Broudy, Harry S. 1965. "A Classical Realist View of Education." In Philip Henry Phenix, ed., *Philosophies of Education: Sketches of Some Contemporary Viewpoints on Education.* New York: John Wiley.

Brousseau, Guy. 1983. "Les obstacles épistémologiques et les problèmes en mathématiques." *Recherche en didactique des mathématiques*, 4:2, pp. 163-197.

Brousseau, Guy. 1989. "Les obstacles épistémologiques et la didactique des mathématiques." In Nadine Bednarz and Catherine Garnier, eds., *Construction des savoirs: Obstacles et conflits*. Montreal: Éditions Agence d'Arc et CIRADE (Centre interdisciplinaire de recherche sur l'apprentissage et le développement en éducation), pp. 41-63.

Brown, Cynthia. 1987. "Literacy in Thirty Hours: Paulo Freire's Process in Northeast Brazil" (Appendix). In Ira Shor, ed., *Freire for the Classroom: A Sourcebook for Liberatory Teaching*. Portsmouth, NH: Boynton/Cook Publishers. pp. 215-231.

Brown, John Seely. 1983. "Learning by Doing Revisited for Electronic Learning Environments." In Mary Alice White, ed., *The Future of Electronic Learning*. Hillsdale, NJ: Lawrence Erlbaum Associates, pp. 13-32.

Brown, John Seely, and Paul Duguid. 1993. "Stolen Knowledge." *Educational Technology*, 33:3 (March), pp. 10-15.

Brown, John Seely, Allan Collins, and Paul Duguid. 1989. "Situated Cognition and the Culture of Learning." *Educational Researcher*, 18:1 (January/February), pp. 32-42.

Brown, John Seely, and D. [Derek] Sleeman. 1982. *Intelligent Tutoring Systems*. London, New York: Academic Press.

Bruner, Jerome S. 1986. *Actual Minds, Possible Worlds*. Cambridge: Harvard University Press.

Buchanan, David. 1993. "Outward Bound Goes to the Inner City." *Educational Leadership*, 50:4 (December/January), pp. 38-41.

Bucke, Richard Maurice. 1901. *Cosmic Consciousness: A Study in the Evolution of the Human Mind*. Reprint, 1989, Secaucus, NJ: Citadel Press.

Bugental, James F.T. 1967. *Challenges of Humanistic Psychology*. New York: McGraw-Hill.

Burrell, Gibson, and Gareth Morgan. 1979. *Sociological Paradigms and Organisational Analysis*. London: Heinemann.

Cantor, Nancy, and John F. Kihlstrom, eds. 1981. *Personality, Cognition, and Social Interaction*. Hillsdale, NJ: Lawrence Erlbaum Associates.

Cantor, Nancy, and Walter Mischel. 1977. "Traits as Prototypes: Effects on Recognition Memory." *Journal of Personality and Social Psychology*, 35:1, pp. 38-48.

Cantor, Nancy, and Walter Mischel. 1979. "Prototypes in Person Perception." In Leonard Berkowitz, ed., *Advances in Experimental Social Psychology*, Vol. 12. New York: Academic Press, pp. 3-52.

Caouette, Charles E. 1992. *Si on parlait d'éducation: Pour un nouveau project de société.* Montreal: VLB Éditeur.

Capra, Fritjof. 1988. *Uncommon Wisdom: Conversations With Remarkable People.* New York: Simon and Schuster.

Carroll, John M. 1984a. *Designing Minimalist Training Material.* Research Report. New York: IBM Watson Research Center.

Carroll, John M. 1984b. "Minimalist Training." *Datamation*, 30:18, pp. 125-136.

Carroll, John M., and Amy Aaronson. 1988. "Learning by Doing With Simulated Intelligent Help." *Communications of the ACM* [Association for Computing Machinery], 31:9 (September), pp. 1064-1079.

Carroll, John M., and Caroline Carrithers. 1984. "Training Wheels in a User Interface." *Communications of the ACM* [Association for Computing Machinery], 27:8 (August), pp. 800-806.

Carroll, John M., and Dana S. Kay. 1988. "Prompting, Feedback and Error Correction in the Design of a Scenario Machine." *International Journal of Man-Machine Studies*, No. 28, pp. 11-27.

Carroll, John M., and Robert L. Mack. 1984. "Learning to Use a Word Processor: By Doing, by Thinking, and by Knowing." In John C. Thomas and Michael L. Schneider, eds., *Human Factors in Computer Systems.* Norwood, NJ: Ablex Publishing. pp. 13-51.

Carroll, John M., Robert L. Mack, Clayton H. Lewis, N.L. Grischkowsky, and S.R. Robertson. 1985. "Exploring a Word Processor." *Human-Computer Interaction*, 1:2, pp. 283-307.

Carroll, John M., and Sandra A. Mazur. 1986. "Lisa Learning." *IEEE Computer*, 19:11 (November), pp. 35-49.

Carroll, John M., and Jean McKendree. 1987. "Interface Design Issues for Advice-Giving Expert Systems." *Communications of the ACM* [Association for Computing Machinery], 30:1 (January), pp. 14-31.

Carroll, John M., Penny L. Smith-Kerker, James R. Ford, and Sandra A. Mazur-Rimetz. 1987-88. "The Minimal Manual." *Human-Computer Interaction*, 3:2, pp. 123-153.

Carugati, Felice, and Gabriel Mugny. 1985. "La théorie du conflit sociocognitif." In Gabriel Mugny, ed., *Psychologie sociale du développement cognitif.* Bern: Peter Lang. pp. 57-71.

Case, Robbie. 1978. "Piaget and Beyond: Toward a Developmentally Based Theory and Technology of Instruction." In Robert Glaser, ed.,

Advances in Instructional Psychology, Vol. 1. Hillsdale, NJ: Lawrence Erlbaum Associates, pp. 167-228.

Castle, Edgar Bradshaw. 1967. *Ancient Education and Today*. Baltimore: Penguin Books.

Cattell, Raymond B. 1966. *The Scientific Analysis of Personality*. Chicago: Aldine Publishing.

Centre Royaumont Pour une Science de l'Homme. 1979. *Théories du langage, théories de l'apprentissage: Le débat entre Jean Piaget et Noam Chomsky*. Organized and compiled by Massimo Piattelli-Palmarini. Paris: Éditions du Seuil.

Chaiklin, Seth, and Jean Lave, eds. 1993. *Understanding Practice: Perspectives on Activity and Learning*. Cambridge, New York: Cambridge University Press.

Chaplin, William F., and Lewis R. Goldberg. 1984. "A Failure to Replicate the Bem and Allen Study of Individual Differences in Cross-Situational Consistency." *Journal of Personality and Social Psychology*, 47:5, pp. 1074-1090.

Charbonneau, Claude, and Michèle Robert. 1977. "Observational Learning of Quantity Conservation in Relation to the Degree of Cognitive Conflict." *Psychological Reports*, 41:3, part 1 (December), pp. 975-986.

Charcot, Jean-Martin. 1991. *Clinical Lectures on the Diseases of the Nervous System. (Leçons sur les maladies du système nerveux, 1887.)* Ruth Harris, ed. London, New York: Routledge.

Château, Jean. 1964. *La culture générale*. Paris: Vrin.

Château, Jean, ed. 1969. *Les grands pédagogues*. Paris: Presses Universitaires de France.

Cherryholmes, Cleo H. 1988. *Power and Criticism: Poststructural Investigations in Education*. New York: Teachers College Press, Columbia University.

Chomsky, Noam. 1965. *Aspects of the Theory of Syntax*. Cambridge: MIT Press.

Chomsky, Noam. 1979. "A propos des structures cognitives et de leur développement: Une réponse à Piaget." In Centre Royaumont Pour une Science de l'Homme. *Théories du langage, théories de l'apprentissage: Le débat entre Jean Piaget et Noam Chomsky*. Paris: Éditions du Seuil.

Churchland, Patricia Smith. 1986. *Neurophilosophy: Toward a Unified Science of the Mind-Brain*. Cambridge: MIT Press.

Clancey, William J. 1992. "Viewpoint: Representations of Knowing: In Defense of Cognitive Apprenticeship." *Journal of Artificial Intelligence in Education*, 3:2, pp. 139-168.

Clifford, James. 1988. *The Predicament of Culture: Twentieth-Century Ethnography, Literature, and Art.* Cambridge: Harvard University Press.

Compayre, Gabriel. 1885. *Histoire critique des doctrines de l'éducation en France depuis le XVIe siècle.* Paris: Hachette.

Conseil Supérieur de l'Education. 1971. *L'activité éducative: Rapport annuel 1969/1970.* Quebec City: Éditeur Officiel.

Conseil Supérieur de l'Education. 1975. *Rapport sur l'état et les besoins de l'enseignement collégial.* Quebec City: Éditeur Officiel.

Conseil Supérieur de l'Education. 1984. *La formation fondamentale et la qualité de l'éducation.* Quebec City: Éditeur Officiel.

Conseil Supérieur de l'Education. 1989. *Le rapport Parent, vingt-cinq ans après: Rapport annuel 1987-1988 sur l'état des besoins de l'éducation.* Quebec City: Éditeur Officiel.

Conseil Supérieur de l'Education. 1990. *La pédagogie, un défi majeur de l'enseignement supérieur.* Quebec City: Éditeur Officiel.

Cooper, James, Susan Prescott, Lenora Cook, Lyle Smith, Randall Mueck, and Joseph Cuseo. 1990. *Cooperative Learning and College Instruction: Effective Use of Student Learning Teams.* Long Beach: California State University Foundation.

Coq, Guy. 1988. "Prolégomènes à une politique de l'éducation." *Esprit*, No. 139 (June), pp. 37-53.

Coulon, Jacques de, Marc-Alain Descamps, Christine Dierkens, and Constantin Fotinas. 1993. *L'éducation transpersonnelle.* Paris: Éditions Trismégiste.

Cox, Murray. 1990. "Interview: Paulo Freire." *Omni*, 12 (April), pp. 74-94.

Cuban, Larry. 1984. *How Teachers Taught: Constancy and Change in American Classrooms, 1890-1980.* New York: Longman.

Cummins, Jim. 1989. *Empowering Minority Students.* Sacramento: California Association for Bilingual Education.

Cunningham, Donald J. 1991. "Assessing Constructions and Constructing Assessments: A Dialogue." *Educational Technology*, 31:5 (May), pp. 13-17.

Darling, F. Fraser, and Raymond F. Dasmann. 1969. "La société humaine vue en écosystème." *Impact: science et société*, 19:2, pp. 121-134.

Davis, Tim R.V., and Fred Luthans. 1980. "A Social Learning Approach to Organizational Behavior." *Academy of Management Review*, 5:2, pp. 281-290.

Deheuvels, Paul. 1988. *L'excellence est à tout le monde: Libres propos sur l'éducation.* Paris: Laffont.

De Ketele, Jean-Marie. 1990. "Le passage de l'enseignement secondaire à l'enseignement supérieur: Les facteurs de réussite." *Vie pédagogique* (Montreal), No. 66 (April), pp. 4-9.

Deleuze, Gilles. 1990. *The Logic of Sense.* (*Logique du sens*, 1969.) Mark Lester and Charles Stivale, trs. Constantin V. Boundas, ed. New York: Columbia University Press.

Deleuze, Gilles, and Felix Guattari. 1977. *Anti-Oedipus: Capitalism and Schizophrenia.* (*Capitalisme et schizophrénie*, 1972.) Robert Hurley, Mark Seem, and Helen R. Lane, trs. New York: Viking Press.

Demolins, Édmond. 1898. *Éducation nouvelle: l'école des Roches.* Paris: Didot.

Desautels, Jacques, and Marie Larochelle. 1989. *Qu'est-ce que le savoir scientifique?* Quebec City: Presses de l'Université Laval.

Deshler, David, ed. 1984. *Evaluation for Program Improvement.* San Francisco: Jossey-Bass.

Dewey, John. 1916. *Democracy and Education: An Introduction to the Philosophy of Education.* New York: Macmillan.

Dewey, John. 1938. *Experience and Education.* 1st ed. New York: Collier.

Dick, Walter, and Lou Carey. 1990. 4th ed. *The Systematic Design of Instruction.* Glenview IL: Scott, Foresman.

Dillon, Ronna F., and Ronald R. Schmeck, eds. 1983. *Individual Differences in Cognition.* New York: Academic Press.

Doise, Willem. 1988. "Régulations sociales des opérations cognitives." In Anne-Nelly Perret-Clermont and Joan Stevenson-Hinde, eds., *Relations interpersonnelles et développement des savoirs.* Cousset (Fribourg): DelVal, pp. 419-440.

Doise, Willem, and Gabriel Mugny. 1979. "Individual and Collective Conflicts of Centrations in Cognitive Development." *European Journal of Social Psychology*, 9:1 (January-March), pp. 105-108.

Doise, Willem, and Gabriel Mugny. 1981. *Le développement social de l'intelligence.* Paris: Interéditions. Translated as *The Social Development of the Intellect.* Angela St. James-Emler and Nicholas Emler, tr., with the collaboration of Diana Mackie. 1st ed. Oxford: Pergamon Press, 1984.

Domenach, Jean-Marie. 1989. *Ce qu'il faut enseigner.* Paris: Éditions du Seuil.

Dreikurs, Rudolf. 1971. *La psychologie adlérienne.* Paris: Bloud et Gay.

Drews, Elizabeth Monroe. 1970. *Policy Implications of a Hierarchy of Values.* Final report on project #6747, prepared for the National Center for Educational Research and Development, Office of Education. Menlo Park, CA: Stanford Research Institute.

D'Souza, Dinesh. 1991. *Illiberal Education: The Politics of Race and Sex on Campus.* New York: Vintage Books.

Dubé, Louis. 1986. *Psychologie de l'apprentissage de 1880 à 1980.* Quebec City: Presses de l'Université du Québec.

Dumouchel, Paul, and Jean-Pierre Dupuy. 1983. *L'auto-organisation: De la physique au politique.* Paris: Éditions du Seuil.

Dunkin, Michael J. 1987. *The International Encyclopedia of Teaching and Teacher Education.* Oxford: Pergamon Press.

Dweck, Carol S., and Ellen L. Leggett. 1988. "A Social-Cognitive Approach to Motivation and Personality." *Psychological Review,* 95:2 (April), pp. 256-273.

Eccles, John C. 1970. *Facing Reality: Philosophical Adventures of a Brain Surgeon.* New York: Springer-Verlag.

Eisner, Elliot W. 1985. *The Educational Imagination: On the Design and Evaluation of School Programs.* 2nd ed. New York: Macmillan.

Eisner, Elliot W., ed. 1985. *Learning and Teaching the Ways of Knowing.* Chicago: National Society for the Study of Education. Distributed by the University of Chicago Press.

Eisner, Elliot W., and Elizabeth Vallance, eds. 1973. *Conflicting Conceptions of Curriculum.* Berkeley, CA: McCutchan Publishing.

Éliade, Mircea. 1965. *Le sacré et le profane.* Paris: NRF. Translated as *The Sacred and the Profane: The Nature of Religion.* Willard R. Trask, trans. New York: Harcourt, Brace, Jovanovich, 1959.

Emerson, Ralph Waldo. 1883. *Essays.* New York: Houghton Mifflin.

Ennis, Robert H. 1991. "Critical Thinking: A Streamlined Conception." Presentation, American Educational Research Association conference, Chicago, April.

Éthier, Girard. 1989. *La gestion de l'excellence en éducation.* Quebec City: Presses de l'Université du Québec.

Feldman, Steven P. 1988. "How Organizational Culture Can Affect Innovation." *Organizational Dynamics,* 17:1 (Summer), pp. 57-68.

Ferguson, Marilyn. 1980. *The Aquarian Conspiracy: Personal and Social Transformation in the 1980s.* Los Angeles: J.P. Tarcher.

Ferrière, Adolphe. 1925. "L'école nouvelle et le bureau international des écoles nouvelles." *Pour l'école nouvelle* (Geneva), No. 15 (April).

Ferrière, Adolphe. 1966. *L'école active.* (7th ed.) Neuchâtel, Switzerland: Delachaux et Niestlé.

Ferry, Gilles. 1983. *Le trajet de la formation: Les enseignants entre la théorie et la pratique.* Paris: Dunod.

Finkielkraut, Alain. 1985. "La défaite de Goethe." *Le temps de la réflexion,* 6, pp. 17-31.

Finkielkraut, Alain. 1988. *La défaite de la pensée.* Paris: Gallimard. Translated as *The Undoing of Thought.* Dennis O'Keeffe, trans. London: Claridge. 1988.

Finn, Chester E., Jr., and Diane Ravitch. 1987. *What Do Our 17-Year-Olds Know?* New York: Harper and Row.

Fisher, Arthur. 1992. "Edutech." *Popular Science,* 241 (October), pp. 68-71.

Fiske, Susan T., and Martha G. Cox. 1979. "Person Concepts: The Effect of Target Familiarity and Descriptive Purpose on the Process of Describing Others." *Journal of Personality,* 47:1 (March), pp. 136-161.

Fiske, Susan T., and Linda M. Dyer. 1985. "Structure and Development of Social Schemata: Evidence From Positive and Negative Transfer Effects." *Journal of Personality and Social Psychology,* 48:4, pp. 839-852.

Flavell, John H. 1963. *The Developmental Psychology of Jean Piaget.* Princeton, NJ: Van Nostrand Reinhold.

Forquin, Jean-Claude. 1991. "Savoirs scolaires, contraintes didactiques et enjeux sociaux." *Sociologie et sociétés,* 23:1 (Spring), pp. 25-39.

Fortin, A. 1954. "Culture classique chrétienne et humanités gréco-latines." In Collège Jean-de-Brébeuf, *Mélanges sur les humanités.* Quebec City: Presses de l'Université Laval; Paris: Vrin.

Fotinas, Constantin. 1990. *Le tao de l'éducation.* Montreal: Libre Expression.

Fotinas, Constantin, and Nicole Henri. 1993. "Vers une pédagogie transpersonnelle à l'université." In Jacques de Coulon, Marc-Alain Descamps, Christine Dierkens, and Constantin Fotinas, *L'éducation transpersonnelle.* Paris: Éditions Trismégiste.

Fotinas, Constantin, and Nicole Henri. 1992. *L'art de vivre en éducation.* Montreal: Laboratoire de recherche Café-école.

Fotinas, Constantin, and Z. Torossian. 1977. *Guide du cours EAV 3352 -- Langage cinématographique en situation d'apprentissage: le film éducatif, production et utilisation.* Montreal: University of Montreal.

Foucault, Michel. 1977. *Discipline and Punish: The Birth of the Prison. (Surveiller et punir.)* Alan Sheridan, trans. New York: Pantheon Books.

Frankenstein, Marilyn. 1987. "Critical Mathematics Education: An Application of Paulo Freire's Epistemology." In Ira Shor, ed., *Freire for the Classroom: A Sourcebook for Liberatory Teaching.* Portsmouth, NH: Boynton/Cook Publishers. pp. 180-210.

Freinet, Célestin. 1990. *Cooperative Learning for Social Change: Selected Writings of Célestin Freinet.* David Clandfield and John Sivell, trs. and eds. Toronto: Our Schools/Our Selves Education Foundation.

Freinet, Célestin. 1969. *Pour l'école du peuple: Guide pratique pour l'organisation matérielle, technique et pédagogique de l'école populaire.* Paris: F. Maspéro.

Freire, Paulo. 1970. *Pedagogy of the Oppressed. (Pedagogia del oprimido.)* Myra Bergman Ramos, trans. New York: Seabury Press. New edition. New York: Continuum, 1993.

Freire, Paulo. 1972. *Cultural Action for Freedom. (Açao cultural para a liberdade.)* Harmondsworth UK: Penguin.

Freire, Paulo. 1973. *Education for Critical Consciousness. (Education as the Practice of Freedom* and *Extension and Communication.) (Educaçao como pratica da liberdade* and *Extension y Comunicacion.)* Myra Bergman Ramos, Louise Bigwood and Margaret Marshall, trans. New York: Seabury Press.

Freire, Paulo. 1978. *Pedagogy in Process: The Letters to Guinea-Bissau. (Cartas a Guine-Bissau.)* Carman St. John Hunter, trans. New York: Seabury Press.

Freire, Paulo. 1985. *The Politics of Education: Culture, Power and Liberation.* (Collection of recent writings.) Donaldo Macedo, trans. South Hadley MA: Bergin and Garvey.

Freire, Paulo, and Antonio Faundez. 1989. *Learning to Question: A Pedagogy of Liberation. (Por uma pedagogia da pergunta.)* Tony Coates, trans. New York: Continuum.

Freire, Paulo, and Donaldo Macedo. 1987. *Literacy: Reading the Word and the World.* South Hadley, MA: Bergin and Garvey.

Fritz, Jane M. 1992. "A Linked Annotation Facility in Hypermedia-Based CAI." *Proceedings of the Seventh Canadian Symposium on Instructional Technology*, May 6-9, Montreal (electronic proceedings).

Fromm, Erich. 1947. *Man for Himself.* New York: Holt, Rinehart and Winston.

Fromm, Erich. 1965. *Escape From Freedom.* New York: Holt, Rinehart and Winston.

Gadbois, Louis. 1988. *La formation fondamentale: La documentation québécoise.* Montreal: Centre d'animation, de développement et de recherche en éducation.

Gadbois, Louis. 1989. "Des classes spéciales pour élèves motivés: Vers la motivation d'une nouvelle élite." *Prospectives*, 25:2 (April), pp. 67-72.

Gagné, Robert Mills. 1966. "Varieties of Learning and the Concept of Discovery." In Lee S. Shulman and Evan R. Keislar, eds., *Learning by Discovery: A Critical Appraisal.* Chicago: Rand McNally, pp. 116-132.

Gagné, Robert Mills. 1974. *Essentials of Learning for Instruction.* New York: Holt, Rinehart and Winston.

Gagné, Robert Mills. 1985. *The Conditions of Learning and Theory of Instruction.* 5th ed. New York: Holt, Rinehart and Winston.

Gagné, Robert Mills, ed. 1987. *Instructional Design: Principles and Applications.* Englewood Cliffs, NJ: Educational Technology Publications.

Gagné, Robert Mills, Leslie J. Briggs, and Walter W. Wager. 1988. *Principles of Instructional Design.* New York: Holt, Rinehart and Winston.

Gardner, Howard. 1987. *The Mind's New Science: A History of the Cognitive Revolution.* Rev. ed. New York: Basic Books.

Gilbert, John K., and D. Michael Watts. 1983. "Concepts, Misconceptions and Alternative Conceptions: Changing Perspectives in Science Education." *Studies in Science Education,* Vol. 10. pp. 61-98.

Gilly, Michel. 1989. "A propos de la théorie du conflit socio-cognitif et des mécanismes psychosociaux des constructions cognitives: perspectives actuelles et modèles explicatifs." In Nadine Bednarz and Catherine Garnier, eds., *Construction des savoirs: Obstacles et conflits.* Montreal: Éditions Agence d'Arc et CIRADE (Centre interdisciplinaire de recherche sur l'apprentissage et le développement en éducation), pp. 162-182.

Gilson, Étienne. 1954. "L'école à la croisée des chemins." In Collège Jean-de-Brébeuf, *Mélanges sur les humanités.* Quebec City: Presses de l'Université Laval; Paris: Vrin.

Gingras, Paul-Émile. 1989. *La formation fondamentale: La documentation anglaise.* Montreal: Centre d'animation, de développement et de recherche en éducation.

Gioia, Dennis A., and Evelyn Pitre. 1990. "Multiparadigm Perspectives on Theory Building." *Academy of Management Review,* 15:4 (October), pp. 584-602.

Giordan, André. 1989. "Vers un modèle didactique d'apprentissage allostérique." In Nadine Bednarz and Catherine Garnier, eds., *Construction des savoirs: Obstacles et conflits.* Montreal: Éditions Agence d'Arc et CIRADE (Centre interdisciplinaire de recherche sur l'apprentissage et le développement en éducation), pp. 240-257.

Giordan, André. 1990. "Le modèle allostérique." Lecture given at the University of Montreal, March 15.

Giordan, André, et al. 1978. *Une pédagogie pour les sciences expérimentales.* Paris: Éditions du Centurion.

Giordan, André, and Y. Girault. 1992. "Un environnement pédagogique pour apprendre: le modèle allostérique." In *Repères: Essais en education* (Université de Montréal, Faculté des sciences de l'éducation), No. 14, pp. 95-124.

Giordan, André, Jean-Louis Martinand, et al. 1983. *L'élève et/ou les connaissances scientifiques: Approche didactique de la construction des concepts scientifiques par les élèves.* Bern: Peter Lang.

Giordan, André, and Girard de Vecchi. 1987. *Les origines du savoir.* Paris: Delachaux.

Giordan, André, Androula Henriques, and Vinh Bang, eds. 1988. *Psychologie génétique et didactique des sciences.* Bern: Peter Lang.

Giordan, André, and Jean-Louis Martinand. 1988. "État des recherches sur les conceptions des élèves en biologie." In André Giordan and Jean-Louis Martinand, eds., *Annales de Didactique des sciences.* Bern: Peter Lang, pp. 29-34.

Giroux, Henry A. 1983a. *Theory and Resistance in Education: A Pedagogy for the Opposition.* South Hadley, MA: Bergin and Garvey.

Giroux, Henry A. 1983b. "Theories of Reproduction and Resistance in the New Sociology of Education: A Critical Analysis." *Harvard Educational Review*, 53:3 (August), 257-293.

Giroux, Henry A. 1985. "Introduction." In Paulo Freire, *The Politics of Education: Culture, Power, and Liberation.* South Hadley, MA: Bergin and Garvey, pp. xi-xxv.

Giroux, Henry A. 1988a. *Schooling and the Struggle for Public Life: Critical Pedagogy in the Modern Age.* Minneapolis: University of Minnesota Press.

Giroux, Henry A. 1988b. "Postmodernism and the Discourse of Educational Criticism." *Journal of Education*, 170:3, pp. 5-30.

Giroux, Henry A., ed. 1991. *Postmodernism, Feminism, and Cultural Politics: Redrawing Educational Boundaries.* New York: Routledge.

Giroux, Henry A. 1992a. *Border Crossings: Cultural Workers and the Politics of Education.* New York: Routledge.

Giroux, Henry A. 1992b. "Resisting Difference: Cultural Studies and the Discourse of Critical Pedagogy." In Lawrence Grossberg, Cary Nelson, and Paula A. Treichler, eds., *Cultural Studies.* New York: Routledge, pp. 199-212.

Giroux, Henry A., and Peter McLaren. 1992. "Leon Golub's Radical Pessimism: Towards a Critical Pedagogy of Representation." In Henry A. Giroux, *Border Crossings: Cultural Workers and the Politics of Education.* New York: Routledge, pp. 207-229.

Giroux, Henry A., and Peter McLaren. 1994. *Between Borders: Pedagogy and the Politics of Cultural Studies.* New York: Routledge.

Goble, Frank. 1970. *The Third Force: The Psychology of Abraham Maslow.* New York: Grossman.

Gohier, Christiane, ed. 1990a. *La formation fondamentale: Actes du XIe Colloque Interdisciplinaire de la Société de Philosophie du Québec.* Montreal: Éditions Logiques.

Gohier, Christiane. 1990b. "En guise de bilan." In Christiane Gohier, ed., *La formation fondamentale: Actes du XIe Colloque Interdisciplinaire de la Société de philosophie du Québec.* Montreal: Éditions Logiques, pp. 389-395.

Goodlad, John I. 1984. *A Place Called School: Prospects for the Future.* New York: McGraw-Hill.

Gorbutt, David. 1972. "The New Sociology of Education." *Education for Teaching,* No. 89 (Autumn), pp. 3-11.

Gore, Jennifer M. 1993. *The Struggle for Pedagogies: Critical and Feminist Discourse as Regimes of Truth.* New York: Routledge.

Grand'Maison, Jacques. 1975. *Le privé et le public.* Vol. 3. Montreal: Leméac.

Grand'Maison, Jacques. 1975. *Des milieux de travail à réinventer.* Montreal: Presses de l'Université de Montréal.

Grand'Maison, Jacques. 1976. *Pour une pédagogie sociale d'autodéveloppement en éducation.* Montreal: Stanké.

Gredler, Margaret E. 1992. *Learning and Instruction: Theory Into Practice.* 2nd ed. New York: Macmillan.

Greene, Maxine. 1986. "In Search of a Critical Pedagogy." *Harvard Educational Review,* 56:4 (November), pp. 427-441.

Greeno, James G. 1988a. "A Perspective on Thinking." *IRL Report 88-0010.* Palo Alto, CA: Institute for Research on Learning.

Greeno, James G. 1988b. "Situations, Mental Models and Generative Knowledge." *IRL Report 88-0005.* Palo Alto CA: Institute for Research on Learning.

Groupe d'Éducation Thérapeutique (GET). 1974. "Pédagogie institution-nelle." In Commission 12, VIe Congrès International des Sciences de l'Éducation, *Psychologie sociale et nouvelles approches pédagogiques.* Paris: Éditions de l'Épi.

Groupe de Rercherche sur les Systèmes Ouverts en Éducation. 1978. *Le Café-École: Vers une libération systémique de l'acte d'aprendre.* Montreal: Université de Montréal, Faculté des sciences de léducation.

Guattari, Felix. 1989. *Les trois écologies.* Paris: Éditions Galilée.

Guigou, Jacques. 1972. *Critique des systèmes de formation.* Paris: Anthropos.

Guiraud, Marc. 1971. "Le rôle de l'enseignant." In Georges Lapassade, ed., *L'autogestion pédagogique.* Paris: Gauthier-Villars, pp. 34-53.

Guitton, Jean. 1960. *Apprendre à vivre et à penser.* 2nd ed. Paris: Payot.

Habermas, Jurgen. 1970. *Toward a Rational Society: Student Protest, Science, and Politics.* (Essays from *Protestbewegung und Hochschulreform* and"Ideologie" from *Technik und Wissenschaft.*) Jeremy J. Shapiro, trans. Boston: Beacon Press.

Habermas, Jurgen. 1989. *The New Conservatism: Cultural Criticism and the Historians' Debate.* (Essays and interviews.) Shierry Weber Nicholsen, trans. and ed. Cambridge: MIT Press.

Hameline, Daniel. 1987. *Du savoir et des hommes.* Paris: Gauthier-Villars.

Hanks, William F. 1991. "Foreword." In Jean Lave and Étienne Wenger, *Situated Learning: Legitimate Peripheral Participation.* Cambridge, New York: Cambridge University Press.

Harman, Willis W. 1972a. "Key Choices of the Next Two Decades (An Exploration of the Future)." *Fields Within Fields ... Within Fields,* 5:1, pp. 82-92.

Harman, Willis W. 1972b. "Changing United States Society: Implications for Schools." In *Alternative Educational Futures in the United States and in Europe: Methods, Issues and Policy Relevance* Paris: Organisation for Economic Co-operation and Development.

Harman, Willis W. 1974. "The Coming Transformation in Our View of Knowledge." *The Futurist,* 8:3 (June), pp. 126-128.

Harman, Willis W. 1988. *Global Mind Change.* Indianapolis: Knowledge Systems.

Heims, Steve J. 1980. *John Von Neumann and Norbert Wiener: From Mathematics to the Technologies of Life and Death.* Cambridge: MIT Press.

Henderson, Hazel. 1991. *Paradigms in Progress: Life Beyond Economics.* Indianapolis: Knowledge Systems.

Henry, Michel. 1987. *La barbarie.* Paris: Grasset.

Hess, Rémi. 1975a. *La socianalyse.* Paris: Éditions universitaires.

Hess, Rémi. 1975b. *La pédagogie institutionnelle aujourd'hui*. Paris: Jean-Pierre Delarge.

Hinde, Robert A., Anne-Nelly Perret-Clermont, and Joan Stevenson-Hinde, eds. 1985. *Social Relationships and Cognitive Development*. Oxford: Clarendon Press; New York: Oxford University Press.

Hirsch, E.D. [Eric Donald]. 1987. *Cultural Literacy: What Every American Needs to Know*. Boston: Houghton Mifflin.

Hoda, M.M. [Mohammad Mansural]. 1973. "Le développement n'est pas une voie à sens unique." *Impact: science et société*, 23:4, pp. 301-314.

Holland, John H., and Keith James Holyoak, Richard E. Nisbett, and P.R. Thagard. 1986. *Induction: Processes of Inference, Learning, and Discovery*. Cambridge: MIT Press.

Holland, James G., and B.F. [Burrhus Frederic] Skinner. 1961. *The Analysis of Behavior: A Program for Self-Instruction*. New York: McGraw-Hill.

Hooper, Simon. 1992a. "The Effects of Peer Interaction on Learning During Computer-Based Mathematics Instruction." *Journal of Educational Research*, 85:3 (January/February), pp. 180-189.

Hooper, Simon. 1992b. "Cooperative Learning and Computer-Based Instruction." *Educational Technology Research & Development*, 40:3, pp. 21-38.

Horton, Myles, and Paulo Freire. 1990. *We Make the Road by Walking: Conversations on Education and Social Change*. Philadelphia: Temple University Press.

Houang, François, and Pierre Leyris. 1979. "Présentation." In Lao-tzu, *La voie et sa vertu*. Paris: Éditions du Seuil, pp. 7-17.

Houssaye, Jean. 1987. *École et vie active: Résister ou s'adapter?* Paris: Delachaux et Niestlé.

Houssaye, Jean. 1988a. *Le triangle pédagogique*. Bern: Peter Lang.

Houssaye, Jean. 1988b. *Pratiques pédagogiques*. Bern: Peter Lang.

Houssaye, Jean. 1992. *Les valeurs à l'école*. Paris: Presses Universitaires de France.

Hutchins, Robert Maynard. 1936. *The Higher Learning in America*. New Haven, CT: Yale University Press.

Hutchins, Robert Maynard. 1943. *Education for Freedom*. Baton Rouge: Louisiana State University Press. Reprint, New York: Grove Press, 1963.

Hutchins, Robert Maynard. 1952. *Some Questions About Education in North America*. Toronto: University of Toronto.

Hutchins, Robert Maynard. 1953. *The Conflict in Education in a Democratic Society*. New York: Harper and Brothers.

Hutchins, Robert Maynard. 1954. *Great Books, The Foundations of a Liberal Education*. New York: Simon and Schuster.

Huxley, Aldous. 1945. *The Perennial Philosophy*. New York: Harper & Brothers.

Icher, François. 1989. *Le campagnonnage*. Paris: Jacques Grancher.

Illich, Ivan. 1971. *Deschooling Society*. New York: Harper & Row.

Inhelder, Bärbel. 1979. "Langage et connaissance dans le cadre constructiviste." In Centre Royaumont Pour une Science de l'Homme. *Théories du langage, théories de l'apprentissage: Le débat entre Jean Piaget et Noam Chomsky*. Paris: Éditions du Seuil, pp. 200-207.

Inhelder, Bärbel, Hermine Sinclair, and Magali Bovet. 1974. *Apprentissage et structure de la connaissance*. Paris: Presses Universitaires de France.

Isen, Alice M. 1984. "Toward Understanding the Role of Affect in Cognition." In Robert S. Wyer, Jr., and Thomas K. Srull, eds., *Handbook of Social Cognition*, Vol. 3. Hillsdale, NJ: Lawrence Erlbaum Associates, pp. 179-236.

James, William. 1890. *The Principles of Psychology*. New York: Henry Holt.

Jantsch, Erich. 1975. *Design for Evolution: Self-Organization and Planning in the Life of Human Systems*. New York: G. Braziller.

Jantsch, Erich, ed. 1981. *The Evolutionary Vision: Toward a Unifying Paradigm of Physical, Biological, and Sociocultural Evolution*. Boulde, COr: Westview Press.

Janvier, Claude. 1992. "Jugement et raisonnement analogique." In Michael Schleifer, ed., *La formation du jugement*. Montreal: Éditions Logiques.

Jodelet, Denise. 1984. "Réflexions sur le traitement de la notion de représentation sociale en psychologie sociale." *Communication Information*, 6:2-3, pp. 15-42.

Johnson, David W., and Roger T. Johnson. 1994. *Learning Together and Alone: Cooperative, Competitive, and Individualistic Learning*. 4th ed. Needham Heights, MA: Allyn and Bacon.

Johnson, David W., and Roger T. Johnson. 1989. *Cooperation and Competition: Theory and Research*. Edina, MN: Interaction Book Co.

Johnson, David W., and Roger T. Johnson. 1990. "Social Skills for Successful Group Work." *Educational Leadership*, 47:4 (January), pp. 29-33.

Johnson, David W., Roger T. Johnson, and Edythe Johnson Holubec. 1988. *Cooperation in the Classroom*. Edina, MN: Interaction Book Co.

Johnson, W. Lewis, and Elliot Soloway. 1987. "PROUST: An Automatic Debugger for Pascal Programs." In Greg Kearsley, ed., *Artificial Intelligence and Instruction: Applications and Methods*. Reading, MA: Addison-Wesley, pp. 49-67.

Joly, Richard. 1981. *Notre démocratie d'ignorants instruits*. Montreal: Leméac.

Joshua, Samuel. 1989. "La perdurance des obstacles épistémologiques: un révélateur de leur nature." In Nadine Bednarz and Catherine Garnier, eds., *Construction des savoirs: Obstacles et conflits*. Montreal: Éditions Agence d'Arc et CIRADE (Centre interdisciplinaire de recherche sur l'apprentissage et le développement en éducation), pp. 110-116.

Joyce, Bruce R., Carlene Murphy, Beverly Showers, and Joseph Murphy. 1989. "School Renewal as Cultural Change." *Educational Leadership*, 47:3 (November), pp. 70-77.

Joyce, Bruce R., Marsha Weil, and Beverly Showers. 1992. *Models of Teaching*. 4th ed. Boston: Allyn and Bacon.

Kaeppelin, Philippe. 1974. *Pratique de l'autogestion éducative: La formation pour adultes*. Paris: Éditions Resma.

Kagan, Spencer. 1990a. "The Structural Approach to Cooperative Learning." *Educational Leadership*, 47:4 (January), pp. 12-15.

Kagan, Spencer. 1990b. *Cooperative Learning Resources for Teachers*. San Juan Capistrano, CA: Resources for Teachers.

Karp, David A., and William C. Yoels. 1987. "The College Classroom: Some Observations on the Meanings of Student Participation." *Sociology and Social Research*, 60, pp. 421-439. Reprinted in Kenneth A. Feldman and Michael B. Paulsen, eds., *Teaching and Learning in the College Classroom*. Needham Heights, MA: Ginn Press, 1994.

Kearsley, Greg, ed. 1987. *Artificial Intelligence and Instruction: Applications and Methods*. Reading, MA: Addison-Wesley.

Kegan, Robert. 1982. *The Evolving Self: Problem and Process in Human Development*. Cambridge: Harvard University Press.

Kennedy, Paul A., and Nancy Feyl Chavkin. 1993. "Interactive Technology Brings Algebra to All." *Educational Leadership*, 50:4 (December/January), pp. 24-28.

Kirkconnell, Watson. 1945. "The Humanities in Our Time." *Canadian School Journal* (April), pp. 140-145, 172.

Kirkwood, Gerri, and Colin Kirkwood. 1989. *Living Adult Education: Freire in Scotland*. Milton-Keynes, England; Philadelphia: Open University Press.

Kirschenbaum, Howard, and Valerie Land Henderson. 1989a. *Carl Rogers: Dialogues*. Boston: Houghton Mifflin.

Kirschenbaum, Howard, and Valerie Land Henderson, eds. 1989b. *The Carl Rogers Reader.* Boston: Houghton Mifflin.

Kneller, George. 1971. *Introduction to the Philosophy of Education*. 2nd ed. New York: John Wiley.

Koerner, James D., ed. 1959. *The Case for Basic Education*. Boston: Little, Brown.

Koestler, Arthur. 1954. *The Invisible Writing*. Vol. 2 of *Arrow in the Blue: An Autobiography*. New York: Macmillan.

Kohlberg, Lawrence. 1981. *Essays on Moral Development*. Vol. 1: *The Philosophy of Moral Development*. New York: Harper & Row.

Köhler, Wolfgang. 1929. *Gestalt Psychology: An Introduction to New Concepts in Psychology*. New York: Horace Liveright.

Kohn, Alfie. 1991. "Group Grading Grubbing Versus Cooperative Learning." *Educational Leadership*, 48:5 (February), pp. 83-87.

Korzybski, Alfred. 1933/1958. *Science and Sanity: An Introduction to Non-Aristotelian Systems and General Semantics*. 4th ed. Lakeville, CT: International Non-Aristotelian Library Publishing Co.

Krathwohl, David R., Benjamin Samuel Bloom, and Bertram B. Masia, eds. 1964. *Taxonomy of Educational Objectives: The Classification of Educational Goals. Handbook II: Affective Domain*. New York: David McKay.

Kreitner, Robert, and Fred Luthans. 1982. "A Social Learning Approach to Behavioral Management: Radical Behaviorists 'Mellowing Out.' " *Organizational Dynamics*, 13:2 (Fall), pp. 47-65.

Krishnamurti, Jiddu. 1969. *Freedom From the Known*. Mary Lutyens, ed. London: Gollancz.

Kuhn, Thomas S. 1962. *The Structure of Scientific Revolutions*. Chicago: University of Chicago Press.

Kurfiss, Joanne Gainen. 1988. *Critical Thinking: Theory, Research, Practice, and Possibilities*. ASHE-ERIC Higher Education Report No. 2. Washington DC: Association for the Study of Higher Education.

Laclau, Ernesto. 1990. *New Reflections on the Revolution of Our Time*. London, New York: Verso Press.

La Garanderie, Antoine de. 1974. *Une pédagogie de l'entr'aide.* Paris: Éditions Ouvrières. Reprint, 1994, Lyon: Chronique Sociale.

La Garanderie, Antoine de. 1980. *Les profils pédagogiques: Discerner les aptitudes scolaires.* Paris: Éditions du Centurion.

La Garanderie, Antoine de. 1982. *Pédagogie des moyens d'apprendre: Les enseignants face aux profils pédagogiques.* Paris: Éditions du Centurion.

La Garanderie, Antoine de. 1984. *Le dialogue pédagogique avec l'élève.* Paris: Éditions du Centurion.

La Garanderie, Antoine de. 1987. *Comprendre et imaginer.* Paris: Éditions du Centurion.

La Garanderie, Antoine de. 1989. *Les profils pédagogiques.* Paris: Éditions du Centurion.

La Garanderie, Antoine de. 1990. *Pour une pédagogie de l'intelligence.* Paris: Éditions du Centurion.

La Garanderie, Antoine de, and Daniel Arquié. 1994. *Réussir, ça s'apprend.* Paris: Bayard Éditions.

Lajoie, Susanne P., Gerard Egan, and Alan M. Lesgold. 1988. "Instructional Strategies for a Coached Practice Environment." In *Proceedings of the Tenth Annual Conference of the Cognitive Society.* New Jersey: Lawrence Erlbaum Associates, pp. 332-339.

Lalande, André. 1962. *Vocabulaire technique et critique de la philosophie.* 9th ed. Paris: Presses Universitaires de France.

Laliberté, Jacques. 1984. *La formation fondamentale: la documentation américaine.* Montreal: CADRE et Ministère de l'Éducation du Québec (Direction générale de l'enseignement collégial).

Laliberté, Jacques. 1988a. "Incidences de la formation fondamentale sur la pédagogie en France et aux États-Unis." *Prospectives,* 24:4 (December), pp. 188-190.

Laliberté, Jacques. 1988b. "Vers l'amélioration de la formation fondamentale en France et aux États-Unis." *Prospectives,* 24:4 (December), pp. 183-188.

Laliberté, Jacques. 1992. "L'école et le développement de la pensée critique." *Vie pédagogique* (Montreal), No. 77 (March), pp. 33-37.

Lampert, Magdalene. 1986. "Knowing, Doing, and Teaching Multiplication." *Cognition and Instruction,* 3:4, pp. 305-342.

Landa, Lev Nakhmanovich. 1974. *Algorithmization in Learning and Instruction. (Algoritmizatsiia v obuchenii.)* Virginia Bennett, trans. Felix F. Kopstein, ed. Englewood Cliffs, NJ: Educational Technology Publications.

Langer, Jonas. 1969. "Disequilibrium as a Source of Development." In Paul H. Mussen, Jonas Langer, and Martin Covington, eds., *Trends and Issues in Developmental Psychology*. New York: Holt, Rinehart and Winston, pp. 22-37.

Langevin, L. 1992. "Stratégies d'apprentissage: Où en est la recherche?" *Vie pédagogique* (Montreal), No. 77, p. 39.

Langley, Pat, Herbert Alexander Simon, G.L. Bradshaw, and Jan M. Zytkow. 1987. *Scientific Discovery: Computational Explorations of the Creative Processes*. Cambridge: MIT Press.

Lao-tzu. 1954. *Tao te ching: The Book of the Way and Its Virtue*. Translated and annotated by J.J.L. [Jan Julius Lodewijk] Duyvendak. 1st ed. London: J. Murray.

Lapassade, Georges. 1967. *Groupes, organisations et institutions*. Paris: Gauthier-Villars.

Lapassade, Georges. 1971a. *L'autogestion pédagogique*. Paris: Gauthier-Villars.

Lapassade, Georges. 1971b. *Le livre fou*. Paris: Éditions de l'Épi.

Lapointe, J. 1990. "Une métavision du processus de la technologie de l'éducation." Unpublished paper, Laval University.

Lapp, Diane, H. Bender, S. Ellenwood, and M. John. 1975. *Teaching and Learning: Philosophical, Psychological, and Curricular Applications*. New York: Macmillan.

Larochelle, Marie, and Jacques Desautels. 1990. "A force de regarder, ça donne toujours la même chose!" Unpublished. Laval University.

Larochelle, Marie, and Jacques Desautels. 1992. *Autour de l'idée de science: Itinéraires cognitifs d'étudiants et d'étudiantes*. Sainte-Foy, PQ: Presses de l'Université Laval; Brussels: De Boeck-Wesmael.

Laszlo, Ervin. 1972. *Introduction to Systems Philosophy: Toward a New Paradigm of Contemporary Thought*. New York: Gordon and Breach.

Lavallée, Micheline. 1992. "La formation fondamentale au primaire et au secondaire." *Vie pédagogique* (Montreal), No. 76 (January-February), pp. 40-41.

Lave, Jean. 1988a. *The Culture of Acquisition and the Practice of Understanding*. IRL Report 88-00087. Palo Alto CA: Institute for Research on Learning.

Lave, Jean. 1991a. "Socially Shared Cognition: Situating Learning in Communities of Practice." In Lauren B. Resnick, John M. Levine, and Stephanie D. Teasley, eds., *Perspectives on Socially Shared Cognition*. Washington DC: American Psychological Association, pp. 63-82.

Lave, Jean. 1991b. *Cognition in Practice: Mind, Mathematics and Culture in Everyday Life.* Cambridge, New York: Cambridge University Press.

Lave, Jean, and Étienne Wenger. 1991. *Situated Learning: Legitimate Peripheral Participation.* Cambridge, New York: Cambridge University Press.

Lawler, Robert W. 1987. "Learning Environments: Now, Then, and Someday." In Robert W. Lawler and Masoud Yazdani, eds., *Artificial Intelligence and Education.* Vol. 1, Norwood, NJ: Ablex Publishing, pp. 1-26.

Lebel, Maurice, ed. 1966. *L'éducation et l'humanisme: Essais.* Sherbrooke, PQ: Éditions Paulines.

Lefebvre-Pinard, Monique. 1985. "La régulation de la communication de l'enfance à l'âge adulte." In Georges Noizet, David Bélanger, and François Bresson, eds., *La communication: Symposium de l'Association de psychologie scientifique de langue française, Montréal 1983.* Paris: Presses Universitaires de France, pp. 107-137.

Lefebvre-Pinard, Monique. 1989. "Le conflit socio-cognitif en psychologie du développement: est-ce toujours un concept heuristiquement valable?" In Nadine Bednarz and Catherine Garnier, eds., *Construction des savoirs: Obstacles et conflits.* Montreal: Éditions Agence d'Arc et CIRADE (Centre interdisciplinaire de recherche sur l'apprentissage et le développement en éducation), pp. 151-155.

Léger, Alain. 1982. *Enseignants du secondaire.* Paris: Presses Universitaires de France.

Legrand, Louis. 1981. *L'école unique: A quelles conditions?* Paris: Éditions du Scarabée.

Legrand, Louis. 1986. *La différenciation pédagogique.* Paris: Éditions du Scarabée.

Le Hénaff, François. 1937. Note from the translator. In Gina Ferrero Lombroso, *L'âme de la femme.* Paris: Payot.

Le Moigne, Jean-Louis. 1977. *La théorie du système général: Théorie de la modélisation.* Paris: Presses Universitaires de France.

Leonard, George B. 1968. *Education and Ecstasy.* New York: Dell.

Leonard, George B. 1978. *The Silent Pulse.* New York: Bantam Books.

Leonard, George B. 1981. *The Transformation: A Guide to the Inevitable Changes in Humankind.* Los Angeles: J.P. Tarcher.

Leonard, George B. 1987. "Playing for Keeps: The Art of Mastery in Sport and Life." *Esquire,* 107:5 (May), pp. 113-116.

Lerbet, Georges. 1980. "L'archéo-pédagogie: Essai d'analyse structuraliste de la genèse du concept pédagogique." *Revue française de pédagogie*, No. 52 (August/September), pp. 4-18.

Leroux, Daniel. 1989. *Risquer le faux pas de la pédagogie institutionnelle.* Montreal: Éditions Agence d'Arc.

Levin, Henry M. 1990. "At-Risk Students in a Yuppie Age." *Educational Policy*, 4:4 (December), pp. 283-295.

Lévy, Bernard-Henri. 1979. *Barbarism With a Human Face.* George Holoch, trans. 1st ed. New York: Harper & Row. trans. of *La barbarie à visage humain.* Paris: B. Grasset, 1977.

Levy-Leblond, Jean-Marc. 1980. "Éloge des théories fausses." In André Giordan, ed., *Approches des processus de construction des concepts en sciences: Journées sur l'éducation scientifique tenues à Chamonix.* Paris: Université de Paris 7, pp. 53-63.

Lewin, Kurt. 1935. *A Dynamic Theory of Personality: Selected Papers.* Donald K. Adams and Karl E. Zener, trs. New York: McGraw-Hill.

Li, Zhongmin. 1992. "Instructional Transaction Shells." *Proceedings of the Seventh Canadian Symposium on Instructional Technology*, May 6-9, Montreal (electronic proceedings).

Li, Zhongmin, and M. David Merrill. 1991. "Transaction Shells: A New Approach to Courseware Authoring." *Journal of Research on Computing in Education*, 23:1 (Fall), pp. 72-86.

Lietz, Hermann. 1910. *Die deutschen Erziehungs-heime: Gedanken und Bilden.* Leipzig: R. Voigtlander.

Lipman, Matthew. 1988. "Critical Thinking — What Can It Be?" *Educational Leadership*, 46:1 (September), pp. 38-43.

Lobrot, Michel. 1972. *La pédagogie institutionnelle.* Paris: Gauthier-Villars.

Lockard, James, Peter D. Abrams, and Wesley A. Many. 1990. *Microcomputers for Educators.* 2nd ed. Glenview IL: Scott, Foresman/Little, Brown.

Lord, Robert G., and Jonathan E. Smith. 1983. "Theoretical, Information Processing, and Situational Factors Affecting Attribution Theory Models of Organizational Behavior." *Academy of Management Review*, 8:1, pp. 50-60.

Lord, Robert G., and Mary C. Kernan. 1987. "Scripts as Determinants of Purposeful Behavior in Organizations." *Academy of Management Review*, 12:2 (April), pp. 265-277.

Lorimier, Jacques de. 1987. *Des stratégies pour la qualité de l'éducation en France: réformes de système et pédagogie différenciée.* Quebec City: Conseil Supérieur de l'Education.

Lourau, René. 1970. *L'analyse institutionnelle et pédagogie.* Paris: Éditions de Minuit.

Lourau, René. 1976. *Sociologue à plein temps.* Paris: Éditions de l'Épi.

Lourau, René. 1979. *Le gai savoir des sociologues.* Paris: Plon.

Lowenthal, Leo. 1961. *Literature, Popular Culture, and Society.* New York: Spectrum Books.

Lupasco, Stéphane. 1969. *La tragédie de l'énergie: Philosophie et sciences du 20e siècle.* Paris: Casterman.

Luthans, Fred. 1989. "Conversation With Edgar H. Schein." *Organizational Dynamics*, 17:4 (Spring), pp. 60-76.

Luthans, Fred, and Nancy C. Morey. 1985. "Refining the Displacement of Culture and the Use of Scenes and Themes in Organizational Studies." *Academy of Management Review*, 10:2 (April), pp. 219-229.

Mack, Robert L., Clayton H. Lewis, and John M. Carroll. 1983. "Learning to Use Word Processors: Problems and Prospects." *ACM Transactions on Office Information Systems* [Association for Computing Machinery], 1:3, pp. 254-271.

Mager, Robert F. 1962. *Preparing Instructional Objectives.* Belmont, CA: Fearon.

Makarenko, Anton Semenovich. 1951. *The Road to Life: An Epic of Education.* (*Pedagogicheskaia poema.*) Ivy Litvinov and Tatiana Litvinov, trans. Moscow: Foreign Languages Publishing House.

Mangieri, John N., ed. 1985. *Excellence in Education.* Fort Worth: Texas Christian University Press.

Manz, Charles C., and Dennis A. Gioia. 1985. "Linking Cognition and Behavior: A Script Processing Interpretation of Vicarious Learning." *Academy of Management Review*, 10:3 (July), pp. 527-539.

Manz, Charles C., and Henry P. Sims. 1981. "Vicarious Learning: The Influence of Modeling on Organizational Behavior." *Academy of Management Review*, 6:1 (January), pp. 105-113.

Marcuse, Herbert. 1964. *One-Dimensional Man.* Boston: Beacon Press.

Marcuse, Herbert. 1968. *Negations: Essays in Critical Theory.* Boston: Beacon Press.

Markle, Susan Meyer. 1978. *Designs for Instructional Designers.* Champaign IL: Stipes Publishing.

Marsolais, Arthur. 1987a. *Le curriculum et les exigences de qualité de l'éducation.* Quebec City: Conseil supérieur de l'éducation.

Marsolais, Arthur. 1987b. *Des stratégies pour la qualité de l'éducation en Grande-Bretagne et aux États-Unis.* Quebec City: Conseil supérieur de l'éducation.

Martinand, Jean-Louis. 1986. *Connaître et transformer la matière: Des objectifs pour l'initiation aux sciences et techniques.* Bern: Peter Lang.

Maslow, Abraham H., ed. 1959. *New Knowledge in Human Values.* New York: Harper & Row.

Maslow, Abraham H. 1970. *The Psychology of Science: A Reconnaissance.* Chicago: H. Regnery.

Maslow, Abraham H. 1976. *The Farthest Reaches of Human Nature.* New York: Penguin Books.

Matthews, Michael R. 1980. *The Marxist Theory of Schooling: A Study of Epistemology and Education.* Atlantic Highlands, NJ: Humanities Press.

McCombs, Barbara L. 1988. "Motivational Skills Training: Combining Metacognitive, Cognitive, and Affective Learning Strategies." In Claire E. Weinstein, Ernest T. Goetz, and Patricia A. Alexander, eds., *Learning and Study Strategies: Issues in Assessment, Instruction, and Evaluation.* New York: Academic Press, pp. 141-169.

McLaren, Peter. 1989. *Life in Schools: An Introduction to Critical Pedagogy in the Foundations of Education.* New York: Longman.

McLaren, Peter. 1993. *Schooling as a Ritual Performance: Towards a Political Economy of Symbols and Gestures.* 2nd ed. New York: Routledge.

McLaren, Peter, and Colin Lankshear, eds. 1994. *Politics of Liberation: Paths From Freire.* New York: Routledge.

McLean, Leslie D. 1988. "Achievement Measures Made Relevant to Pedagogy." *McGill Journal of Education*, 23:3 (Fall), pp. 243-252.

McMahon, Harry, Bill O'Neill, and Donald Cunningham. 1992a. "'Open' Software Design: A Case Study." *Educational Technology*, 32:2 (February), pp. 43-55.

McMahon, Harry, Bill O'Neill, and Donald Cunningham. 1992b. "Bubble Dialogue: A New Tool for Instruction and Assessment." *Educational Technology Research & Development*, 40:2, pp. 59-67.

Meirieu, Philippe. 1991. *Le choix d'éduquer: Éthique et pédagogie.* 2nd ed. Paris: Éditions Sociales Françaises.

Miller, Gary E. 1988. *The Meaning of General Education: The Emergence of a Curriculum Paradigm.* New York: Columbia University, Teachers College Press.

Milner, Jean-Claude. 1984. *De l'école.* Paris: Éditions du Seuil.

Ministère de l'Éducation du Québec. 1971. *L'Opération Départ.* 5 vols. Montreal: Ministère de l'Education.

Ministère de l'Enseignement supérieur et de la Science du Québec. 1993. *Des collèges pour le Québec du XXIe siècle.* Quebec City: Éditeur officiel.

Ministère de l'Enseignement supérieur et de l'Éducation. 1993. *Des collèges pour le Québec du XXIe siècle.* Quebec City: Ministère de l'Enseignement supérieur et de l'Éducation.

Minsky, Marvin Lee. 1967. *Computation: Finite and Infinite Machines.* Englewood Cliffs, NJ: Prentice-Hall.

Mischel, Walter, and Philip K. Peake. 1982. "Beyond Déjà Vu in the Search for Cross-Situational Consistency." *Psychological Review,* 89:6 (November), pp. 730-755.

Moll, Luis C., ed. 1990. *Vygotsky and Education: Instructional Implications and Applications of Sociohistorical Psychology.* Cambridge: Cambridge University Press.

Mongin, Olivier. 1987. "Déclin de la culture et rhétoriques du déclin." *Esprit,* No. 132 (November), pp. 60-74.

Montessori, Maria. 1913. *Pedagogical Anthropology.* (Lectures given at the University of Rome.) Frederic Taber Cooper, trans. New York: F.A. Stokes, 1913.

Morin, Edgar. 1977/1992. *The Nature of Nature.* (*La méthode.* Vol. 1: *La nature de la nature.*) J.L. Roland Belanger, trans. New York: P. Lang.

Morin, Edgar. 1989. "Pour une nouvelle conscience planétaire." *Le monde diplomatique,* No. 427 (October), pp. 18-19.

Morin, Lucien, and Louis Brunet. 1992. *Philosophie de l'éducation: Les sciences de l'éducation.* Sainte-Foy, PQ: Presses de l'Université Laval.

Mugny, Gabriel, ed. 1985. *Psychologie sociale du développement cognitif.* Bern: Peter Lang.

National Commission on Excellence in Education. 1983. *A Nation at Risk: The Imperative for Educational Reform.* Washington DC: U.S. Government Printing Office.

Neill, A.S. [Alexander Sutherland]. 1960. *Summerhill: A Radical Approach to Child Rearing.* New York: Hart.

Neill, A.S. [Alexander Sutherland]. 1966. *Freedom — Not License!* New York: Hart Publishing Co.

Neill, A.S. [Alexander Sutherland]. 1975. *A Dominie's Log* (1915). In *The Dominie Books of A.S. Neill.* New York: Hart Publishing Co.

Newmann, Fred M., and Judith A. Thompson. 1987. *Effects of Cooperative Learning on Achievement in Secondary Schools: A Summary of Research.*

Madison, WI: National Center on Effective Secondary Schools; Wisconsin Center for Education Research, University of Wisconsin-Madison.

Nielsen, Jakob. 1990. *Hypertext and Hypermedia.* Boston: Academic Press.

Not, Louis. 1979. *Les pédagogies de la connaissance.* Toulouse: Privat.

Novak, Joseph D., ed. 1987. *Proceedings of the Second International Seminar"Misconceptions in Science and Mathematics."* Ithaca, NY: Cornell University Press.

Oakes, Jeannie. 1985. *Keeping Track: How Schools Structure Inequality.* Boston: Houghton Mifflin.

Ogilvy, James. 1979. *Many Dimensional Man: Decentralizing Self, Society, and the Sacred.* New York: Harper Colophon Books.

Ornstein, Robert E., and Paul Ehrlich. 1990. *New World, New Mind: Moving Toward Conscious Evolution.* 1st ed. New York: Doubleday.

Ortega y Gasset, José. 1939. *Ideas y creencias y otros ensayos de filosofia.* Buenos Aires, Mexico City: Espasa-Calpe Argentina.

Ortega y Gasset, José. 1960. *The Revolt of the Masses. (La rebelion de las masas.)* trans. anonymous. New York: W.W. Norton & Co.

O'Shea, Tim, and John Self. 1983. *Learning and Teaching With Computers: Artificial Intelligence in Education.* Englewood Cliffs, NJ: Prentice-Hall.

Otto, Rudolf. 1958. *The Idea of the Holy: An Inquiry Into the Non-Rational Factor in the Idea of the Divine and Its Relation to the Rational. (Das Heilige.)* John W. Harvey, trans. New York: Oxford University Press.

Oury, Fernand, and Jacques Pain. 1972. *Chronique de l'école- caserne.* Paris: F. Maspéro.

Oury, Jean. 1973. "Exercices sur la psychothérapie institutionnelle." *Connexions,* No. 7, pp. 17-27.

Ouvry-Vial, Brigitte. 1987. "L'excellence: Une valeur pervertie." *Autrement,* No. 86 (January), pp. 8-11.

Ozmon, Howard A., and Samuel M. Craver. 1986. *Philosophical Foundations of Education.* 3rd ed. Columbus OH: Merrill Publishing.

Pagès, Max. 1965. *L'orientation non-directive en psychothérapie et en psychologie sociale.* Paris: Dunod.

Palincsar, Annemarie Sullivan, and Ann L. Brown. 1984. "Reciprocal Teaching of Comprehension-Fostering and Comprehensive-Monitoring Activities." *Cognition and Instruction,* 1:2, pp. 117-175.

Papert, Seymour. 1980. *Mindstorms: Children, Computers, and Powerful Ideas.* New York: Basic Books.

Papillon, Simon, Romain Rousseau, Yolande Tremblay, and Pierre Potvin. 1987. "Les orientations de la recherche en éducation dans les constituantes de l'Université du Québec." *Revue des sciences de l'éducation*, 13:1, pp. 51-68.

Paquette, Claude. 1976. *Vers une pratique de la pédagogie ouverte.* Laval, PQ: Éditions NHP.

Paquette, Claude. 1985a. *Intervenir avec cohérence.* Montreal: Québec-Amérique.

Paquette, Claude. 1985b. *Pédagogie ouverte et autodéveloppement.* Laval: Éditions NHP.

Paquette, Claude. 1991. *Éducation aux valeurs et projet éducatif.* Vol. 1: *L'approche.* Vol. 2: *Démarches et outils.* Montreal: Québec-Amérique.

Paquette, Gilbert. 1988. "Le développement d'outils intelligents d'apprentissage pour le traitement des connaissances." *Intelligent Tutoring Systems: Actes du colloque ITS-88*, Montreal, June 1-3, pp. 75-81.

Paquette, Gilbert. 1992. "Le logiciel éducatif et de formation dans la société cognitive." *Proceedings of the Seventh Canadian Symposium on Instructional Technology*, May 6-9, Montreal (electronic proceedings).

Paré, André. 1976. "Quelques propos sur l'apprentissage." *Pédagogie Ouverte*, 1:2.

Paré, André. 1977. *Créativité et pédagogie ouverte.* Laval, PQ: Éditions NHP.

Parsons, Talcott. 1954/1964. *Essays in Sociological Theory.* 2nd ed. New York: The Free Press.

Parsons, Talcott, and Edward A. Shills, ed. 1951/1962. *Toward a General Theory of Action.* 2nd ed. New York: Harper & Row.

Paul, Richard W. 1992. *Critical Thinking.* 2nd ed. Santa Rosa, CA: Foundation for Critical Thinking.

Pavlov, Ivan Petrovich. 1955. *Selected Works.* S. Belsky, trans. J. Gibbons, ed. Moscow: Foreign Languages Publishing House.

Pavlov, Ivan Petrovich. 1966. *Essential Works of Pavlov.* Michael Kaplan, ed. New York: Bantam Books.

Pea, Roy D. 1988. "Distributed Intelligence in Learning and Reasoning Processes." Presentation, Tenth Annual Conference of of the Cognitive Science Society, Montreal, Aug. 17-19.

Peretti, André de. 1974. *Pensée et vérité de Carl Rogers.* Toulouse: Privat.

Perrenoud, Philippe. 1984. *La fabrication de l'excellence scolaire, du curriculum aux pratiques d'évaluation: Vers une analyse de la réussite, de l'échec et des inégalités comme réalités construites par le système scolaire.* Geneva: Droz.

Peters, Thomas J., and Nancy Austin. 1985. *A Passion for Excellence: The Leadership Difference*. New York: Random House.

Peters, Thomas J., and Robert H. Waterman, Jr. 1982. *In Search of Excellence: Lessons From America's Best-Run Companies*. New York: Harper & Row.

Petitjean, Armand. 1989. "Pour un contrat de l'homme avec la Nature." *Le Monde diplomatique*, No. 426 (September), p. 19.

Piaget, Jean. 1963. *The Psychology of Intelligence*. (*La psychologie de l'intelligence*.) Malcolm Piercy and D.E. Berlyne, trs. Paterson, NJ: Littlefield, Adams.

Piaget, Jean. 1980. *Adaptation and Intelligence: Organic Selection and Phenocopy*. (*Adaptation vitale et psychologie de l'intelligence: Sélection organique et phénocopie*.) Stewart Eames, trans. Chicago: University of Chicago Press.

Piaget, Jean. 1978. *Behavior and Evolution*. (*Le comportement moteur de l'évolution*.) Donald Nicholson-Smith, trans. New York: Pantheon Books.

Piaget, Jean. 1971. *Biology and Knowledge: An Essay on the Relations Between Organic Regulations and Cognitive Processes*. (*Biologie et connaissance: Essai sur les relations entre les régulations organiques et les processus cognitifs*.) Beatrix Walsh, trans. Chicago: University of Chicago Press.

Piaget, Jean. 1979. "La psychogénèse des connaissances et sa signification épistémologique." In Centre Royaumont Pour une Science de l'Homme, *Théories du langage, théories de l'apprentissage: Le débat entre Jean Piaget et Noam Chomsky*. Paris: Éditions du Seuil, pp. 53-64.

Piaget, Jean, and Bärbel Inhelder. 1969. *The Psychology of the Child*. (*La psychologie de l'enfant*.) Helen Weaver, trans. New York: Basic Books.

Pinar, William F. 1989. "A Reconceptualization of Teacher Education." *Journal of Teacher Education*, 40:1 (January-February), pp. 9-12.

Pirsig, Robert M. 1975. *Zen and the Art of Motorcycle Maintenance: An Inquiry Into Values*. New York: Bantam Books.

Pocztar, Jerry. 1989. *Analyse systémique de l'éducation: Essai*. Paris: Éditions Sociales Françaises.

Poeydomenge, Marie-Louise. 1984. *L'éducation selon Rogers*. Paris: Dunod.

Polak, Fred [Frederik Lodewijk]. 1973. *The Image of the Future*. (*De Toekomst is verleden tijd*). Elise Boulding, trans. and ed. San Francisco: Jossey-Bass.

Pontalis, J.-B. 1985. "La culture défaite." *Le temps de la réflexion*, 6, pp. 34-36. [Response to Alain Finkielkraut, "La défaite de Goethe."]

Power, Edward J. 1982. *Philosophy of Education: Studies in Philosophies, Schooling, and Educational Policies.* Englewood Cliffs, NJ: Prentice-Hall.

Pratte, Richard. 1971. *Contemporary Theories of Education.* Scranton, PA: Intext Educational Publishers.

Prégent, Richard. 1994. *Charting Your Course: How to Prepare to Teach More Effectively.* Marcia Parker, trans. (*La préparation d'un cours*, 1992.) Madison, WI: Magna Publications.

Prégent, Richard. 1993. "La planification de l'enseignement en milieu universitaire." In Rolland Viau, ed., *La planification de l'enseignement: Deux approches? deux visions?* Sherbrooke, PQ: CRP, School of Education, University of Sherbrooke, pp. 39-62.

Prigogine, I. [Ilya]. 1980. *From Being to Becoming: Time and Complexity in the Physical Sciences.* San Francisco: Freeman.

Ravitch, Diane. 1985. *The Schools We Deserve: Reflections on the Educational Crises of Our Times.* New York: Basic Books.

Régnier, Louise, and J.-L. Ricci. 1988a. "Pour une formation courte et efficace des étudiants aux logiciels outils." Presentation, Colloque de l'Association Internationale de Pédagogie Universitaire. University of Montreal, May.

Régnier, Louise, and J.-L. Ricci. 1988b. "How to Train Engineering Students to Use Application Software." Presentation, Canadian Conference of Engineering Education. University of Manitoba, May.

Reboul, Olivier. 1971. *La philosophie de l'éducation.* Paris: Presses Universitaires de France.

Reddie, Cecil. 1900. *Abbotsholme, 1889-1899, or Ten Years' Work in an Educational Laboratory.* London: G. Allen.

Resnick, Lauren B. 1987. "Learning in School and Out." *Educational Researcher*, 16:9 (December), pp. 13-20.

Resnick, Lauren B., John M. Levine, and Stephanie D. Teasley, eds. 1991. *Perspectives on Socially Shared Cognition.* Washington, DC: American Psychological Association.

Rest, James R., Elliot Turiel, and Lawrence Kohlberg. 1969. "Level of Moral Development as a Determinant of Preference and Comprehension of Moral Judgments Made by Others." *Journal of Personality*, 37:11, pp. 738-748.

Robert, F. 1960. *Culture générale et enseignement européen.* Actes du Congrès de l'Association des Universitaires d'Europe, Trieste, 1955. Paris: Librairie générale de droit et de jurisprudence.

Robert, J.M. 1985. "Learning by Exploration." *IFAC Man-Machine Systems* [International Federation of Automatic Control], pp. 189-193.

Robert, J.M. 1989. "Learning a Computer System by Unassisted Exploration, An Example: the Macintosh." In F. [Friedhart] Klix, Norbert A. Streitz, Yvonne Waern, and H. [Hartmut] Wandke, eds. *MACINTER II — Man-Computer Interaction Research.* Amsterdam: Elsevier, pp. 461-479.

Robin, Jacques. 1989a. *Changer d'ère.* Paris: Éditions du Seuil.

Robin, Jacques. 1989b. "Le choix écologique." *Le Monde diplomatique*, No. 424 (July), pp. 1, 16-17.

Rogers, Carl R. 1942. *Counseling and Psychotherapy: Newer Concepts in Practice.* Boston: Houghton Mifflin.

Rogers, Carl R. 1951. *Client-Centered Therapy: Its Current Practice, Implications, and Theory.* Boston: Houghton Mifflin.

Rogers, Carl R. 1961. *On Becoming a Person: A Therapist's View of Psychotherapy.* Boston: Houghton Mifflin.

Rogers, Carl R. 1969. *Freedom to Learn: A View of What Education Might Become.* Columbus, OH: C.E. Merrill Publishing.

Rogers, Carl R. 1970. *Carl Rogers on Encounter Groups.* New York: Harper & Row.

Rogoff, Barbara, and Jean Lave, eds. 1984. *Everyday Cognition: Its Development in Social Context.* Cambridge: Harvard University Press.

Roman, Leslie G., Linda K. Christian-Smith, and Elizabeth Ellsworth, eds. 1988. *Becoming Feminine: The Politics of Popular Culture.* New York: Falmer Press.

Romiszowski, A.J. [Alexander Joseph]. 1986. *Developing Auto-Instructional Materials: From Programmed Texts to CAL and Interactive Video.* London: Kogan Page; New York: Nichols Publishing.

Rosaldo, Michelle Zimbalist. 1984. "Toward an Anthropology of Self and Feeling." In Richard A. Shweder and Robert A. Le Vine, eds. *Culture Theory: Essays on Mind, Self, and Emotion.* Cambridge, New York: Cambridge University Press, pp. 137-158.

Rosch, Eleanor, and Barbara B. Lloyd. 1978. *Cognition and Categorization.* Hillsdale, NJ: Lawrence Erlbaum Associates.

Rosenblueth, Arturo, Norbert Wiener, and Julian Bigelow. 1943. "Behavior, Purpose and Teleology." *Philosophy of Science*, 10:1 (January), pp. 18-24.

Rosnay, Joël de. 1979. *The Macroscope: A New World Scientific Vision.* (*Le Macroscope: Vers une vision globale*, 1975.) Robert Edwards, trans. New York: Harper and Row.

Rosnay, Joël de. 1983. *Les chemins de la vie.* Paris: Éditions du Seuil.

Rousseau, Jean-Jacques. 1974. *Emile.* (*Émile, ou l'éducation.*) Barbara Foxley, trans. New York: E.P. Dutton.

Rousseau, Jean-Jacques. 1950. *The Social Contract, and Discourses.* (*Du contrat social and Discours.*) G.D.H. Cole, trans. New York: E.P. Dutton.

Roux, Jean-Paul, Michel Gilly, Brigitte Rohrer, and Sophie Verlynde. 1984. "Aide apportée par le marquage social dans use procédure de résolution chez des enfants de 12-13 ans: Données et réflexions sur les mécanismes." *Bulletin de psychologie,* Vol. 38 (November-December), pp. 145-155.

Rowan, John. 1976. *Ordinary Ecstasy: Humanistic Psychology in Action.* London: Routledge & Kegan Paul.

Rowell, J.A., and C.J. Dawson. 1983. "Laboratory Counterexamples and the Growth of Understanding in Science." *European Journal of Science Education,* 5:2, pp. 203-215.

Rudhyar, Dane. 1977. *The Planetarization of Consciousness.* New York: ASI Publishers.

Rumelhard, Guy. 1986. *La génétique et ses représentations dans l'enseignement.* Bern: Peter Lang.

Ryan, Lucie Léveillé. 1990. "La mutualité et la réciprocité du rapport éducateur-éduqués dans une approche écologique et humaniste en éducation créatrice." In Association Internationale de Pédagogie Expérimentale de Langue Française, *Les modèles en éducation.* Montreal: Éditions Noir sur Blanc, pp. 328-334.

Sabouret, Jean-François. 1985. *L'Empire du concours: Lycéens et enseignants au Japon.* Paris: Éditions Autrement.

Saint-Arnaud, Yves. 1970. *Essai sur les fondements psychologiques de la communauté.* Montreal: Éditions du Centre interdisciplinaire de Montréal.

Sandberg, Jacobin, Yvonne Barnard, and Paul Kamsteeg. 1992. "Student Modelling: A Broader Perspective." *Proceedings of the Seventh Canadian Symposium on Instructional Technology,* May 6-9, Montreal (electronic proceedings).

Sandberg, Jacobin, and Bob Wielinga. 1992. "Situated Cognition: A Paradigm Shift?" *Journal of Artificial Intelligence in Education,* 3, pp. 129-138.

Sapon-Shevin, Mara, and Schniedewind, Nancy. 1991. "Cooperative Learning as Empowering Pedagogy." In Christine E. Sleeter, ed., *Empowerment Through Multicultural Education.* Albany, NY: State University of New York Press, pp. 159-178.

Schaffer, Carrie, and Sidney Blatt. 1990. "Interpersonal Relationship and the Experience of Perceived Efficacy." In Robert J. Sternberg and John Kolligian, Jr., eds., *Competence Considered*. New Haven CT: Yale University Press, pp. 229-246.

Scherer, Marge. 1993. "On Savage Inequalities: A Conversation With Jonathan Kozol." *Educational Leadership*, 50:4 (December/January), pp. 4-9.

Schmalhofer, Franz, and Otto Kühn. 1988. "Acquiring Computer Skills by Exploration Versus Demonstration." In *Proceedings of the Tenth Annual Conference of the Cognitive Science Society. Hillsdale, NJ: Lawrence Erlbaum Associates*, pp. 724-730.

Schmeck, Ronald R., ed. 1988. *Learning Strategies and Learning Styles*. New York: Plenum.

Schniedewind, Nancy, and Ellen Davidson. 1983. *Open Minds to Equality: A Sourcebook of Learning Activities to Promote Race, Sex, Class, and Age Equity*. Englewood Cliffs, NJ: Prentice-Hall.

Schunk, Dale H. 1989. "Self-Efficacy and Cognitive Skill Learning." In Carole Ames and Russell Ames, eds., *Research on Motivation in Education*, vol. 3: *Goals and Cognitions*. New York: Academic Press, pp. 13-44.

Science Council of Canada. 1984. *Science Education in Canadian Schools*. Ottawa: Science Council of Canada.

Science Council of Canada. 1984. *Science for Every Student: Educating Canadians for Tomorrow's World*. Ottawa: Science Council of Canada.

Scriven, Michael, and Richard W. Paul. 1993. "Defining Critical Thinking." Handout distributed at a regional workshop by the National Council for Excellence in Critical Thinking. Boston, January.

Self, John. 1988. "Student Models: What Use Are They?" In Paolo Ercoli and Robert Lewis, eds., *Artificial Intelligence Tools in Education: Proceedings of the IFIP TC3 Working Conference, Frascati, Italy, May 26-28, 1987*. Amsterdam, New York: Elsevier Science Pub, pp. 73-87.

Seymour, Jim. 1993. "Making Multimedia Work." *PC Magazine*, 12:2 (Jan. 26), pp. 99-100.

Sharan, Shlomo, ed. 1990. *Cooperative Learning: Theory and Research*. New York: Praeger.

Sharan, Yael, and Shlomo Sharan. 1990. "Group Investigation Expands Coperative Learning." *Educational Leadership*, 47:4 (January), pp. 17-21.

Sharan, Shlomo, Peter Kussell, Rachel Hertz-Lazarowitz, Yael Bejarano, Shulamit Raviv, and Yael Sharan. 1985. "Cooperative Learning Effects on Ethnic Relations and Achievement in Israeli Junior-High-School Classrooms." In Robert E. Slavin, Shlomo Sharan, Spencer Kagan, Rachel Hertz-Lazarowitz, Clark Webb, and Richard Schmuck, eds., *Learning to Cooperate, Cooperating to Learn*. New York: Plenum Press, pp. 313-344.

Shor, Ira. 1980. *Critical Teaching and Everyday Life*. Boston: South End Press.

Shor, Ira. 1992a. *Culture Wars: Schools and Society in the Conservative Restoration, 1969-1991*. Chicago: University of Chicago Press.

Shor, Ira. 1992b. *Empowering Education: Critical Teaching for Social Change*. Chicago: University of Chicago Press.

Shor, Ira, ed. 1987. *Freire for the Classroom: A Sourcebook for Liberatory Teaching*. Portsmouth, NH: Boynton/Cook.

Shor, Ira, and Paulo Freire. 1987. *A Pedagogy for Liberation: Dialogues on Transforming Education*. South Hadley, MA: Bergin and Garvey.

Shulman, Lee S., and Evan R. Keislar, eds. 1966. *Learning by Discovery: A Critical Appraisal*. Chicago: Rand McNally.

Sierpinska, Anna. 1989. "Sur un programme de recherche lié à la notion d'obstacle épistémologique." In Nadine Bednarz and Catherine Garnier, eds., *Construction des savoirs: Obstacles et conflits*. Montreal: Éditions Agence d'Arc et CIRADE (Centre interdisciplinaire de recherche sur l'apprentissage et le développement en éducation), pp. 130-147.

Sigel, Irving E. 1969. "The Piagetian System and the World of Education." In David Elkind and John H. Flavell, eds., *Studies in Cognitive Development: Essays in Honor of Jean Piaget*. New York: Oxford University Press, pp. 465-489.

Simon, Roger I. 1992. *Teaching Against the Grain: Texts for a Pedagogy of Possibility*. South Hadley, MA: Bergin and Garvey.

Sims, Henry P., Jr., and Dennis A. Gioia, et al. 1986. *The Thinking Organization*. San Francisco: Jossey-Bass.

Sims, Henry P., Jr., and Peter Lorenzi. 1992. *The New Leadership Paradigm: Social Learning and Cognition in Organizations*. Newbury Park, CA: Sage Publications.

Sims, Henry P., Jr., and Charles C. Manz. 1981/1982. "Social Learning Theory: The Role of Modeling in the Exercise of Leadership." *Journal of Organizational Behavior Management*, 3:4, pp. 55-63.

Sirotnik, Kenneth A. 1989. "What Goes On in Classrooms? Is This the Way We Want It?" In Landon E. Beyer and Michael W. Apple, eds.

The Curriculum: Problems, Politics, and Possibilities. Albany, NY: State University of New York Press, pp. 56-70.

Siviter, Douglas, and Keith Brown. 1992. "Hypercourseware for Users of Distributed Computer Systems." *Proceedings of the Seventh Canadian Symposium on Instructional Technology*, May 6-9, Montreal (electronic proceedings).

Skidelsky, Robert. 1969. *English Progressive Schools*. London: Penguin Books.

Skinner, B.F. [Burrhus Frederic]. 1954. "The Science of Learning and the Art of Teaching." *Harvard Educational Review*, 24 (Spring), pp. 86-97.

Skinner, B.F. [Burrhus Frederic]. 1968. *The Technology of Teaching*. New York: Appleton-Century-Crofts.

Slavin, Robert E. 1987. "Cooperative Learning and the Cooperative School." *Educational Leadership*, 45:3 (November), pp. 7-13.

Slavin, Robert E. 1990a. "Here to Stay — or Gone Tomorrow?" *Educational Leadership*, 47:4 (January), p. 3.

Slavin, Robert E. 1990b. "Research on Cooperative Learning: Consensus and Controversy." *Educational Leadership*, 47:4 (January), pp. 52-54.

Slavin, Robert E. 1991. "Synthesis of Research on Cooperative Learning." *Educational Leadership*, 48:5 (February), pp. 72-82.

Slavin, Robert E. 1991. "Are Cooperative Learning and 'Untracking' Harmful to the Gifted?" *Educational Leadership*, 48:6 (March), pp. 68-71.

Slavin, Robert E., Nancy L. Karweit, and Barbara A. Wasik. 1993a. "Preventing Early School Failure: What Works?" *Educational Leadership*, 50:4 (December/January), pp. 10-18.

Slavin, Robert E., Nancy L. Karweit, and Barbara A. Wasik, eds. 1993b. *Preventing Early School Failure: Research on Effective Strategies: Research, Policy, and Practice*. Boston: Allyn and Bacon.

Slavin, Robert E., Shlomo Sharan, Spencer Kagan, Rachel Hertz-Lazarowitz, Clark Webb, and Richard Schmuck, eds. 1985. *Learning to Cooperate, Cooperating to Learn*. New York: Plenum Press.

Sleeter, Christine E., ed. 1991. *Empowerment Through Multicultural Education*. Albany, NY: State University of New York Press.

Smullyan, Raymond M. 1977. *The Tao Is Silent*. New York: Harper & Row.

Snyders, Georges. 1971. *Pédagogie progressiste*. Paris: Presses Universitaires de France.

Snyders, Georges. 1973. *Où vont les pédagogies non-directives?* Paris: Presses Universitaires de France.

Solomon, Cynthia. 1987. *Computer Environments for Children: A reflection on Theories of Learning and Education.* Cambridge: MIT Press.

Solorzano, Daniel G. 1989. "Teaching and Social Change: Reflections on a Freirean Approach in a College Classroom." *Teaching Sociology,* 17 (April), pp. 218-225.

Spady, William G., and Gary Marx. 1984. *Excellence in Our Schools: Making It Happen.* Arlington, VA: American Association of School Administrators.

Stanley, William B. 1992. *Curriculum for Utopia: Social Reconstructionism and Critical Pedagogy in the Postmodern Era.* Albany, NY: State University of New York Press.

Sternberg, Robert J., and John Kolligian, Jr., eds. 1990. *Competence Considered.* New Haven: Yale University Press.

Stolovitch, Harold D., and Gabriel La Rocque. 1983. *Introduction à la technologie de l'instruction.* St-Jean-sur-Richelieu, PQ: Éditions Préfontaine.

Stone, Jeanne. 1989. *Cooperative Learning and Language Arts: A Multi-Structural Approach.* San Juan Capistrano, CA: Resources for Teachers.

Strain, John Paul. 1971. *Modern Philosophies of Education.* New York: Random House.

Strain, John Paul. 1975. "Idealism: A Clarification of an Educational Philosophy." *Educational Theory,* 25:3, pp. 263-271.

Strike, Kenneth A., and George J. Posner. 1982. "Conceptual Change and Science Teaching." *European Journal of Science Education,* 4:3, pp. 231-240.

Suchman, Lucille Alice. 1987. *Plans and Situated Actions: The Problem of Human-Machine Communication.* Cambridge, New York: Cambridge University Press.

Sullivan, Edmund V. 1967. *Piaget and the School Curriculum: A Critical Appraisal.* Ontario Institute for Studies in Education, Bulletin No. 2. Toronto: OISE.

Suppes, Patrick. 1988. "The Future of Intelligent Tutoring Systems: Problems and Potential." *Intelligent Tutoring Systems: Actes du colloque ITS-88,* Montreal, June 1-3, pp. 24-32.

Suzuki, Daisetz Teitaro. 1957. *Mysticism: Christian and Buddhist.* New York: Harper & Row.

Suzuki, Daisetz Teitaro. 1959. "Human Values in Zen." In Abraham H. Maslow, ed. *New Knowledge in Human Values.* New York: Harper & Row, pp. 94-106.

Suzuki, Daisetz Teitaro. 1983. *The Zen Doctrine of No-Mind: The Significance of the Sutra of Hui-neng (Wei-Lang).* H. Benoit, trans. Christmas Humphreys, ed. London: Rider.

Tardif, Jacques. 1992. *Pour un enseignement stratégique: L'apport de la psychologie cognitive.* Montreal: Éditions Logiques.

Taurisson, Alain. 1988. *Les gestes de la réussite en mathématiques à l'élémentaire.* Montreal: Éditions Agence d'Arc.

Thelen, Herbert Arnold. 1960. *Education and the Human Quest.* New York: Harper & Row.

Thomas, R. Murray, ed. 1990. *The Encyclopedia of Human Development and Education: Theory, Research, and Studies.* New York, Oxford: Pergamon Press.

Thomas, Russell. 1992. "The Humanities." In *The Idea and Practice of General Education: An Account of the College of the University of Chicago, by Present and Former Members of the Faculty.* Reprint of 1950 edition. Chicago: University of Chicago Press, pp. 103-122.

Thorndike, Edward L. 1913. *Educational Psychology.* New York: Teachers College Press, Columbia University.

Tickton, Sidney G., ed. 1971. *To Improve Learning: An Evaluation of Instructional Technology.* New York: R.R. Bowker.

Tiberghien, Andrée. 1989. "Difficulté dans l'apprentissage de la physique: la structuration du monde matériel en physique et dans la vie quotidienne." In Nadine Bednarz and Catherine Garnier, eds., *Construction des savoirs: Obstacles et conflits.* Montreal: Éditions Agence d'Arc et CIRADE (Centre interdisciplinaire de recherche sur l'apprentissage et le développement en éducation), pp. 228-239.

Toffler, Alvin. 1970. *Future Shock.* New York: Random House.

Toffler, Alvin, ed. 1974. *Learning for Tomorrow: The Role of the Future in Education.* New York: Random House.

Toffler, Alvin. 1980. *The Third Wave.* New York: Morrow.

Toffler, Alvin. 1983. *Previews and Promises: An Interview With the Author of* Future Shock *and* The Third Wave. New York: W. Morrow.

Toffler, Alvin. 1990. *Powershift: Knowledge, Wealth, and Violence in the 21st Century.* New York: Bantam Books.

Trentowski, Bronislaw Ferdynand. 1843. *Stosunek Filozofii do Cybernetyki.* (The Relation Between Philosophy and Cybernetics.) Poznan: J.K. Zupanski.

Turiel, Elliot. 1969. "Developmental Processes in the Child's Moral Thinking." In Paul H. Mussen, Jonas Langer, and Martin Covington, eds., *Trends and Issues in Developmental Psychology*. New York: Holt, Rinehart and Winston, pp. 92-133.

Turner, Victor Witter. 1982. *From Ritual to Theater: The Human Seriousness of Play*. New York: Performing Arts Journal Publications.

UNESCO. 1981. *A Systems Approach to Teaching and Learning Procedures: A Guide for Educators*. Paris: UNESCO.

Vallance, Elizabeth. 1986. "A Second Look at *Conflicting Conceptions of Curriculum*." *Theory Into Practice*, 25:1 (Winter), pp. 24-30.

Vallet, Odon. 1988. *Culture générale*. Paris: Masson.

Van Doren, Mark. 1959. *Liberal Education*. Boston: Beacon Press.

Varela, Francisco, Humberto R. Maturana, and R. Uribe. 1974. "Autopoiesis: The Organization of Living Systems, Its Characterization and a Model." *Bio Systems*, Vol. 5, p. 187.

Varela, Francisco J., Evan Thompson, and Eleanor Rosch. 1991. *The Embodied Mind: Cognitive Science and Human Experience*. Cambridge: MIT Press.

Vasquez, Aïda, and Fernand Oury. 1966. *Vers une pédagogie institutionnelle?* Paris: F. Maspéro.

Vasquez, Aïda, and Fernand Oury. 1971. *De la classe coopérative à la pédagogie institutionnelle*. Paris: F. Maspéro.

Vecchi, Girard de, and André Giordan. 1989. *L'enseignement scientifique: Comment faire pour que"ça marche"?* Nice: Z'Éditions.

Viau, Rolland, ed. 1993. *La planification de l'enseignement: Deux approches? deux visions?* Sherbrooke, PQ: CRP, School of Education, University of Sherbrooke.

Viau, Rolland. 1994. *La motivation en contexte scolaire*. Montreal: Le Renouveau Pédagogique.

Voss, James F. 1989. "Problem Solving and the Educational Process." In Alan M. Lesgold and Robert Glaser, eds., *Foundations for a Psychology of Education*. Hillsdale, NJ: Lawrence Erlbaum Associates, pp. 251-295.

Viennot, Laurence. 1989a. "Obstacle épistémologique et raisonnements en physique: tendance au contournement des conflits chez les enseignants." In Nadine Bednarz and Catherine Garnier, eds., *Construction des savoirs: Obstacles et conflits*. Montreal: Éditions Agence d'Arc et CIRADE (Centre interdisciplinaire de recherche sur l'apprentissage et le développement en éducation), pp. 117-129.

Viennot, Laurence. 1989b. "Tendance à la réduction fonctionnelle: obstacle au savoir scientifique et objet de consensus." In Nadine Bednarz and Catherine Garnier, eds., *Construction des savoirs: Obstacles et conflits*. Montreal: Éditions Agence d'Arc et CIRADE (Centre interdisciplinaire de recherche sur l'apprentissage et le développement en éducation), pp. 84-92.

Vygotsky, L.S. [Lev Semenovich]. 1934/1978. *Mind in Society: The Development of Higher Psychological Processes*. Michael Cole *et al.*, eds. Cambridge: Harvard University Press.

Vygotsky, L.S. [Lev Semenovich]. 1934/1986. *Thought and Language*. (*Myshlenie i rech'*.) Eugenia Hanfmann and Gertrude Vakar, trs. and eds. Alex Kozulin, ed. Cambridge: MIT Press.

Wager, Walter W., J. Applefield, R. Earl, and J. Dempsey. 1990. *A Learner's Guide to Accompany Principles of Instructional Design*. New York: Holt, Rinehart and Winston.

Walker, John E. 1982. "Who Gives Public Schools A-B Ratings?" *The Clearing House*, 56:3, pp. 136-140.

Walsh, James, ed. 1981. *Cloud of Unknowing*. New York: Paulist Press, 1981.

Ward, F. Champion, ed. *The Idea and Practice of General Education: An Account of the College of the University of Chicago, by Present and Former Members of the Faculty*. 1950. Reprint, 1992. Chicago: University of Chicago Press.

Watts, Alan. 1957. *The Way of Zen*. New York: Vintage Books.

Watts, Alan. 1940. *The Meaning of Happiness: The Quest for Freedom of the Spirit in Modern Psychology and the Wisdom of the East*. New York: Harper & Row.

Weil, Marsha, Bruce R. Joyce, and Bridget Kluwin. 1978. *Personal Models of Teaching*. Englewood Cliffs, NJ: Prentice-Hall.

Wertsch, James V. 1985a. *Vygotsky and the Social Formation of Mind*. Cambridge, New York: Cambridge University Press.

Wertsch, James V., ed. 1985b. *Culture, Communication, and Cognition: Vygotskian Perspectives*. Cambridge, New York: Cambridge University Press.

Wexler, Philip. 1990. *Social Analysis of Education: After the New Sociology*. London, New York: Routledge and Kegan Paul.

Whitaker, Elizabeth T., and Ronald D. Bonnell. 1992. "A Blackboard Model for Adaptive and Self-Improving Intelligent Tutoring Systems." *Journal of Artificial Intelligence in Education*, 3:1, pp. 3-27.

Wiener, Norbert. 1948. *Cybernetics, or Control and Communication in the Animal and the Machine*. New York: John Wiley.

Wilder, Raymond L. 1981. *Mathematics as a Cultural System*. Oxford, New York: Pergamon Press.

Wong, Martin R., and John D. Raulerson. 1975. *A Guide to Systematic Instructional Design*. Englewood Cliffs, NJ: Educational Technology Publications.

Woodhead, Neville. 1991. *Hypertext and Hypermedia: Theory and Applications*. Wokingham, UK; Reading MA: Addison-Wesley.

Wyer, Robert S., Jr., and Donald E. Carlston. 1979. *Social Cognition, Inference, and Attribution*. Hillsdale, NJ: Lawrence Erlbaum Associates.

Wyer, Robert S., Jr., and Thomas K. Srull, eds. 1984. *Handbook of Social Cognition*. Vol. 3. Hillsdale, NJ: Lawrence Erlbaum Associates.

Young, Michael F.D., ed. 1971. *Knowledge and Control: New Directions for the Sociology of Education*. London: Collier Macmillan.

Young, Michael F.D. 1991. "Programmes d'études et démocratie: Quelques leçons à tirer de l'expérience de la 'nouvelle sociologie de l'éducation.' " *Sociologie et Sociétés*, 23:1 (Spring), pp. 189-200.

Yovits, Marshall C., George T. Jacobi, and Gordon D. Goldstein. 1962. *Self-Organizing Systems*. Washington DC: Spartan Books.

Yovits, Marshall C., and Scott Cameron, eds. 1960. *Self-Organizing Systems*. Proceedings of the Interdisciplinary Conference on Self-Organizing Systems (Chicago, 1959).

Zeleny, Milan, ed. 1980. "Autopoiesis: A Paradigm Lost?" In Milan Zeleny, *Autopoiesis, Dissipative Structures, and Spontaneous Social Orders*. Boulder, CO: Westview Press, pp. 3-43.

Zimmerman, Barry J. 1990. "Self-Regulated Learning and Academic Achievement: An Overview." *Educational Psychologist*, 25:1 (Winter), pp. 3-17.

INDEX

A

academic theories (aka traditionalist, generalist, classic) 5.1, ch. 7, Chart
academism 7.3.1
Acker, Sandra 6.3.3
Ada, Alma Flor 6.3.2
Ada and Olave 6.3.2
Adler, Alfred 2.3.1, Chart
Adler, Mortimer 7.1.1, 7.2, 7.3.1, 7.3.2, Chart
Adorno, Theodor W. 6.3.3
allosteric model 3.2.4
Althusser, Louis 6.3.3
Alvès, Pojé-Crétien, and Maous-Chassagny 5.4.1
Analyse systémique de l'éducation (Pocztar) 4.3.1
Angers, Pierre 2.1.2, 2.4.2, 7.4.2, Chart
Ansbacher and Ansbacher 2.3.1
anthropology 6.3.3, Chart
Apple, Michael 6.3.3, 8.2, Chart
Apprendre à vivre et à penser (Guitton) 7.3.1
Ardoino, Jacques Introduction, 2.6, 6.2, 6.2.2
Aristotelianism 7.3.1
Aristotle 7.3.1
Aronowitz, Stanley 6.3.3, 8.2, Chart
Aronowitz and Giroux 6.3.3, 8.2
Arshad and Ward 4.4.3
artificial intelligence Chart
Aspen Institute for Humanistic Studies 7.3.2
Audio-Visual Instruction (journal) 4.3.1
Augusteijn, Broome, Kolbe, and Ewell 4.4.2
Augustine, Gruber, and Hanson 5.6.1, 5.6.2
Ausubel, David Paul 3.2.2
Ausubel, Novak, and Hanesian 4.5
authentic activities 5.5.3
Avanzini, Guy Introduction

B

Bachelard, Gaston 3.2.1, 3.2.2, 3.3.1, 3.4, Matrix

Back to Basics 7.5
Banathy, Bela H. 4.3.2
Bandura, Albert 5.1, 5.2.1, 5.2.2, 5.2.3, 5.7, 6.3.1, Matrix
Banks, James 6.3.2
Barbier, René 6.2, 6.2.4
Barel, Yves 4.3.1
Barker, Philip 4.4.2
basics 7.5, Matrix
Baudelot and Establet 7.1.1
Baudrillard, Jean 6.3.3
Baveja, Showers, and Joyce 5.6.3
Bednarz, Nadine 3.2.1, Matrix
Bednarz and Garnier 5.3.1, 5.3.2
behaviorism 1.4.1, 4.4.1, 5.2.1, Matrix
Bennett, Kathleen 5.6.1
Bergeron, Anne 4.4.2
Bergeron and Bordier 4.4.2
Bergson, Henri 1.3
Bertalanffy, Ludwig von 4.3.1, Matrix
Bertrand, Michel 5.6.1
Bertrand, Yves 5.2.2
Bertrand and Guillemet 7.4.2
Bertrand and Valois 1.2, 1.3, 6.5, 8.2
Beyer, Landon E. 6.3.3
Beyou, Claire 4.4.2, 4.4.3
Bigelow, Julian 4.4.1
Blaye, Agnès 5.3.1
Bloom, Allan 7.1.1, 7.2, 7.3.1, 7.4.2, Matrix
Bloom *et al.* 4.4.1
Border Crossings (Giroux) 6.3.3
Bordier, Jacques 3.2.1, Matrix
Bourdieu, Pierre Matrix
Bourdieu and Passeron 6.2.4, 6.3.3
Bowers, C.A. 6.1
Bowles and Gintis 6.3.3
Bradford, Gibb, and Benne 2.1.1
Brickman, William W. 7.3.2
Briggs, Leslie J. 4.3.2, Matrix
Brodinsky, Ben 7.5
Broudy, Harry S. 7.1.1
Brousseau, Guy 3.2.1, 3.4
Brown, John Seely 4.5, 5.5.1, Matrix
Brown, Collins, and Duguid 4.4.2, 5.5.1, 5.5.2, 5.5.3, 6.3.2

Bruner, Jerome S. 5.4.1, 5.4.3, Matrix
Bubbles project 4.4.3
Bucke, Richard Maurice 1.2, 1.4.1, Matrix
Buddhism Matrix
Budé, Guillaume 7.3.1
Burroughs, William S. 1.2

C

Cantor, Nancy 5.2.1
Capra, Fritjof Matrix
Carey, Lou Matrix
Carroll, John M. 4.5, Matrix
Carroll and Aaronson 4.5
Carroll and Kaye 4.5
Carroll, Mack, Lewis, Grischkowsky, and
    Robertson 4.5
Carroll and McKendree 4.5
Carugati and Mugny 5.3.1
Center for Critical Thinking and Moral
    Critique 7.4.2, 7.4.3
Chaiklin, Seth 5.5.1
Charcot, Jean Martin 3.3.1
Matrixing Your Course (Prégent) 4.3.1
Cherryholmes, Cleo H. 6.3.3
Clancey, William 4.4.2, 5.5.1, 5.5.2, 5.5.3,
    Matrix
classical literature Matrix
classical realism 7.3.1, Matrix
cognitive apprentice 5.5.3
cognitive conflict 3.2.4, 3.4
cognitive disequilibrium 3.4, 5.3.2
cognitive development 5.3.1, 5.3.2, Matrix
cognitive nature 3.4
cognitive psychology Matrix
Collins, Allan 5.5.1, Matrix
Commission des Écoles Catholiques de
    Montréal 7.4.2
Commission on Instructional Technology
    4.1
communication theory Matrix
competency training Matrix
computer-assisted instruction 4.4.1,
    Matrix
conceptual change (models) 3.2.5
conceptual complexification 3.2.5
conflict, cognitive 3.2.4, 3.4
conflict, social interactional 5.3.2
conscientization 6.1
conscientization pedagogies 6.3, 6.3.1,
    6.3.2
Conseil supérieur de l'éducation
    (Quebec) 2.4.1, 7.1.1, 7.4.2, 7.4.3

constructivist cognitive theories 4.4.1
constructivist epistemology Matrix
constructivism 3.1, 3.2.1, 5.1, 5.3.1, 5.3.2
Cooper, James Matrix
Cooper *et al.* 5.6.2, 5.6.3
Cooperative Learning (journal) 5.6.1
cooperative learning 5.6.1, Matrix
cooperative teaching 5.6.1, Matrix
cosmic consciousness 1.2, 1.4.1, Matrix
Cox, Martha G. 5.2.1
critical teaching Matrix
critical theory Matrix
critical thinking 6.3.3, 7.4.2, Matrix
critical pedagogy 6.3.3
Cuban, Larry 6.3.3
cultural agent 6.3.3
cultural metaphor 6.3.3
cultural studies 6.3.3
culture Matrix
culture, industry of 6.3.3
culture, mass 6.3.3
culture, organizational 6.2.4
culture, technocratic 6.3.3
Culture générale et enseignement européen
    (Robert) 7.3.1
Cummins, Jim 6.3.2
Cunningham, Donald J. 4.4.2, 4.4.3, Matrix
cybernetics 4.3.1, 4.4.1, 4.6, Matrix
*Cybernetics, or Control and Communication
    in the Animal and the Machine* (Wiener)
    4.4.1

D

D'Aguesseau, Henri François 7.3.1
D'Souza, Dinesh 7.3.1
Davidson, Ellen 6.3.2
Davis, Tim 5.2.1
Deshler, David 5.2.1
Design for Education (Jantsch) 6.4.2
Deleuze, Gilles 6.3.3
democracy 6.3.1, 6.3.3
Demolins, Edmond 2.1.1
Desautels, Jacques 3.2.1
Desautels and Larochelle 3.4
developmental psychology Matrix
Dewey, John Matrix, 5.1, 6.3.2
Dick, Walter Matrix
Dick and Carey 4.3.1, 4.3.2
Doise, Willem 5.3.1, Matrix
Doise and Mugny 5.3.2
Domenach, Jean-Marie 7.1.1, 7.3.1, 7.3.2,
    7.5, Matrix

Dreikurs, Rudolf 2.3.1, 2.3.2
Duguid, Paul 5.5.1, Matrix
Dweck and Leggett 5.6.3

E

Eastern philosophies Matrix
Eccles, John C. 6.4.2
Eckhart, Meister 1.2, 1.4.2
École et sociétés (Bertrand and Valois) 8.2,
    8.3
École et vie active (Houssaye) 7.3.1
école nouvelle (new school) 2.1.1
École Polytechnique de Montréal 4.5
ecology 6.4.1, Matrix
eco-social theories 6.1, 6.4
ecosociety 6.4.1
ecstatic theory 1.4.3
Educaçao como pratica da liberdade (Freire)
    6.3.1
Éducation et l'humanisme, L' (Lebel) 7.3.1
Educational Imagination, The (Eisner) 4.1
Educational Technology (journal) 4.3.1
Eisner, Elliot 4.1, 7.3.2
Eisner and Vallance Introduction
electronic scenario 4.5
Éliade, Mircea 1.1, 1.3, 1.4.1, Matrix
Ellsworth, Elizabeth 6.3.3
Emerson, Ralph Waldo 1.3, Matrix
empowering education 6.3.2, 6.3.3, Matrix
endoscopy 2.3.3
environmental sciences Matrix
epistemological disturbance 3.2.5
epistemological obstacle 3.3, 3.4
epistemological profile 3.3
Erasmus 7.3.1
essentialism 7.3.1, 7.5, Matrix
Éthier, Girard 7.4.2, Matrix
EVE project 4.4.3
evocation 3.3.2
experiential education 6.4.2
extrinsic learning 1.4.1

F

Feldman, Steven P. 5.2.1
feminist studies 6.3.3, Matrix
Ferguson, Marilyn Introduction, 1.2, 1.3,
    1.4, 1.4.4, Matrix
Ferrière, Adolphe 2.1.1
Finkielkraut, Alain 7.3.1, 7.3.2
Finn and Ravitch 7.2
Fisher, Arthur 4.4.3

Fiske, Susan T. 5.2.1
Flavell, John H. 3.2.1
Forquin, Jean-Claude Matrix
Fortin, A. 7.3.1
Fotinas, Constantin Introduction, 1.4,
    1.4.5, 1.5, 2.1.2, 2.3.2, 2.3.3, 2.6, Matrix
Fotinas and Henry 1.2, 1.3, 1.4.5, 2.3.3
Fotinas and Torossian 2.3.2
Foucault, Michel 6.3.3
Frankenstein, Marilyn 6.3.2
Frankfort School 6.3.3
Freie-Schulgemeinden 2.1.1
Freinet, Célestin 5.6.1, 6.2
Freire, Paulo 6.1, 6.3, 6.3.1, 6.3.3, 8.2,
    Matrix
Freire and Faundez 6.3.1
Freire and Macedo 6.3.1
Freud, Sigmund 2.3.1, 5.2.2, Matrix
Fritz, Jane M. 4.4.2
Fromm, Erich 2.3.1, 6.3.3
fundamental education 7.4.2
Future Shock (Toffler) 6.4.3

G

Gadbois, Louis 7.4.2, Matrix
Gagné, Robert Mills Introduction, Matrix
Gagné, Briggs, and Wager 4.3.1, 4.3.2, 4.5
Garnier, Catherine 3.2.1
general education 7.4, 7.4.1, 7.4.2, Matrix
General System Theory (Bertalanffy) 4.3.1
gestalt psychology 5.4.1
gestalt therapies Table 1.1
Gilly, Michel 5.3.1, 5.3.2, Matrix
Gilson, Étienne 7.1.1, 7.3.1, 7.3.2, 7.5,
    Matrix
Gingras, Paul-Émile 7.3.3
Ginsberg, Allen 1.2
Gioia, Dennis A. 5.2.1
Giordan, André 3.2.1, 3.2.2, 3.2.3, 3.2.4,
    3.4, 5.3.1, Matrix
Giordan and Vecchi 3.2.3
Giroux, Henry A. 6.1, 6.3, 6.3.3, 8.2, Matrix
Glaser, Robert Matrix
Goble, Frank 2.3.1
Gohier, Christiane 7.4.2
Goodlad, John I. 6.3.3
Gorbutt, David 6.3.3
Gore, Jennifer 6.1
Grand'Maison, Jacques 6.1, 6.3.4, Matrix
Greco-Roman humanism 7.3.1, 7.3.3, 7.5,
    Matrix

Gredler, Margaret E. 5.2.1, 5.2.2, 5.2.3, 5.4.3, Matrix
Greeno, J.G. 5.5.1
group therapies Table 1.1
Guattari, Felix 6.3.3, 6.4, 8.2
Guide to Systematic Instructional Design, A (Wong and Raulerson) 4.3.1
Guidebook to Learning, A (Adler) 7.3.2
Guigou, Jacques 6.2
Guiraud, Marc 6.2.3
Guitton, Jean 7.3.1

H

Habermas, Jurgen 6.3.3
Hameline, Daniel Introduction
Harman, Willis W. Introduction, 1.2, 1.3, 1.4, 1.4.2, 1.5, Matrix
Henderson, Hazel 1.2, 1.3, Matrix
Henry, Michel 7.1.1, 7.3.1, 7.3.2, Matrix
hermeneutics Matrix
Hess, Rémi 6.2
Hirsch, E.D. [Eric Donald] 7.2
Hooper, Simon 4.4.2, 5.6.3
Horton, Myles 6.3.2
Houang and Leyris 1.2
Houssaye, Jean Introduction, 5.6.2, 7.3.1, 7.5, 8.2, Matrix
humanism Matrix, 7.5
humanistic psychology Matrix
humanistic theories 5.2.1, 6.2.3
humanities 7.4.2, Matrix
Hutchins, Robert Maynard 7.1.1, 7.2, 7.3.1, Matrix
Huxley, Aldous 1.2, 1.3, 1.4.1, 1.4.2
Hypercard 4.4.2, 4.4.3
hypercourseware 4.4.2, Matrix
hypermedia (technological) 4.2, 4.4, 4.4.1, 4.4.2, 4.4.3, 4.6
hypermedia theories 4.2, 4.4.1
hypnosis Table 1.1

I

IBM 4.5
Illich, Ivan 6.4.1, Matrix
industrial paradigm 1.2, 6.1
Information Modelling Programme, Leeds University (UK) 4.4.3
Institute for Research on Learning 5.1, 5.5.1
institutional pedagogies 6.1, 6.2, 6.2.2, 6.2.3, 6.2.4

institutional psychotherapy 6.2, 6.2.2
instructional design Matrix
Instructional Design: Principles and Applications (Briggs) 4.3.1
Instructional Systems (Banathy) 4.3.1
instructional technology 4.1
intelligent learning environment Matrix
intelligent systems of instruction 4.4.1
intelligent tutoring systems 4.4.2
intrinsic learning (self-actualization) 1.4.1
Isen, Alice M. 5.2.1
ITS Challenger 4.4.2

J

James, William 5.4.2
Jantsch, Erich 6.1, 6.4, 6.4.2, 6.5, Matrix
Janvier, Claude 3.2.1
Jaspers, Karl 6.3.1
Jesuits (Society of Jesus) 7.3.1
Jodelet, Denise 3.2.2
Johnson and Johnson 5.6.1, 5.6.3, Matrix
Johnson, Johnson, and Holubec 5.6.3
Joly, Richard 7.1.1
Joyce, Bruce Matrix
Joyce, Showers, and Murphy 5.6.3
Joyce and Weil 3.2.1, 5.1
Joyce, Weil, and Showers 5.1, 5.6.1, 5.6.2, 6.3.3
Jung, Carl Matrix

K

Kaeppelin, Philippe 6.2
Kagan, Spencer 5.6.2, Matrix
Karp and Yoels 5.6.1
Kearsley, Greg 4.4.1
Kegan, Robert 3.2.1
Kerouac, Jack 1.2
Kirkconnel, Watson 7.1.1
Kirkwood and Kirkwood 6.3.2
Kirschenbaum and Henderson 2.6
knowledge acquisition *in situ* 5.5.1
Koerner, James D. 7.5
Koestler, Arthur 1.2, 1.4.2
Kohlberg, Lawrence 3.2.1
Köhler, Wolfgang 5.4.1
Kohn, Alfie 5.6.3
Korzybsky, Alfred 3.2.1
Kozol, Jonathan 8.1
Krathwohl, Bloom, and Masia 4.4.1
Kreitner, Robert 5.2.1
Krishnamurti, Jiddu 1.1, 1.4.3, 1.5

Kuhn, Thomas S. 6.4.2

L

Laclau, Ernesto 6.3.3
La Garanderie, Antoine de 3.3.1, 3.3.2, 3.4, Matrix
Lajoie, Eggan, and Lesgold 4.5
Laliberté, Jacques 7.4.2, Matrix
Land-Erziehungsheime 2.1.1
Landa, Lev Nakhmanovich 4.4.1, Matrix
Langer, Jonas 5.3.1
Language Development and Hypermedia Research Group, University of Ulster 4.4.3
Lao-Tzu 1.2, Matrix
Lapassade, Georges 2.6, 6.2, 6.2.1, 6.2.3, Matrix
Lapointe, J. 4.1, 4.3.1
Lapp, Bender, Ellenwood, and John Introduction, 7.3.2
Larochelle, Marie 3.2.1
Larochelle and Desautels 3.2.2, 3.2.3, 3.2.5, 5.3.1, Matrix
Laszlo, Ervin 6.4.2
Lavallée, Micheline 7.4.3, Matrix
Lave, Jean 5.5.1, 5.5.2, Matrix
Lave and Chaiklin 5.5.1
Lave and Wenger 5.5.1
Lawler, Robert W. 4.4.1
Le Moigne, Jean-Louis 4.3.1
Le nouvel éducateur (journal) 5.6.1
Learning for Tomorrow (Toffler) 6.4.3
learning styles/profiles:
    auditory 3.3.2
    visual 3.3.2
Lebel, Maurice 7.1.1, 7.3.1, 7.5
Lefebvre-Pinard, Monique 5.3.1, 5.3.2, Matrix
Léger, Alain 7.1.1
Leonard, George B. Introduction, 1.2, 1.3, 1.4, 1.4.3, 1.5, Matrix
Lerbet, Georges Introduction
Léveillé-Ryan, Lucie (Ryan, Lucie Léveillé) 2.1
Levi-Leblond, Jean-Marc 3.2.1
Levin, Henry M. 5.6.1, 6.3.2
Lévy, Bernard-Henri 7.1.1
Lewin, Kurt 2.1.1, 2.6, Matrix
Li, Zhongmin 4.4.2
liberal arts 7.4.2, Matrix
liberal education 7.4.2

liberatory education (aka pedagogy of liberation, empowering education) 6.3.2, Matrix
Lietz, Hermann 2.1.1
Lobrot, Michel 6.2, 6.2.1, 6.2.3
LOGO language 4.2
Lombroso, Cesare 2.1.1
Lord, Robert G. 5.2.1
Lorimier, Jacques de 7.4.2
Lourau, René 6.2, 6.2.1, 6.2.2
Lowenthal, Leo 6.3.3
Lupasco, Stéphane 3.2.1
Luthans, Fred 5.2.1

M

Mack, Lewis, and Carroll 4.5
Mager, Robert F. 4.4.1, Matrix
Makarenko, Anton [Semenovich] 6.2
Mangieri, John N. 7.4.2
Manz, Charles C. 5.2.1
Marcuse, Herbert 6.3.3
Markle, Susan Meyer 4.5
Marsolais, Arthur 7.4.2, Matrix
Martinand, Jean-Louis 3.2.1
Marxism 6.2.1, 6.3.3, Matrix
Maslow, Abraham H. Introduction, 1.4, 1.4.1, 1.4.3, 2.1.1, 2.3.1, 2.4.2, Matrix
McCarthy, Sen. Joseph 6.3.3
McCombs, Barbara L. 5.2.1
McLaren, Peter 6.3.3, Matrix
McLean, Leslie D. 5.6.3, 5.7, Matrix
McMahon, Harry Matrix
McMahon, O'Neill, and Cunningham 4.4.3
meditation Table 1.1
Meirieu, Philippe 2.1
metacognition 5.2.2
meta-needs 1.4.1
metaphysical theory (transpersonal) 1.4.5
metaphysics Matrix
Miller, Gary E. 7.1.1
minimal manual 4.5
minimal training 4.5, Matrix
Ministère de l'Enseignement supérieur et de la science du Québec 7.2, 7.4.2
Mischel, Walter 5.2.1
modernity 6.3.3
Moll, Luis C. 5.4.3
Montessori, Maria 2.1.1
Morin, Edgar 4.3.1, 6.1, 6.4, 6.5
Morin and Brunet 7.1.1, 7.2
Mugny, Gabriel 5.3.1, Matrix

Mugny and Doise 5.3.2
multicultural democracy Matrix
mysticism Matrix

N

NASA 4.5
Nation at Risk, A (National Commission on Excellence in Education) 7.1.1, 7.4.2
National Commission on Excellence in Education 7.4.2
National Training Laboratory (NTL) 2.1.1
naturalism Matrix
Neill, A.S. [Alexander Sutherland] 2.1.1, 2.6, 6.2, Matrix
neo-Marxism 6.3.3
neo-Piagetian thought 5.3.1, 5.3.2
neurolinguistic programming theories 5.2.2
New School 2.1.1
new sociology of education (NSE) 6.3.3
new theater Table 1.1
Newmann and Thompson 5.7
Nielsen, Jakob 4.4.2
non-deterministic free school Matrix
Not, Louis Introduction
Novak, Joseph D. 3.2.2

O

O'Neill, Bill Matrix
Oakes, Jeannie 6.3.2
Olave, Maria del Pilar de 6.3.2
Ontario Institute for Studies in Education 5.6.3
open education Matrix
open system 4.3.1
Opération Départ 2.4.1, 2.4.2
operative conditioning 4.4.1
Ordinary Ecstasy (Rowan) 1.5
organizational culture 6.2.4
Ornstein and Ehrlich 6.4, 6.5
Ortega y Gasset, José 7.1.1, 7.3.2
Otto, Rudolf 1.4.1
Oury, Fernand 6.2
Oury, Jean 6.2.2
Ouvry-Vial, Brigitte 7.4.2
Ozmon and Craver 6.3.3

P

Pagès, Max 2.1.1, 2.2.1
paideia (Athens) 1.4.4, 7.3.2, 7.5
Paideia (Adler) 7.3.2, 7.5

Paideia Problems and Possibilities (Adler) 7.3.2
Paideia Program, The (Adler) 7.3.2
Paideia Proposal, The (Adler) 7.3.2
Palenque (multimedia program) 4.4.3
Palincsar, Annemarie Sullivan Matrix
Palincsar and Brown 5.4.3
Papert, Seymour 4.2, 4.4.2
Paquette, Claude 2.1.2, 2.5.1, 2.5.2, Matrix
Paquette, Gilbert 4.4.2, Matrix
Paré, André Matrix, 2.1.2, 2.5.1, 2.5.2, 2.6
Passeron, Jean-Claude Matrix
Paul, Richard W. 7.4, 7.4.1, 7.4.2, Matrix
Pavlov, Ivan Petrovich 5.4.1
Pea, Roy D. 5.5.1, Matrix
peak experience 1.4.1
pedagogical drama 5.4.1
pedagogical profile 3.1, 3.3.2
pedagogy of liberation 6.3.1, 6.3.2
perennial philosophy (eternal philosophy, *philosophia perennis*) 1.3, Matrix
Perret-Clermont, Anne-Nelly 5.3.1
personalism Matrix
personalist theories (aka humanistic, libertarian, non-directive, organic, pulsional, free, open) 5.2.2, Chapter 2, Matrix
Peters and Waterman 7.4.2
Petitjean, Armand 6.4
Petrarch 7.3.1
phenomenology 6.3.3
philosophy Matrix
Piaget, Jean 3.2.1, 3.2.2, 4.2, 4.4.2, 5.3.2, 5.4.2, Matrix
Piaget and Inhelder 5.3.2
Piagetian psychology Matrix
Pinar, William 6.3.3
Pirsig, Robert M. 8.2
Plato 1.4.2, 7.3.2, 7.3.3
Pocztar, Jerry 4.3.1
Poeydomenge, Marie-Louise 2.6
Poggio 7.3.1
political science Matrix
Polak, Frederik Lodewijk 6.3.3
Pontalis, J.-B. 7.4.2
postmodernity 6.3.3
potential zone of development (aka zone of potential development and proximal development zone) 5.4.1, 5.4.2
Power, Edward J. 7.3.1, 7.5
Pratte, Richard 7.1.1, 7.3.1
Prégent, Richard 4.3.1, 4.3.2, Matrix

Previews and Promises (Toffler) 6.4.3
Prigogine, Ilya 6.4.2
Principles of Instructional Design (Gagné, Briggs, and Wager) 4.3.1
prior conception 3.1, 3.4, 5.3.1
progressive education Matrix
proximal development zone (aka potential zone of development and proximal development zone) 5.3.2, 5.4.1, 5.4.2
psychedelic drugs Table 1.1
psychoanalysis Matrix
psychoanalytical trend 6.2.2
psychocognitive theories - Chapter 3, 5.1, Matrix
psychodrama Table 1.1
psychodynamic psychology 5.2.2
psychodynamic theories 5.2.2
psychosociological approaches 6.2.1
psychosociology Matrix

R

Reddie, Cecil 2.1.1
reflexology 5.4.1
Régnier, Louise 4.5
Régnier and Ricci 4.5
religions Matrix
Research Society for Creative Altruism 1.4.1
Resnick, Levine, and Teasley 5.5.1
Rest, Turiel, and Kohlberg 5.3.1
Revue française de sociologie (journal) 4.3.1
Robert, F. 7.3.1
Robert, J.M. 4.5, 7.3.1
Rogers, Carl Introduction, 1.1, 2.1.2, 2.2.1, 2.2.2, 2.2.3, 2.3.1, 2.4.2, 2.5.2, 2.6, 4.2, 6.2.1, 6.2.2, 6.2.3, 8.2
Roman, Leslie G. 6.3.3
romantic humanism Matrix
Romiszowski, A.J. [Alexander Joseph] 4.3.2
Rosch, Eleanor 5.2.1
Rosenblueth, Arturo 4.4.1
Rosnay, Joël de 4.3.1, 6.1, 6.4, 6.4.1, 6.4.2, 6.5, Matrix
Rousseau, Jean-Jacques 2.1.1, 2.6
Roux, Jean-Paul 5.3.1
Rowan, John 1.2, 1.4.3, 1.5
Rowell and Dawson 3.4
Ryan, Lucie Léveillé 2.1

S

Saint-Arnaud, Yves 2.4.2
Sandberg, Barnard, and Kamsteeg 4.4.2
Sandberg and Wielinga 4.4.2
Sapon-Schevin, Mara 6.3.2
Sapon-Schevin and Schniedewind 6.3, 6.3.2
Sartrian existentialism 1.4.1
Scherer, Marge 8.1
Schmalhofer and Kühn 4.5
Schniedewind, Nancy 6.3.2
Schniedewind and Davidson 5.6.1, 6.3.2
scholasticism 7.3.1
school for excellence 7.4.2
Schooling in Capitalist America (Bowles and Gintis) 6.3.3
Schunk, Dale 5.2.1, 5.2.2
Science Council of Canada 5.6.3
Scriven, Michael Matrix
Scriven and Paul 7.4.2
self-awareness exercises Table 1.1
self-management pedagogies 6.1, 6.2, 6.2.1
sensitivity training Table 1.1
sensorial awareness Table 1.1
Seymour, Jim 4.4.2
Sharan, Shlomo 5.6.2, Matrix
Sharan, Kussell, Hertz-Lazarowitz, Bejarano, Raviv, and Sharan 5.6.3
Sharan and Sharan 5.1
Shor, Ira 5.6.1, 5.6.2, 6.1, 6.3, 6.3.2, 6.3.3, 8.2, 8.3, Matrix
Shor and Freire 6.3.1, 6.3.2, 6.3.3
Sierpinska, Anna 3.4
Sigel, Irving E. 3.2.1
Simon, Roger I. 6.3.3
Sims, Henry P., Jr. 5.2.1, Matrix
Sims and Lorenzi 5.2.2
Sirotnick, Kenneth A. 6.3.3
Siviter and Brown 4.4.2
Skinner, B.F. 4.2, 4.4.1, 5.2.1, 5.2.2, Matrix
Slavin, Robert E. 5.6.1, 5.6.3, 5.7, Matrix
Sleeter, Christine E. 6.3.2, Matrix
Snyders, Georges Introduction, 7.5
social cognitive conflict 5.3.1, 5.3.2
social cognitive theories - Chapter 5, 6.3.1, Matrix
social theories - Chapter 6, Matrix
social transactional dynamism 5.2.2
social values 6.3.3
sociohistorical psychology 5.1, 5.4.3, 5.7
sociology Matrix

Solomon, Cynthia 4.4.1
Sophocles 7.3.3
South Bank Polytechnic School (London) 4.4.2
Spady and Marx 7.1.1, 7.4.2
spiritualistic theories (aka metaphysical, transcendental) - Chapter 1, Matrix
Srull, Thomas K. 5.2.1
stages of knowledge (Koestler) 1.4.2
Stanley, William B. 6.3, 6.3.3, 8.2, Matrix
Stolovitch, Harold D. Matrix
Stolovitch and La Roque 4.1
Strike and Posner 3.2.5
structuralism 6.3.3
Sullivan, Edmund V. 3.2.1
Summerhill 8.2
Suppes, Patrick 4.4.2
Suzuki, Daisetz Teitaro 1.4.1, Matrix
symbolic violence 6.2.4
Systematic Design of Instruction, The (Dick and Carey) 4.3.1
systemics (technological) 4.2, 4.3, 4.3.1, 4.3.2, 4.6, Matrix
systemic education 6.4.1
systems theory 4.2, Matrix

T

T-Group (training group) 1.4.2, 2.1.1
Taoism Matrix
Tardif, Jacques 5.1
Taurisson, Alain 3.2.1, 3.3.2, Matrix
technocratic culture 6.3.3
technological theories (technosystemic, systemic) - Chapter 4, Matrix
Temps de la réflexion, Le (journal) 7.3.1
Thelen, Herbert Arnold 5.1
theories:
    Academic (traditionalist, generalist, classic)- Chapter 7, Matrix
    Personalist (humanistic, libertarian, non-directive, organic, impulsive, free, open) - Chapter 2, Matrix
    Psychocognitive - Chapter 3, Matrix
    Social - Chapter 6, Matrix
    Social Cognitive - Chapter 5, Matrix
    Technological (technosystemic, systemic) - Chapter 4, Matrix •
    Spiritualistic (metaphysical, transcendental) - Chapter 1, Matrix
Third Wave, The (Toffler) 6.4.3
Thomas, Russell 7.4.2
Thomism 7.3.1

Thoreau, Henry Matrix
Thorndike, Edward L. 5.4.1
Tickton, Sidney G. 4.1
Tieberghen, Andrée 3.2.1
Toffler, Alvin 6.1, 6.4, 6.4.2, 6.4.3, 6.5, Matrix
training groups (T groups) Table 1.1
transcendental theory 1.3
transpersonal theory (metaphysical) 1.4.5
Turiel, Elliot Matrix

U

underground press Table 1.1
Université de Montréal 7.4.2
University of Chicago 7.4

V

Valla, Lorenzo 7.3.1
Vallance, Elizabeth Introduction, 7.3.2
Valois and Bertrand Introduction
Van Doren, Mark 7.1.1
Vasquez, Aïda 6.2
Vasquez and Oury 6.2.2
Viau, Rolland 5.2.1, Matrix
Vygotsky, L.S. [Lev Semenovich] 5.1, 5.3.2, 5.4.1, 5.4.2, 5.4.3, 5.7, Matrix

W

Walker, John E. 7.2
Watts, Alan 1.4.3, 1.5
Weil, Joyce, and Kluwin 2.1.2
Weil and Showers Introduction
Wenger, Étienne 5.5.1
Wertsch, James V. 5.4.3
Wexler, Philip 6.3.3
Whitaker and Bonnel 4.4.1
Wiener, Norbert 4.4.1
Wilson, Kathy (Bank Street College of Education, New York) 4.4.3
Windows on Science 4.4.3
Wong and Raulerson 4.3.2
Woodhead, Nevill 4.4.2
Wyer, Robert S. 5.2.1

Y

yoga Table 1.1
Young, Michael F.D. 6.3.3, Matrix

Z

Z theory 1.4.1
Zen 1.3, 1.4.1
Zen and the Art of Motorcycle Maintenance (Pirsig) 8.2
Zimmerman, Barry J. 5.2.1

zone of potential development (aka potential zone of development, proximal development zone) 5.4.1, 5.4.2

zone of proximal development (aka zone of potential development, potential zone of development, proximal development zone) 5.3.2, 5.4.1, 5.4.2